DATE DUE

SEP 29 1989			

HIGHSMITH 45-220

QUALITY CIRCLES

QUALITY CIRCLES

A GUIDE TO PARTICIPATION AND PRODUCTIVITY

OLGA L. CROCKER
Professor, Faculty of Business Administration, University of Windsor
Adjunct Professor, Institute for Personal and Career Development,
Central Michigan University

JOHNNY SIK LEUNG CHIU

and CYRIL CHARNEY
Management Consultant, Thorne, Stevenson and Kellogg

Facts On File Publications

New York, New York ● Bicester, England

Quality Circles: A Guide to Participation and Productivity

Copyright © 1984 by Methuen Publications
A Division of the Carswell Company Limited

Published in the United States of America by Facts on File, Inc., 460 Park Avenue South, New York, NY 10016.

Published in Canada by Methuen Publications, 2330 Midland Avenue, Agincourt, Ontario M1S 1P7.

ISBN 0-8160-1161-3

Cover design: Don Fernley
Text design: The Dragon's Eye Press

Printed and bound in the United States of America
1 2 3 4 5   84   89 88 87 86 85

To our families

NATHAN, KEVIN, GERRI, TERENCE, and GINGER

MR. and MRS. SHU-CHONG CHIU

and

RHONA, DANEAL, THALIA, and DAVIN

PREFACE

The purpose of this book is to introduce the reader to the concept of quality circles and to compare quality control circles in Japan with those in the United States (and by projection, those in Canada). It is hoped that through an identification of the differences between these two countries and an analysis of the reasons behind these differences, an isolation of the effects that quality circles have on productivity and on worker motivation can be made. The study is important for another reason. At present, literature is replete with articles emphasizing the desirability of introducing Japanese-type quality circles to North American industry; no analysis of the differences and similarities between the two countries, however, is usually given.

The book is written for five types of audiences. First it is written for the practitioner — that man or woman who is participating or is trying to decide whether or not to participate in quality circles. It is hoped that both blue- and white-collar circle members will find the book a useful and complete guide.

Second, it is written for my students and those of other professors. Many have taken courses in innovative methods of resolving labour–management conflict and are expected to apply in the "real world" what they have learned or should have learned. The book answers an often-heard plea of many of them: How do I start and what do I do?

The third audience is those students who are still in the classroom and have aspirations of becoming employed in areas in which they can use their knowledge of team processes and productivity improvements. Perhaps a book such as this will help in teaching the fundamentals and will serve as a useful everyday reference when these students leave their academic institutions.

Fourth, it is written for facilitators and coordinators who have been trained in group processes but have not been trained in quality circle processes. This group may obtain ideas and assurance that they are on the right track.

The fifth audience is the managerial one — those people who want a quick overview of what their personnel are doing, and who must be knowledgeable in spite of the fact that time is at a premium.

To the extent that the book meets the needs of any and all of these groups it is a success.

Many people have participated in bringing this book to completion. Special thanks are extended to those people who read the book and provided many useful comments: Dr. Pierre DuBois of the consulting firm of Woods Gordon; L. M. Galicinski, Qualitran Professional Services, Stroud, Ontario; Prof. Kevin B. Crocker of College-University of Cape Breton, Sydney, Nova Scotia; and Ginger Grant. And to Ginger, many thanks for the technical assistance.

Thanks also go to: Mr. and Mrs. Dan Connor; Mr. and Mrs. Tse; Brenda Butler, Manager, General Planning, Aetna Canada; Donna M. Hornsby, Secretary–Director of Maintenance, Air BC; Peter R. Leslie, Supervisor, Employee Relations, Allis-Chambers Canada Inc.; Anne S. Connor, Meeting Planner Program Manager, AMR International, Inc; R. H. Bettinger, Supervisor, Reliability Programs, American Airlines, Maintenance & Engineering Centre; Yvonne Horvath, Administrative Assistant, American Society for Quality Control; Zenon Onufryk, Bonar Packaging Ltd.; J. W. Cormier, Specialist, Union Relations, Canadian General Electric; Nestor Chyz, The Canadian Salt Company Limited; Jacquie Taylor, Coordinator, Cariboo Management Centre, Cariboo College; Joseph H. Martin, President, Conestoga College; Jan Shuckard, Assistant Vice President Corporate Services, Constellation Assurance Company; Laurie A. Hirsch, Corporate Quality Circle Facilitator, Continental Illinois Bank and Trust Company of Chicago; E. L. Marr, Crush Canada Ltd.; Garry S. Kissuk, Manager, Human Resource Planning, Dome Petroleum Limited; Linda Lehtonew, QC Coordinator, Dominion Life Assurance Co. Ltd.; K. McCullough, Manager, Engineering, Dover Elevator; G. J. Peterson, Human Resources Manager, Esso Chemical Canada; Philip C. Hassen, Executive Vice President, Foothills Hospital.

Cam Prymak; Gary Lesperance, EI Program Coordinator, Windsor Operations; Rudy Orgis, Processing Engineer; Gary H. Blevins, Forward Planning and Analysis Department, Labour Relations Staff; William Johnston, Manager of Labour Relations and Hourly Personnel, Windsor Operations (all of the Ford Motor Co. of Canada Ltd.); Jerry W. Dillard, Manager, Corporate Safety, Ford Motor Co.; and Stephen Barney, World Headquarters, Ford Motor Co.

Michael Nastanski of General Dynamics; Ed J. Taylor, Associate Manager, Productivity Services, Great West Life; John T. Rooney, Commercial Services Manager, National Quality Team/Steering Committee Chairman, Hewlett Packard Canada Ltd.; S. Cairns, Vice President Operations, Hostess Food Products Ltd.; J. Al Spence, President, Hussman Store Equipment Limited; Larry S. Kacher, Manager, Organization Development, Corporate Human Resource Development Department, Honeywell, Inc.; S. Takeda, Publicity, Hotel Okura, Tokyo, Japan; Robert Collier, Executive Director of International Association of Quality Circles; J. E. Vereshack, Senior Information Representative, Information Department IBM (Canada) Ltd.; Tsunetaka Irei, Okinawa, Japan; Joji Arai, Director, Japan Productivity Center; Japan Trade Centre Office; W. Alan Lewis, Vice-President and General Manager, Knape & Vogt Canada Inc.; Audrey LaPointe, Controller, *Mainland* Magazine; Dr. Stanley Stark, Professor, Department of

Management, Michigan State University; Jack Germain, Vice-President and Director of Quality, Motorola, Inc.; Don L. White, Vice President Operations, Motorways Limited; J. J. Zeyen, Vice President–Manufacturing, Nashua Canada Ltd.; R. M. Cuddy, Vice-President, Manufacturing, Northern Telecom Canada Limited, Islington, Ontario; Robert I. Patchin, Director of Productivity Improvement Programs, Northrup Corporation, Aircraft Division; Bob Ackerman, Omark Canada Ltd., Guelph, Ontario; Art Van Pelt, Employee Relations Manager, Overwaitea Foods; Bruce Fuller, Vice-President Corporate Affairs, The Jim Pattison Group; Robert J. Shaw, Principal, Peat, Marwick, Mitchell & Co.; Stan Jarovi, Price Waterhouse Limited.

Donald Young, PSI Coordinator and Director of Governmental Affairs; Bob Brown; John Olaja, Director of Advertising; and Derek Millet, Engineer and Team Captain; all of Vickers World headquarters.

R. C. Sinclair, Coordinator, Quality Programme Project, Toronto-Dominion Bank; Ed Artuso, QCC Facilitator, Tridon Limited; Ray Wakeman, Curtis Davidson, Frank Morand, and members of UAW Local 200 for their help in the completion of the Ford Motor Co. survey; Dr. Vedanand, Faculty of Administrative Studies, Department of Marketing, University of Manitoba; Dr. Robert E. Cole, Professor, University of Michigan; Dr. Akira Kubota, Political Science Department, University of Windsor.

Guy Cassady, Clara Chai, Patrick Chee, Albert Pak Choong, Garry Swee Foo, Thomas Ho, Vincent Lam, Thomas Ng, Shih Yuan Wong, Marianne Wylupek, and Alfred Yau, all students at the University of Windsor, and Jo Ann Sokkar, Senior Associate Librarian, Graduate School of Business Administration Library, University of Windsor.

K. B. Nisbet, Director, Corporate Affairs, Westinghouse Canada, Inc.; Ralph J. Barra, Director of Corporate Quality, Westinghouse Electric Corporation; Dean J. Alex Murray and Dr. Hans J. Bocker, Wilfred Laurier University; and Dr. Charles J. McMillan, Professor, Faculty of Administrative Studies, York University.

Special thanks are given to the Faculty typists and the women at the Word Processing Centre who helped bring this work to a readable conclusion: Catherine Walker, Suzanne Patterson, Sandra Van Zetten, Pat Awid, Barbara Faria, Lucia Brown, Roni Burleigh, Carmela Papp, Lyn LaPorte and Nancy Dawid.

Last, but not least, Dr. Eric West, Dean, Faculty of Business Administration, University of Windsor, and Methuen's executive editor, Herb Hilderley, and assistant editor, Catherine Munro, without whose support and assistance this project would have been much more difficult.

CONTENTS

PART II
THE IMPLEMENTATION PROCESS

PART III
STATISTICAL ANALYSIS AND EVALUATION

PART I

JAPAN AND
NORTH AMERICA

1 The Concept of Quality Circles

The 1970s have been riddled with one crisis after another—wars, political problems and the energy crisis. Not the least was the economic crisis created by the enormous influx of Japanese goods on the Canadian and American markets. North America in the 1980s is in a period of record high inflation and record high unemployment.

Many analysts argue that high unemployment is attributable to a "productivity crisis." On the surface, the solution appears simple—increase employee productivity. Productivity can be defined as the ratio of what goes into the production process (inputs) to what comes out (outputs). But the inputs and outputs of even the most simple production process are many. As a consequence, many different approaches are suggested to accomplish increased productivity.

Some analysts attribute high unemployment and low productivity to the gap in wage rates between North American workers and workers in other parts of the world, particularly Japan. The figure depends on who does the calculation, but generally it is estimated that North American workers cost about $25 per hour whereas Japanese workers cost about $12 per hour, a substantial difference of $13 per hour. Therefore, some claim, the answer to productivity problems is to slash labour costs drastically.

This measure, of course, would be easier than tackling the productivity problems that exist. Labour costs could be reduced to the level of those in Japan if, as a society, Americans were prepared to allow their standard of living to regress to that of the Japanese. Some other issues also must be considered. If the United Auto Workers (UAW; the union which represents automotive industry blue-collar employees) is typical of North American unions, it is doubtful that, over the long term, American workers would be prepared to tolerate "clawbacks." Nor would American workers and unions accept the ramifications associated with a labour cost–cutting contest with workers in other parts of the world. It appears, then, that this solution is impractical.

Labour's answer to the problems facing the domestic market is to avoid the question of productivity but invoke protectionist measures. This could take the form of stringent import quotas or content legislation or both. However, there could be a price to pay for such a move.

First, invoking protectionist legislation would invite retaliation from countries that import North American goods. For Canada, which exports more to Japan than it imports, such a move would have a net negative effect. This also would go against world pressures to ease import restrictions and promote fair trade between countries.

Second, protectionism, over time, tends to make the protected industry inefficient. Economists argue that with protectionism there is a substitution of legislation for natural market forces. This in turn puts the economy and the marketplace, which are in delicate balance, into a state of disequilibrium. If this is so, in the long run protectionism would do more harm than good to the economy.

The government's answer to the problem includes wage or price controls or both, nationalization, government grants, loans and subsidies. But these partial solutions have also been very inefficient in the long run and are expensive or politically unacceptable.

Within industry, in the past, the answer has been increased job specialization. But it is probable that very little further increase in productivity can be accomplished by breaking down jobs into tasks that are even simpler and more repetitive. Too, it is doubtful that the better-educated workers of the 1980s and '90s will be willing to do more menial tasks merely to increase productivity. This partial solution is ineffective and unacceptable.

The Japanese have utilized robots to increase productivity and to do the more repetitive, dangerous and less desirable jobs. But in North America, it has been argued that the application of such technology would result in the loss of jobs, and that robots do not buy cars and other consumer goods. It is probably true that the use of robots in production processes can displace workers. The development, manufacture and servicing of robots, however, will create many more new jobs and preserve existing ones. In any case, the introduction of robts to industry in North America has met with considerable resistance, and their application here has been slower than in Japan.

It appears that workers in North America will not work for Japanese wages. Protectionist legislation would be a step in the wrong direction and, like government grants, loans and subsidies, would be very inefficient and unacceptable. Breaking existing jobs down into more simple repetitive tasks also would be counterproductive. Lastly, the introduction of robots to industry has been and will probably continue to be slower in North America than in Japan. A remaining possibility, however, is the human factor in productivity. Can employees be managed in such a manner that they are more satisfied, more motivated and more productive? The key may be the involvement of employees at all levels within the organization in the decision-making process. One such approach is quality circles.[1]

Possible answers to productivity problems:
* lower wages
* protectionist measures
* wage and price controls
* increased job specialization
* more robots

These ideas are impractical, politically unwise or inefficient.

The answer: more motivated and more productive workers through quality circle programs.

The words "quality circle" or "quality control circle" mean different things to different people. Additionally, they suggest that quality control (the improvement of quality within an organization) and quality circles (participative decision-making groups) are one and the same. Although quality circles generally do focus on quality control, the two concepts are not synonymous.

In Japan, quality control circles are organized within a department or work area for the purpose of studying and eliminating production-related problems. They are problem-solving teams which use simple statistical methods to research and decide on solutions to workshop problems. Similar types of activities are known by many names, such as: *Ai* (chemical industry—all members' ideas) movements; big brother or big sister groups; JK *(jishu kanri,* in the steel industry); level-up movements; management by objectives; mini–think tanks; new-life movements; no-error movements; productivity committees; safety groups; suggestion groups; workshop involvement groups; workshop talk groups; and ZD (zero defect) movements.[2]

Presently, in Japan, quality circles and other small group activities have expanded beyond the manufacturing sector, especially into the sales and marketing fields. They focus on more than quality and productivity improvement. Employee development and the improvement of communication and morale among co-workers also are important.

Quality circles in North America are similar to Japanese circles in spite of the fact that each may emphasize a particular function such as problem solving, team building or quality control. In many cases, each company (and representative union) has its own unique name for the circle activity. For example, Ford Motor Co. and the United Auto Workers have EI (Employee Involvement); Vickers, Inc. has PSI (People Seeking Improvement); and American Motors Corporation and the United Auto Workers have PIP (Partners in Progress) and JEEP (Joint Effort Employing People); the Toronto-Dominion Bank's circles are EWG (Employee Work Groups). Frequently an individual circle within a particular company will give its team a name. Ford Motor Co. and the United Auto

Workers in Windsor, Ontario, for example, has SOS (Save Our Stampings) and TOPP (Total Opportunity for Plant Participation).

Canadian and U.S. quality circles, although concerned with quality and productivity, also study the improvement of life at the job site. It is not unusual for QC members to tackle such issues as carpooling, busing, absenteeism and child care. Also, the idea has expanded beyond the manufacturing sector into the service sector, particularly into retailing, finance, education and transportation.

The quality circle concept is the result of the interaction between the American statistical method of quality control and Japanese organizational practices. The Japanese adopted the concept of quality control, which originated in the United States, and developed it pragmatically into quality control circles. In the Japanese reinterpretation, each and every person in the organizational hierarchy, from top management to rank-and-file workers, receives training on statistical quality control concepts and techniques. Workers and supervisors participate jointly in small groups to upgrade quality control practices. In this context, quality control shifts from being the prerogative of a minority of engineers with limited shop experience to being the responsibility of each employee. As Norihiko Nakayamo, manager of Fujitsu subsidiaries, stated recently at a seminar in New York City:

Quality Control is not just a little room adjacent to the factory floor, whose occupants make a nuisance of themselves to everyone else. It is a state of mind and a matter of leadership with everyone from the president to production trainee involved.[3]

Underlying the QC concept is the assumption that the causes of quality or productivity problems are unknown to workers and to management. It is also assumed that shop-floor workers have hands-on knowledge, are creative, and can be trained to use this natural creativity in job problem solving. Quality circles, however, are a people-building, rather than a people-using, approach. They aim at making every worker a decision maker concerning his or her own work.

Characteristics of Quality Circles

Quality circles are a formal, institutionalized mechanism for productive and participative problem-solving interaction among employees.[4] Small groups of workers engage in a continuing cooperative study process to uncover and to solve work-related problems. Each circle also acts as a surveillance mechanism which assists the organization in adapting to its environment and in monitoring opportunities. It "scans the environment for opportunities, does not wait to be activated by a problem, and does not stop its activities when a problem has been found and solved."[5] It follows that, for greatest organizational benefit, quality circles should function continuously and be independent of the production process.

The number of members within any one circle differs depending on the policies of the organization. Usually the number is in the three-to-twenty-employee range, with the average circle having eight to ten members. Members get together regularly to learn interpersonal skills and statistical methods associated with problem solving and to select and solve real problems. Meetings are conducted both during regular working hours, with the approval of supervisors, and outside of regular working hours, on the workers' own initiative. Membership in circles is voluntary.

Meetings are chaired by a group leader. In most cases, the role is assumed by the first-line supervisor. In the context of the circle, the leader is not in an authority position over the other members but is a discussion moderator who facilitates the problem-solving process. It is this person's task to keep the group directed toward accomplishing its agenda and to ensure that everyone participates. In the words of one manager, the task is one of "complementing one another's work rather than managing it." In this sense, a circle leader has no authority but is a coordinator in the real sense of the word.

Most organizations also employ a facilitator. The facilitator develops training programs, provides continuing training and guidance to team leaders and, on request, offers training programs for team members. When the number of circles becomes large, some organizations also use a coordinator. This individual acts as a liaison between the facilitators and the quality circle steering committee and middle management.

Each circle is formally independent but may meet with other circles in the company to work jointly on common problems. At each meeting, all members are given assignments which they are expected to complete, on company and non-company time, by the next meeting. These assignments commonly involve first-hand observation of specific phenomena in the workplace and the collection and analysis of data. At the quality circle meeting itself, the brainstorming approach operates; each member is encouraged to participate and put forward ideas. A more detailed summary of the characteristics of quality circles is given in Table 1–1.

TABLE 1–1
Typical Characteristics of Quality Circles

Objectives
- To improve communication, particularly between line employees and management.
- To identify and solve problems.

Organization
- The circle consists of a leader and eight to ten employees from one area of work.
- The circle also has a coordinator and one or more facilitators who work closely with it.

Selection of Circle Members
- Participation of members in circle is voluntary.
- Participation of leaders may or may not be voluntary.

Scope of Problems Analyzed by Circles
- The circle selects its own problems.
- Initially, the circle is encouraged to select problems from its immediate work area.
- Problems are not restricted to quality, but also include productivity, cost, safety, morale, housekeeping, environment and other spheres.

Training
- Formal training in problem-solving techniques is usually a part of circle meetings.

Meetings
- Usually one hour per week.

Awards for Circle Activities
- Usually no monetary awards are given.
- The most effective reward is the satisfaction of the circle members from solving problems and observing the implementation of their solutions.

The Myths and Facts of Quality Circles

A number of myths have grown up around quality circles and act as obstacles to utilizing worker creativity on the job. Among the most common are that quality circles are used solely to solve product quality problems, that there is a need to train only shop-floor employees because managers and supervisors already have the needed training, that the quality circle concept requires copying of every detail of the Japanese practice, and that workers in successful quality circle projects must be compensated by large financial rewards. Juran (1980) has analyzed a number of these myths and identified the associated factual situation (Table 1–2).

TABLE 1–2
The Myths and Facts about Quality Circles

Myths	Facts
The QC is to be used solely to solve problems in product quality.	QCs can be used (and are being used) to solve problems in productivity, safety and cost as well as quality. The original preoccupation with quality was for reasons unique to Japan during the 1960s.
The QC concept is applicable anywhere provided the workers are trained in problem solving.	The QC concept involves a significant amount of worker participation in decision making on matters previously regarded as solely the responsibility of supervisors. Managers must be willing to accept such participation.

The need is to train only the workers. The managers and supervisors already have all the training needed.

The training of managers and supervisors must precede that of the workers. This training is not only in the techniques but in the entire idea of how to work with QCs.

The QC is the only way ever invented to make use of the education, experience and creativity of the worker.

Nonsense. Pride in crafts and skills dates back many centuries to the days of the guilds. Even in Taylor system–type factories, ways were found to secure worker participation before the QC concept was invented, for example, the "Scanlon Plan."

Adoption of the QC concept requires copying the Japanese practice on details of application; for example, should training be done outside or during working hours; what amount of payment should be made for time spent working on projects, etc.

The need is to establish practices which are compatible with the culture. The Japanese practice evolved in response to the nature of their unique culture.

Workers associated with successful QC projects must be rewarded specially, just as in the case of useful employee suggestions.

The rewards, if any, whether financial or non-financial, must be responsive to the cultural realities.

The QC can make a major contribution to solution of the company's quality problems.

The contribution can be significant but not major. Most of the company's quality problems must be solved by the managers, supervisors and professional specialists.

Source: Adapted from J.M. Juran, "International Significance of the QC Circle Movement," *Quality Progress* 13 (November 1980): 21.

If there is only one thing that can be learned from Juran's work, it is that the Japanese quality control circles concept cannot be transplanted to other countries without modification. In fact, it requires significant modification to ensure its applicability.

In summary, quality circles are not a new panacea to cure all industrial ailments. They are a mechanism for creating the type of organization and the type of people-oriented philosophy that is needed if North American corporations are to compete successfully in world markets in the future.

Quality circle definition:
- Small group of workers.
- Group has a leader.
- Organized by work area.
- Solves problems of that area.

Assumptions underlying quality circles:
- Causes of quality or productivity problems are unknown to workers and management.
- Workers can help to solve these problems.
- Must be a people-building, not a people-using, approach.

Characteristics:
- Formal mechanism for participation of employees in problem solving.
- Helps organization to adapt to its environment.
- Eight to ten members in each circle.
- Meets regularly.
- Leader is not in an authority position.
- Facilitator assists in training and coordination.

Myths corrected:
- Not a panacea.
- Can be used to solve all types of problems.
- Training of managers and supervisors must precede that of workers.
- Only one of the many methods available that can be used to tap the creativity of the worker.
- Quality circle practices must be compatible with the culture.

2 *Quality Control Circles in Japan*

This chapter explores the development of the quality control circle (QCC) movement in Japan, its salient characteristics and particularly the underlying factors that have contributed to its success.

Since the late 1950s, Japanese companies have expended considerable effort in formulating small group teams among their workers. These have played a vital role in raising productivity, creating a workplace which is fulfilling to workers, and improving labour–management relations. Quality control circles have been one of these informal small group team concepts. Other circle activities have dealt with such objectives as zero defects, suggestions, safety and recreation. Presently 77 percent of Japanese companies with more than 10,000 employees have some type of small group team activities.[1]

Before discussing Japanese QCCs, it would be wise to remember that postwar Japan was a country which had been virtually destroyed and which had a reputation for producing cheap, poor quality products. The government was determined to change the countryside and the image: to rebuild the country into a strong nation (by reconstructing the economy based on industrial production) and to secure a competitive edge in international markets through uniformly high-quality products. This conviction, shared by some influential industrialists with foresight, was to become the driving force behind the QCC movement. Seven events made the quality control circles concept the workable and pragmatic idea that it is today:

1. The introduction of statistical quality control methods.
2. The founding of the Japanese Union of Scientists and Engineers (JUSE).
3. The Industrial Standardization Law.
4. The consulting work of Dr. W.E. Deming (see Deming's principles in Chapter 4).
5. The lectures of Dr. J.M. Juran.
6. Publication of the *Gemba* (Supervisor's Guide) to Quality Control.
7. The first International Conference on Quality Control was held in Japan.

The QC movement began during the Allied occupation years. W.G. Magil of the Civilian Telecommunications Section of the office of the Supreme Commander for the Allied Powers (SCAP) introduced statistical quality control concepts to manufacturers in the electrical communication section. The idea caught on and other members of SCAP continued to promote wide-scale adoption of quality control practices.[2]

In 1946, the Japanese Union of Scientists and Engineers (JUSE) was founded. JUSE was, and is, dedicated to studying foreign technology, launching research studies and implementing training programs. Today, it continues to be the major organizational instrument for diffusing quality control practices in Japan. It also serves as a major liaison between the manufacturing and academic sectors.

Also, under the Allied occupation, Walter Shewhart, one-time head of technical staff, Bell Telephone Laboratories, Inc., and Dr. W.E. Deming, Harvard professor and chief statistician for the U.S. Bureau of Census, were called in as consultants to assist in the reconstruction of Japanese industries. Deming's work is well cited in other publications and will not be repeated here. Suffice it to say that the Deming Prize was instituted by JUSE to commemorate Dr. Deming's contribution.[3]

The Japanese government strongly supported the quality movements. As a result, The Industrial Standardization Law was passed in July 1949. Under this law, companies that are successful in meeting quality requirements prescribed by the Minister of International Trade and Industry are authorized to use a special label on their products. Also, because of this law, the Japanese Standards Association, a strong force for quality control, was established.[4]

A short time later, in 1954, Dr. J.M. Juran, international consultant and lecturer, visited Japan to give lectures on the managerial aspects of quality control. He emphasized management's role in quality control. Influenced by his teachings, Japanese companies adopted a newer orientation. Quality control became an integral part of the management function and was practised throughout the entire organization. In effect, quality control mobilized ordinary workers into participating in the operational decision-making process.

In 1962, JUSE published the *Gemba* to Quality Control (*Quality Control for Foremen*). The publication put particular emphasis on using case studies to train supervisors. The event was significant in that it coincided with a pan-industrial[5] move for the adoption of the QCC concept. In the same year, JUSE set up the QCC head office and named its founder, Dr. Kenichi Koyanagi, as the first director. Currently, the head office administers eight chapters in eight regions and sponsors QCC conferences, seminars and company visits to promote nationwide activities.

Significant too was the first International Conference on Quality Control, held in 1969 in Tokyo. It led to the inauguration, in 1970, of the Japanese Society for Quality Control, which had as one of its prime responsibilities the strengthening of cooperation between the industrial and academic sectors. Gradually, through this society, the foundation for the organized movement was solidified, and the number of QCCs registered with JUSE grew phenomenally (from a total of 1,000 in 1964 to 115,254 in December 1980.[6] (See Table 2–1.) Indeed, in

TABLE 2–1

Number of Members and Quality Control Circles in Japan (By Selected Years)*

	Circles		*Participants*	
Year	Number	Percent Increase Over Previous Three-Year Period	Number	Percent Increase Over Previous Three-Year Period
1962	23			
1965	4,930	21,334.8	70,920	
1968	17,416	253.3	212,134	199.1
1971	42,366	143.3	472,421	122.7
1974	65,477	54.6	664,458	40.6
1977	86,189	24.0	836,448	25.9
1980	115,254	33.7	1,062,759	27.6

*Note: Data are as of December. Raw figures have been provided by Japanese trade consulate.

1982 it was estimated that as many as one out of every eight Japanese employees was participating in a QCC or some small-group activities.

QCCs in Japan have not only proliferated but have also been fruitful. The QCC movement has significantly improved product quality and spurred productivity. Juran (1980) summarizes the results thus:

Collectively, the millions of improvement projects have saved enormous sums of money, running into many billions [milliards] of dollars. These same projects have significantly improved the saleability of Japanese product [sic] by removing numerous sources of customer dissatisfaction. Through such great saleability, the companies become more competitive, which makes the workers' jobs more secure.[7]

This achievement is reflected in the Japanese world-wide industrial trade surplus of over $76 billion in 1981. During the same year, the U.S. had a deficit of $28 billion.[8] Japan has succeeded because there is an all-out effort to seize world leadership in quality, and this, in no small measure, is attributable to the QCC movement.

People, Organizations, and Events Which Have Made QCCs Workable
- Introduction of quality control methods
- Japanese Union of Scientists and Engineers (JUSE)
- Industrial Standardization Law
- Dr. W.E. Deming
- Dr. J.M. Juran
- *Gemba*
- First International Conference on Quality Control

The Characteristics of Japanese Quality Control

The preceding section has examined briefly the development of quality control and quality control circle activities in Japan following the war. This section will examine the unique characteristics of the concept. Ishikawa, founding father of the quality control circle movement, describes six salient features of Japanese quality control. These are: (1) company-wide quality control, (2) emphasis on education and training, (3) QCC activities, (4) application of statistical methods, (5) the quality control audit, and (6) nation-wide quality control promotion activities.[9] Each of these concepts is described in more detail below.

Company-Wide Quality Control and Total Quality Control

Total Quality Control (TQC), proposed in 1961 by V.A. Feigenbaum, Secretary, Quality Control Coordinating Committee of General Electric, is "religion" in Japanese firms. As one Japanese executive commented: "QCC are not effective without TQC; 'circles' must be a way of life, not something extra." Unlike traditional statistical quality control, the TQC concept posits the overall management of quality control. Thus TQC embraces product design and development, sales and after-sale servicing. In fact, the proper objective of TQC is to eliminate quality control, that is, to have quality control "built in" and not "inspected in."[10]

To meet this objective, quality control policies are specified as corporate strategy. They are

reflected in the way top management policies are transmitted and implemented throughout the organization . . . . Once top management policies are established . . . the policy is deployed down to the lowest level, and its progress is checked, on a regular basis, again using the common statistical and factual data.[11]

In other words, quality control involves all facets of design and production and all employees in upgrading quality and maximizing corporate resources.

An Emphasis on Training

Japanese companies train workers to do the quality control checks. The training is given by company instructors. The in-house training sessions are specifically aimed at different company echelons such as middle management, engineers, supervisors and operators. As an example, Appendix 2 illustrates a breakdown of a quality control training program in Toyota Motor Company.

JUSE, the Japanese Standards Association, the Japanese Management Association, the Japanese Productivity Center, and several other organizations conduct seminars on quality control. In addition to regular technical training and education, some companies sponsor trips and sessions whereby supervisors, senior workers and new employees participate in exchanging views and examining new ideas.

Japanese companies place particular emphasis on training supervisors. The content of these training programs (as summarized by Ishikawa, 1968) includes:
* administrative training (an integral part of the in-company training program which is given to all employees)
* simple statistical methods for analyzing and carrying out shop improvements
* an emphasis on practical (as opposed to academic) training and the study of real cases
* teaching that is tied closely to the given firm's own technology
* participative management techniques.[12]

The absence of professional quality control experts in Japan makes training extremely important. Since quality control is not an established profession, it is very difficult, if not impossible, to assign experts to all departments actually involved in the implementation of quality control. Furthermore, most companies refrain from using experts to solve work group problems because work groups are regarded as independent social entities and are endowed with considerable autonomy in decision making. The use of experts would be regarded as outside interference and would undermine employee morale and leadership. All employees therefore are taught quality control methods. This, in turn, diminishes the need for specialists or industrial engineers.

Quality Control Circle Activities

A large number of Japanese workers have had twelve years of formal education (nine are compulsory). No real differences exist, therefore, in the basic skills of employees among the major Japanese companies. How adequately a firm can draw on the capabilities of workers depends on the personnel policy of that organization and upon the leadership exhibited by management. QCC activities make employee motivation and commitment a reality at the actual working level. This is achieved through company-wide instruction and training of employees at all levels within the organization.

Most Japanese companies organize quality control circles as shown in Figure

FIGURE 2–1

Typical Quality Circle Organization in Japan

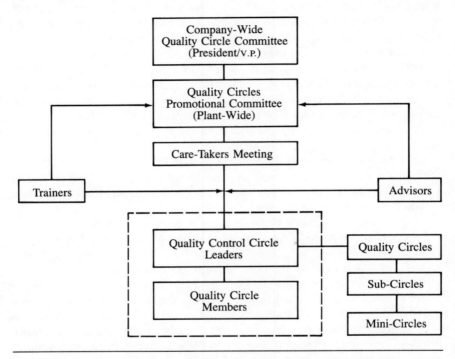

Source: Sud Ingle, *Quality Circles Master Guide* (Englewood Cliffs, NJ: Prentice-Hall, 1982): 19.

2–1. There is a quality control circle committee which is headed by the president or vice-president, a plant-wide promotional committee, a care-takers group, advisers and trainers. Supervisors are generally quality control circle team leaders. It is not unusual to have mini-circles working on one specific aspect of a problem nested within sub-circles which work on some broader aspect, nested within the QCC as a whole, which works on the total problem. For example, the circle may be working on rust prevention of a particular area on a car, the sub-circle may decide to examine the corrosibility of the various metals used, and the mini-circle may be studying the impact of a particular acid on one metal.

An example, Sankyo Seiki Manufacturing Company, is given in Figure 2–2. This company sets up a formal hierarchy to administer small group activities. The hierarchy is composed of four committees—the standardization committee, the rust-prevention committee, the training committee and the quality control circle offices. Each division has its quality control organization which is chaired by the divisional manager and which is under the overall supervision of the

FIGURE 2–2

Q C C Organization of Sankyo Seiki Manufacturing Company

At present, a company-wide Standardization Conference is being formed outside the Q C C.

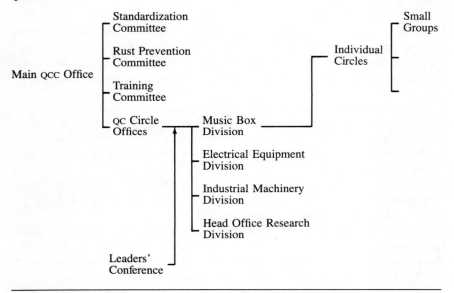

Source: Toshiharu Yokosawa, "The QC Circle Movement Applied to Shop Requirement," in *Japan Quality Control Circles* (Tokyo: Asian Productivity Organization, 1982): 192.

quality control circle office. Further, each division forms its own QCC, which is supervised by a section chief.

Application of Statistical Methods

To minimize quality problems, it is necessary to observe the relevant phenomena closely and to analyze objectively the relationship between the numerous factors affecting product quality and any changes in that quality. For this purpose, statistical methods can be used extensively as an analytical tool and therefore are included in quality control training programs. (According to the authors of Toyota's and JUSE's training programs, for example, statistical methodology is one of the most important parts of quality control training.)

Like quality problems, other job-related troubles may be caused by managerial ignorance, misunderstanding or faulty analysis. Statistical methods are again crucial in the diagnosis of symptoms and identification of problems. Highly sophisticated statistical methods are not needed. In fact, most Japanese companies use comparatively simple methods like the "seven basic tools of quality control"—(1) Pareto diagrams, (2) cause-and-effect diagrams, (3) histograms, (4) check sheets, (5) graphs, (6) scatter diagrams, and (7) control charts—to solve workshop problems.

Quality Control Audits

In Japan it is quite usual for top management, especially the presidents and general managers, to provide leadership in quality aspects of production. Accordingly, large Japanese companies normally establish a quality control audit committee at the strategic apex to review comprehensively policy matters such as:

- What should be the quality mission of the company?
- What are the key product qualities (as seen by clients?)
- As to these key qualities, what is the company's competitive position?
- What opportunities does the company have for quality improvement and reduction of quality-related costs?
- What can be done to make better use of the human resources within the company?
- What competitive threats are developing?[13]

In the structural sense, the committee is simply an integrating mechanism designated to coordinate QC activities, to scan environmental opportunities and threats, and finally to promote liaison contacts within the organization. As a result, the company can achieve synergistic effects in production.

Nation-Wide Quality Control Promotion

Japan is not endowed with natural resources. It also is harassed by typhoons, earthquakes and tidal waves. The Japanese see themselves as a "ship at sea" and feel that they must work together to keep the ship afloat. Both government and enterprise recognize that the improvement of productivity is the key to survival in international competition. Indeed, John McAllister (staff executive for product quality at General Electric), who participated in a Technology Transfer Institutes exchange in 1979, claims:

The only way it [Japan] can survive is by importing its food and resources and exporting high contributed-value goods. To do that, its products have to be regarded as of high quality . . . . [This] is a strategic requirement for national as well as business success.[14]

This urge for international survival is an instigating factor in forcing Japan to make an all-out effort to seize world leadership in quality. Quality control circles are a key activity in this effort.

CHARACTERISTICS OF JAPANESE QUALITY CONTROL

Total company commitment to quality.

Promoted nation-wide.

Emphasis on training:
• All workers learn to perform quality control checks.
• Supervisors are especially important.

All workers learn statistical control methods.

Management performs frequent quality audits.

QCC activities are well organized.

Factors Contributing to QCC Success

What is the secret of QCC success? Many factors are involved: (1) the culture, (2) the national and organizational structure, (3) the industrial relations and personnel systems, (4) the extensive educational and training programs, and (5) the technology. Figure 2–3 uses an Ishikawa diagram to illustrate these factors.

Japanese Culture and Society

Japan has been characterized as collectivity-oriented or group-minded (*Bonsai*). Traditionally, the individual and the contribution of the individual have been de-emphasized. This is founded on the conviction that the energy produced by the collectivity brings the most effective results. Because the overriding principle of teamwork is *Bonsai* (harmony), employees share *Gemeinschaft* (group values) and strive for *Ikiga* (a worthwhile life) while achieving company goals.[15]

Japan is also a paternalistic society. The nature of this paternalism can be more fully expressed by two Japanese expressions—*Kigyō ikka* (one family enterprise) and *Kigyō wa unmei kyodotai de aru* (the enterprise and its employees share a common destiny). Japan's culture is built on the teachings of Confucius—respect for parents and ancestors, kindliness, faithfulness, intelligence and proper behaviour—and the philosophy of *amae*, a nurturance and dependency relationship between superiors and subordinates. Thus large organizations are concerned about the welfare of all employees.[16]

These paternalistic practices mean committed employees. Workers develop a company spirit, identify with the company, and are loyal to it. As Reischauer observes:

FIGURE 2–3
Factors Which Contribute to Success of the Japanese QCC Movement

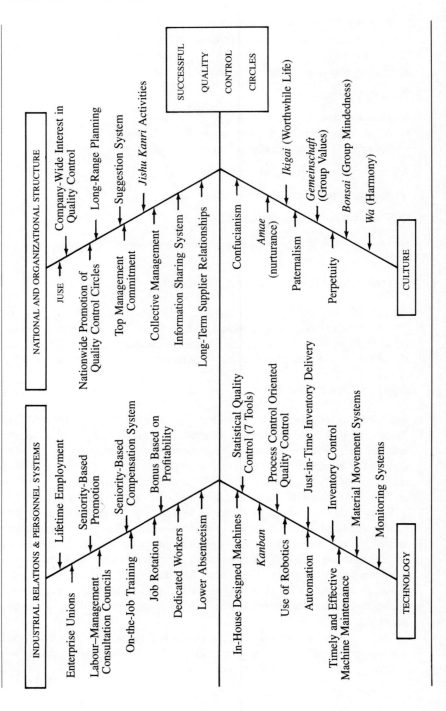

There is little of the feeling, so common in the West, of being an insignificant and replaceable cog in a great machine. In other words, there is no loss of identity but rather a gaining of pride for both workers and executives through their company, particularly if it is large and famous.[17]

The company is a familial social group to which employees have total emotional and psychological commitment.[18] It is this culture, this collectivism and this commitment and loyalty to the organization that sustain and expand the QCC movement.

The National and Organizational Structure

National structures exist which encourage quality control and quality circles. There is a nationwide promotion of the concepts. The Japanese Union of Scientists and Engineers awards the Deming and other prizes for outstanding company achievement. Among companies, including competitors, there is a sharing of information regarding new techniques and methods. For most large companies, a long-term relationship with suppliers exists. Suppliers are expected to meet specific standards but, in exchange, have a guaranteed long-term commitment. At the organizational level, there is company-wide interest in quality control. This results in quality circles, *jishu kanri* and other small group activities, and in the promotion of various types of employee suggestion systems.[19]

The *ringi* system of decision making is utilized: consensus is sought among all those who are affected by a decision prior to its implementation. Once consensus occurs implementation of a change is very quick.[20] In North America, on the other hand, it takes a considerable length of time to introduce a change.

Senior managers also are committed to quality control. They ensure that long-range planning and the enforcement of quality control practices occur on a company-wide basis. Support is not of a token nature. In fact, no money or effort is spared in this cause. The efforts, commitment and experiences of top management are translated into daily activities. At Meindensha, for example, both the president and board chairperson took part in study sessions on the subject of quality control circles before the concept was instituted. Their attitude clearly showed to the entire body of employees what the company was doing and the direction in which it was heading. Similar leadership of QCC movements is shown by other top Japanese executives.

The Industrial Relations and Personnel Systems

Japan has unique industrial relations and personnel systems. There is no inherited class-conscious union militancy, like that which is found in the United Kingdom. Unions generally are cooperative in promoting quality control and quality circles within the work setting. Although they have very little input into the decision-making process, union leaders seldom adopt adversarial positions. A number of factors may contribute to this.

First, although Japanese unions are patterned after those in the United States, there are some differences. One important difference is that Japanese unions are enterprise unions, that is, they are organized by company rather than around crafts or industries. Each business enterprise has its own union. Larger industrial federations do exist; their activities, however, are mostly limited to distributing information and coordinating the bargaining policies of their affiliated unions for the Spring Wage Offensive (*Shunto*).[21]

Second, in order to moderate the labour movement, management encourages foremen,[22] supervisors, and white-collar workers below the managerial level to join unions. This has narrowed the gap between management and the rank-and-file worker, and thereby the gap between management and union.

The Japanese style of "bottom-up management," where decisions are made primarily by employees and junior managers and handed up the hierarchy, instead of being made by top management and handed down, is another key factor. Union members are not as removed from the source of decision-making power. In fact, managers may have been union members just a few years previously and therefore are much better able to understand the union's situation. Additionally, there are fewer levels within the hierarchy than in most large North American corporations.

A fourth important factor that affects the union–management relationship is the nature of Japanese management philosophy. A key part of this philosophy is a concern for the welfare of employees. As Jiro Tokuyama, Director of Nomura Research Institute, commented, "Japanese management is more personalized. On many occasions, management will do more for the employees than it has to do—more than the contract requires."[23]

A key aspect of this philosophy is the lifetime employment system. Layoffs or dismissals of permanent employees are rare. When business slows, permanent employees are kept on the job. If necessary, companies obtain monetary assistance from the government. Also, employees displaced by new technology are retrained for new jobs.[24]

Japan's personnel policies might seem strange to North Americans. In addition to lifetime employment, there is seniority-based promotion and seniority-based remuneration in the early years of an employee's career. Wages depend not only on level within the organization and seniority but also on need. A married man who has a large family to support receives, at least in theory, more financial remuneration than one with no family, even if they are both at the same hierarchical level and have equivalent seniority.[25] (In reality, the dependency allowances are likely to be small.)[26] There is also a bonus system which is based on the profitability of the company. The Japanese believe in training generalists rather than specialists. Job rotation, therefore, is frequent. As a consequence of these personnel policies, employees are more committed and absenteeism is low.

This job security has other important implications. It is possible that in return for lifetime employment and other benefits, workers generally do not insist as strongly on other rights. Other observers of the Japanese environment argue that this kind of commitment to the worker has earned the trust and loyalty of employees, and that this trust consequently is the reason why unions do not insist on a greater role in decision making. As Bryon (1981) notes, ''The workers trust their bosses to make the right decisions because there is a pervasive sense that both labor and management are working together.''[27]

The feelings of cooperation and trust and the lack of alienation among employees may be attributable to the relatively homogeneous and classless society that exists. According to opinion polls conducted by the Prime Minister's office in 1980, 90 percent of Japanese consider that they are middle class. Four percent identify themselves as upper class; and about 6 percent feel they belong to the lower class.[28] Much of the cooperation and trust in labour relations may be associated with this social stability.

Also, there is little class consciousness in Japanese labour–management relations. This is reflected in the fact that the union leaders often become executives in later years. Indeed, a position as a union officer is seen by many as a way to demonstrate the leadership ability needed to become a good manager. As the 1981 Nikkeiren report, based on a survey of 313 corporations, shows, one out of six Japanese executives once served as a leader of an employees' union. Of the 6,121 executives, 992 or 16.2 percent were previously union leaders.[29]

In summary, the structure of unions and union membership, together with paternalistic management and personnel practices, tend to lessen the militancy of unions. Second, cultural homogeneity and bottom-up decision making have helped diminish the feelings of powerlessness and alienation that could lead to employee demands for a larger role in the decision-making process.

Extensive Educational and Training Programs

In Japan, it is widely believed that the success of small group activities has been achieved through the improvement of the educational level of the workforce (94 percent have graduated from senior high school; 36 percent from colleges and universities).[30] Both government and enterprises have expended considerable effort in providing training courses. For example, the Japan Productivity Center has been conducting ''productivity seminars'' for youth leaders. Some unions even use productivity seminars as part of their training programs for union executives.

Japanese companies also concentrate on training junior leaders. Every year, the Junior Executive Council of Japan conducts a ''sea cruise training session.'' Fumio Imamura, managing director of the Council, explains why such training is important:

A good piece of fabric is always made of two threads—the warp and the woof, the horizontal and vertical threads. Similarly, a healthy organization must have both formal and informal threads. The vertical threads are the managerial hierarchy . . . . The informal or horizontal are represented by voluntary participation in the numerous small groups of which the company is comprised. It is at this level that corporate policy is discussed and implemented. That is why we need to develop junior leaders who can induce participation and commitment from other members.[31]

Furthermore, Japanese workers often take the initiative to participate in training programs. For instance, several hundred workers of Matsushita gave up a day of their own time, without being paid, to attend lectures sponsored by Kanto Subdivision on how to improve quality control.

The massive training effort is not only a salient characteristic of Japanese quality control circle movements, but also is a decisive factor in making them successful.

Technology

The use of technology is important to Japanese industrial success. Four approaches contribute to this technological effectiveness: attitudes toward robots; machine design and upkeep; inventory delivery and control; and statistical controls.[32]

First, machines are designed in-house. Quality control circles suggest required tolerances and the necessary capabilities of robots and other automated equipment. They also request that robots replace workers so that more effective production can occur.

Every member is responsible for minor machine maintenance and for ensuring that major problems are corrected quickly. Timely and effective maintenance of all equipment is key.

The inventory delivery and control system is very different. Suppliers bring raw materials and parts to the plants three or four times per day, that is, through a *kanban*[33] re-order system just in time to be used within the production process. Parts are perfect or near perfect; little allowance is made for variance from the required tolerance levels. (Defects are measured in parts per million.) The movement of materials within the plant is watched closely to ensure that shortages or product build-up do not occur.

Circles are involved in these activities and in the correction of malfunctioning processes.

Other Advantages of Quality Circles

Small group activities have other advantages, namely:
1. Setting group objectives creates a sense of teamwork.
2. Group members share and coordinate their respective roles better.

3. Communication is improved between labour and management, as well as between workers of different ages.
4. Morale is greatly improved.
5. Workers can acquire new skills and knowledge and develop more cooperative attitudes.
6. The group is self-initiating and undertakes problem-solving tasks which would otherwise be left up to management.
7. Labour–management relations are greatly improved.[34]

QCC management also achieves the following effects:

- People grasp the real issues more rapidly.
- More emphasis is placed on the planning phase.
- A process-oriented way of thinking is encouraged.
- People concentrate on the more important issues.
- Everybody participates in building the new system.[35]

To assist members to perform their duties, workers learn process control and monitoring and the seven tools of statistical control. Skills are reinforced within the circles.

WHY ARE QCCs SUCCESSFUL IN JAPAN?

Culture
- Collectivism
- Paternalism

Nation-wide promotion of concept

Unions
- Company, not craft or industry.
- Include supervisors and white-collar workers.
- Participate in decision making.
- Union leaders often become managers.

Management philosophy

Practice of lifetime employment

Training of junior leaders

Members involved in technological decisions

And the Shortcomings?

No business endeavour is perfect, and the Japanese QCC approach does have shortcomings. In principle, participation in a circle is voluntary, but in many companies, peer and management pressure pushes participation rates for workers to 90 percent or more. Cole, commenting on this problem, states:

[I]t is known that there is tremendous variation among companies and industries in how voluntary those activities are; in most companies with circles, there is strong pressure on all workers to belong to quality circles. Not to do so would suggest to management a lack of commitment to corporate goals and thereby damage one's promotion prospects. There are companies that have quota systems—so many suggestions per circle, so many suggestions per month—which are hardly models of voluntarism.[36]

When this occurs, QCCs become a burden rather than a motivational scheme. There is a lack of spontaneity; the circle becomes unproductive and inactive.[37]

Other problems also exist. In some companies, QCC participants complain that the involvement of quality control or production engineers is excessive. Moreover, some companies place greater emphasis on productivity than they do on the development of worker potential.

Another significant problem is that participation tends to become ritualistic once it loses its spontaneity. As time passes, it becomes more difficult for group members to identify new problems to attack. As a solution, some Japanese companies, such as Suzuki Motor Company, have introduced evaluation systems to revitalize QCC activities and to promote worker participation (see Chapter 11).[38]

The last problem is that unions have not become involved in the group activities. In most instances, unions act only as monitors of the movement. Thus, in the future, as QCCs become more established and as the results of their efforts are more difficult to quantify, activities may need to be monitored more closely or promoted with the positive participation of company unions.

This chapter has presented a study of how the Japanese have skilfully woven modern Western industrial methods into the technical fabric of quality control and quality circles. From all these movements, a pattern of industrial strategy has emerged which is uniquely Japanese.

SHORTCOMINGS IN SOME ENTERPRISES

Participation is not always voluntary in every firm.

Involvement of production engineers may be excessive.

Participation becomes ritualistic.

Unions are not involved.

3 *Quality Circles in North America*

During the past ten years in North America, companies have been plagued with problems of stagnating productivity, unemployment and job insecurity, consumer dissatisfaction, worker alienation and low morale. On the surface, none of these problems seems to be directly related to product quality. So why a quality control circle movement?

The "catching up with the Japanese" syndrome serves as one of the major catalysts of the movement. As North American industries lag in productivity, especially in the automobile industry, American managers search for clues by looking at the techniques used by their Japanese competitors. They focus upon Japanese-style management with its stable labour–management relations, high labour productivity, superb quality control and the like. In this sense, American managers recognize the underlying benefits of involving workers in the workplace and the implications of involvement for motivation. On the surface, it becomes sensible to emulate Japan's productivity tour de force.

Other American observers are still skeptical about the practicability of quality circles in U.S. industries. They speculate that the quality circle (QC) movement is only a fad. As Edgar H. Schein explains:

One of the greatest strengths of U.S. society is our flexibility, our ability to learn. When we see a problem, we tinker with it until we have it solved, and we seem to be willing to try anything and everything. One of our greatest weaknesses, on the other hand, is our impatience and short-run orientation. This leads to fads, a pre-occupation with instant solutions, a blind faith that if we put in enough effort and money anything is possible.

Institutionalization of QCs requires long-term commitment, resolute implementation and patience. In this chapter, an examination of the development of quality circles in North America is made. The history and salient features are described and the basic reasons that have led to these conditions are examined. The chapter also indicates some of the problems that might be encountered when companies install quality circles.

The Developmental Pattern of Quality Circles

Although quality circles are rapidly gaining momentum in U.S. industries, the literature tends to be more popular than documentary. The first U.S. firms to adopt the full QC concept were Lockheed Missile & Space Co. Inc., a Sunnyvale, California division of Lockheed Aircraft Corporation,[2] and Honeywell Corporation.[3]

At Lockheed, after learning about the concept from a visiting Japanese team and consulting with Dr. J.M. Juran, international consultant, Missile System Division Manufacturing Manager Wayne Ricker arranged for a number of employees to tour eight Japanese firms. They were impressed and reported that quality circles were effective in motivating workers by enriching their jobs and increasing their sense of participation. The report also noted the strong support which senior management gave to the program and the involvement and commitment of workers in the plant. As a result, Lockheed established the first circle in October 1974. By the end of 1975, there were fifteen circles, and by 1977, thirty were to be found in production, research and development, machine, electronic and composite shops.

Although some managers and workers were reluctant to participate, those who did were generally enthusiastic. The results were impressive. By 1977, Lockheed estimated that circles had saved them $3 million. The number of defects per 1,000 hours caused by the manufacturing process declined by two-thirds. Late in 1976, the firm conducted a survey of members of two circles. They found that morale and job satisfaction had improved.

Honeywell too established its first circle in 1974. Since 1974, about 400 such groups have operated—mostly in an effort to improve quality of working life. The results indicate that both financial and human gains have occurred. An extensive 1982 study of seven divisions of the company found that there is improved communication between employees and supervisors, an interest in working toward organizational goals, a commitment to the organization, and an increased sense of individual self-worth. The study also suggests that professional quality circles tend to be less successful and that participants who have experienced failure tend to be more reluctant to participate in additional circles.[4] On the whole, QCs at Honeywell have worked well.

Since that time, other companies of different sizes, industries, and technologies have accepted the circle idea. Among the early pioneering companies were Metaframe Corporation, Smithline Instruments Inc. and the United States Envelope Company. Growth of the circle movement in America started slowly; only about twenty-five companies were involved in 1978. The rate of growth increased, and the number of organizations that were exploring circles leaped (see Appendix 3). By 1980, there were at least 6,000 circles in the United States and signs that many people were viewing circles as a panacea (which they are not). In Canada, the institution of quality circles is just beginning (see Appendix 4).

In truly American fashion, a variety of consultants has sprung up to implement quality circles, and the circle philosophy is now a regular feature of seminars offered by leading management organizations. The International Association of Quality Circles was set up exclusively to promote the spread of the concept. It is currently being restructured to carry out these activities in a more professional manner, with a Board of Directors composed primarily of company representatives from user organizations. As of winter 1982, the Association has some 5,400 members who represent individual member companies and seventy-three chapters. Its various training programs, conferences and publication activities have provided a major source of information to those who want to learn about quality circles.

The American Society of Quality Circles (ASQC) and the Technology Transfer Institute (TTI) are also rapidly moving toward a stronger commitment in supporting quality circle activities. In particular, TTI serves to facilitate the exchange of technical information and professional skills between Japanese and American businesses, and also sponsors international study missions to Japan to provide Americans with first-hand information on quality control and quality circle activity. In short, the publicity campaigns which diffuse quality circle practice are beginning to develop and accumulate momentum.

As the movement is still in a developmental stage, it is too soon to try to determine its significance. Despite numerous reports that quality circles are beneficial, it is felt, in view of the short time that has elapsed, that the findings are incomplete and perhaps even inconsequential. Any conclusions could be premature, controversial and misleading.

HISTORY OF QUALITY CIRCLES IN THE U.S. AND CANADA

1974—Lockheed Missile & Space Co. sets up its first quality circle.

1974—Honeywell Corporation establishes its first quality circle.

1980—There are over 6,000 circles in the United States.

1984—In Canada, nation-wide spread of idea is just beginning.

Organizations committed to spreading the concept:
• American Society of Quality Circles
• Technology Training Institute
• International Association of Quality Circles

The Characteristics of North American Quality Circles

Americans have "reborrowed" the Japanese quality control concept and have adapted it to fit the unique business environment in North America. During the adaptation process, some notable features have evolved. These are: (1) QC organization and structure, (2) the use of facilitators, (3) union involvement, (4) voluntary participation, (5) extensive use of external consultants and (6) white-collar circles.

QC Structure vs. the Formal Hierarchical Structure

In the developmental phase, in order to ensure that resistance to change will not develop, management may introduce few major changes. There may be no radical organizational or managerial innovations. Quality circles are established as a number of committees or task forces. Although orientation and training in the concept increases, these activities generally are perceived as a normal function of all organizations. As the process evolves, however, a separate organizational structure is required if the program is to be responsive and if it is to maintain its vitality and continuity. What emerges is a formal quality circle organization which exists alongside the formal bureaucratic structure (Figure 3–1).

The typical hierarchical organization has a series of functional leadership levels which range from presidential to unit supervisor ranks. Each level is assigned authority, and has responsibility, for work performed by employees at levels subordinate to it. The quality circle organizational structure, on the other hand, is much flatter. It is administered and coordinated by a steering committee whose members include middle management (directors, functional managers and departmental managers), union leaders and, in a liaison position, at least one facilitator or coordinator. At the second hierarchical level are facilitators who, as the name implies, assist but have no authority over, or responsibility for, the core people in quality circles—the circle leaders and the circle members.

The contrast between the two can be better understood through an examination of Stein and Kanter's parallel-structure concept (Figure 3–2). The hierarchical bureaucratic structure is geared to routine operations, that is, it focuses primarily on functional mass-production activities in which employees perform fixed job assignments according to objectives established by senior management. They are competent for these jobs prior to assignment. For this, they are provided with limited developmental and promotional opportunities but receive reasonably generous compensation in the form of pay and benefits. Leadership in this organization is based on level within the organization.

By contrast, the parallel structure is that adopted by quality circles. It is, ideally, a

vehicle for creating new ways of flexibly grouping people providing the possibility of

FIGURE 3–1

Quality Circle Structure Compared to the Formal Hierarchical Structure of a Typical North American Company

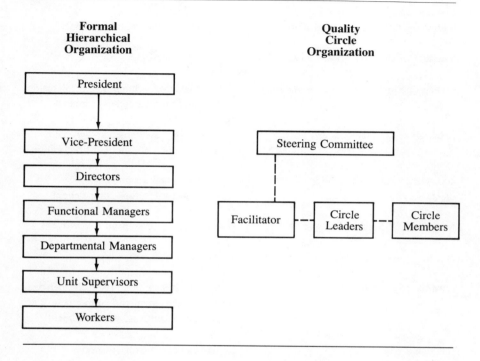

challenge, learning and growth [opportunity] and for opening access to resources, support, and recognition.[5]

It focuses on the non-routine and on high uncertainty. Circle members have flexible job assignments and identify, develop and solve those problems that are important to them and their work tasks. Ideally, objectives or specifications are also bottom-up; there is little or no chain of command. The assignment has expandable learning opportunities and the circle members are able to increase their competencies as the situations demand. Rewards are both extrinsic (financial incentives) and intrinsic (recognition, visibility by more senior management, an ability to learn new skills, personal growth and development, and self-fulfill-ment). Leaders are those who have the expertise or who have been chosen or recognized by the group.

It must be pointed out that the quality circle organization is not an ad hoc committee. It exists as part of the total organization, yet operates independently

---

FIGURE 3–2
Characteristics of Bureaucratic and Parallel Organizations

Bureaucratic Organization	Parallel Organization
routine operations; low uncertainty	problem-solving; high uncertainty
focused primarily on "production"	focused primarily on "organization"
limited opportunities (e.g., promotion)	expandable opportunities [e.g., decision making within the quality circles]
fixed job assignments	flexible [job assignments]—problem identification and [problem] prevention
competency established before assignment	developmental assignment [assignment develops competency]
long chain of command	short chain of command
objectives usually top-down	objectives also bottom-up
rewards: pay and benefits	rewards: recognition, visibility, personal growth, development learning new skills, financial incentives, self-fulfillment
functionally specialized	diagonal slices—mix functions
leadership is a function of level	leadership drawn from any level

---

Source: B.A. Stein and R.M. Kanter, "Building the Parallel Organization: Creating Mechanisms for Permanent Quality of Work Life," *The Journal of Applied Behavioral Science* 16 (1980): 385.

and continuously to achieve its designated goals and purposes. Furthermore, it is organic in nature; workers temporarily group together to study work-related problems. Participants are not limited by their positions and occupations. Circles may be dissolved or organized at any time. In an effort to encourage dialogue between management and workers, a new set of organizational relationships and a new reporting system is established. The comunication structure is modified so that information flows up as regularly and freely as it does down; power is redistributed to give workers more decision making in areas which concern them. In sum, the quality circle organizational structure is designed to be adaptive and responsive to both internal and external environments.

FIGURE 3–3
Quality Circles Organization

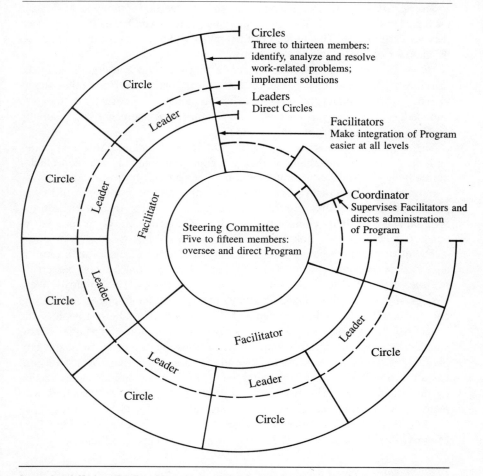

Circles
Three to thirteen members:
identify, analyze and resolve
work-related problems;
implement solutions

Leaders
Direct Circles

Facilitators
Make integration of Program
easier at all levels

Coordinator
Supervises Facilitators and
directs administration
of Program

Steering Committee
Five to fifteen members:
oversee and direct Program

Source: Joseph Hanley, "Our Experience with Quality Circles," *Quality Progress* 13 (February 1980): 24.

The Organization of Quality Circles

North American companies normally organize quality circles in the manner
depicted in Figure 3–3. This usually includes a steering committee, coordinator,
facilitators, leaders and circle members. The *steering committee* is the focal point
or central hub. Under its direction, policies and procedures for the program are
established and implemented. The committee then oversees the operation period.

The committee is normally composed of management and union. For example, at Cordis Dow, the steering committee includes two department managers, a union leader, group leaders, production workers and an engineer.[6]

The *facilitators* are the liaison between the steering committee and circle leaders. They oversee and keep abreast of all activities within the circle for which they are responsible. The number of facilitators within the company depends on the number of circles within the plant.

Circle leaders are responsible for conducting meetings and coordinating the activities of the individual circle. In most cases, under the facilitator's supervision, leaders conduct the training of circle members to ensure that they are knowledgeable in the various methods of identifying, analyzing and resolving problem situations brought before them.

The *coordinator's* position is generally the last to be added. Most companies omit this position, especially if their programs are limited. The coordinator normally supervises the facilitators and provides administrative backing.

Industrial engineers and plant managers continue to have a dominant role in production planning, quality control and coordination. The quality circle organization and the quality control department work together closely in an effort to ameliorate conflict and to attain synergistic results.

The quality circle organization of the Toronto-Dominion Bank, in Toronto, is an excellent example (Figure 3–4). The president, R.W. Korthals, personally oversees the overall activities of the T.D. quality program. The Employee Work Groups (EWG) are coordinated through the steering committee. A full-time coordinator, Ron Sinclair, has been added to assist in the administration of the program. The division support team serves as the in-house consulting team, which is responsible for promoting EWG among management and bank employees. Each branch (such as Bathurst and Steeles of the Metro West Division) has a full-time facilitator to provide training, information and resources needed by the groups. Each EWG is made up of six to ten volunteer members who meet, with the group leader, for one to one-and-a-half hours every week.[7]

More detailed studies of two other successful quality circle organizations, Ford Motor Co. of Canada and Vickers, Inc., appear in Chapters 12 and 14.

Involvement of the Union

Because the relationship between companies and unions has been traditionally adversarial, most management teams do not proceed with the implementation of quality circles without consulting and getting the support of the union. To do so would defeat the participative principles which the program is attempting to promote and invite a confrontational approach on cooperative issues. The consultation and involvement begins with the planning phase. Union leaders are invited to encourage their members to join the circles. The majority of union executive officers also provide valuable contributions to make the endeavour successful. Some union officials, however, are cautious about endorsing the

FIGURE 3–4

Toronto-Dominion Bank Quality Program Organizational Chart

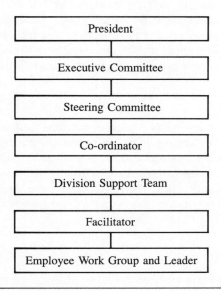

```
┌─────────────────────────────────────┐
│             President               │
└─────────────────────────────────────┘
                  │
┌─────────────────────────────────────┐
│        Executive Committee          │
└─────────────────────────────────────┘
                  │
┌─────────────────────────────────────┐
│         Steering Committee          │
└─────────────────────────────────────┘
                  │
┌─────────────────────────────────────┐
│            Co-ordinator             │
└─────────────────────────────────────┘
                  │
┌─────────────────────────────────────┐
│        Division Support Team        │
└─────────────────────────────────────┘
                  │
┌─────────────────────────────────────┐
│             Facilitator             │
└─────────────────────────────────────┘
                  │
┌─────────────────────────────────────┐
│   Employee Work Group and Leader    │
└─────────────────────────────────────┘
```

Source: *Toronto-Dominion Quality Programme Introductory Kit* (Toronto: Toronto-Dominion Bank of Canada, 1982): 10.

plan. They feel that, historically, management almost always has been concerned with increasing productivity and net output. New ideas have been used as gimmicks to trap workers into greater productivity. Management and unions alike, however, do see the importance of a cooperative effort to meet foreign competition, especially that of the Japanese. Because their welfares are intimately intertwined, both groups are more willing to work together. Generally, there is agreement that ''something must be done to close the chasm between management and labor in this country. It is an adversarial and counter-productive atmosphere . . . .''[8] Essentially these joint efforts help institutionalize quality circles and protect against their discontinuity.

In a number of companies, management installed circles with only a bare minimum of consultation with unions. When this occurred, union leaders put pressure on workers not to cooperate, and the circle either did not get off the ground or collapsed soon after it had started. On this point, Widtfeldt of Honeywell notes: '' . . . we never go into a plant without explaining thoroughly to everyone, union and rank-and-file workers, what QC are all about. There really is nothing about QCC that impinges on the negotiating process in any case.''[9] Union participation is critical in making the program successful.

Voluntary Participation

Worker membership in most American quality circles usually is voluntary, but supervisors who appear to have potential as circle leaders are encouraged to participate. In some companies, during pilot runs, management invites selected workers to become members to ensure that the first few circles are successful. Generally there are more than enough initial and new volunteers. At the present time, there is seldom peer pressure to join, as there is in Japan.

Extensive Use of Consultants

In forming quality circles, many American companies ask external management consultants to help in planning, in designing training packages and in providing training for circle facilitators and leaders. Sometimes consultants may act as the "buffer" between management and union in establishing communication and facilitating reconciliation. In a recent survey by the American Management Association, 65 percent of companies surveyed had employed consultants to help on a portion or on all of the circle activity.[10]

White-Collar Circles

A number of firms are experimenting with quality circles for staff, office and professional personnel. Others are establishing union–management circles. Westinghouse, for example, has set up ten white-collar quality circles under the construction group in which controllers, personnel directors and marketing directors discuss common problems with their counterparts in other units. The details of an engineering quality circle at Vickers Inc. are given in Chapter 14.

The concept is even being used in banks. Continental Illinois National Bank and Trust Company of Chicago established a management circle or "horizontal team circle" for managers of eleven divisions to address problems on a departmental scale. These management circles have four main advantages. They:
1. Serve as a model to demonstrate management support.
2. Provide managers with a problem-solving structure.
3. Address problems that cannot be resolved at lower circle levels.
4. Communicate corporate-level goals.[11]

CHARACTERISTICS OF THE QUALITY CIRCLES PROGRAM

Both a quality circle structure and a formal hierarchical structure exist side by side.

Quality circle structure:
• flat

- flexible job assignments
- short chain of command
- bottom-up objectives
- leadership drawn from any level
- rewards are intrinsic

Is part of the total organization but operates independently.

Is organic.

Organization includes:
- steering committee
- facilitator
- circle leader
- circle members
- perhaps a coordinator if there are many circles

Union must be involved.

Participation is voluntary.

External consultants are used frequently.

Staff, office and professional circles function in North America.

Factors Contributing to Problems

If there is only one lesson which companies using quality circles have learned, it is that Japanese methods do not work in North America. In order to make the concept workable, adaptation is required. Problems generally occur for one or more of the following reasons: lack of senior management commitment, lack of support of middle management, an adversary relationship between union and management, a poor implementation process, an inadequate clarification of objectives and roles, and inadequate feedback to employees.

Lack of Senior Management Commitment

To every manager who is judged by the bottom line, the idea of improving profits and productivity is tremendously appealing. Companies too frequently seek an elixir. Success stories regarding quality circles suggest that they may be a magic potion which need only be imbibed. So, a management announcement states that Jason Williams will be in charge of the quality circle program. A bewildered but pleased Williams searches the literature and phones his more knowledgeable friends and acquaintances. The anticipated or fantasized results fail to materialize. Management blames Williams and the program is allowed to die a slow death.

This situation recurs far too frequently. Commitment is more than the budgeting of monies, establishment of committees or recruitment of people to oversee and participate in the meetings. It involves time, interest, a specific management philosophy regarding the worth of employees, and last, but most important, patience.

Many writers have suggested that the key is Theories X and Y versus Theory Z. Theory X and Theory Y are two different beliefs about human nature that *influence* managers to adopt one strategy of managing people rather than another. Theory Z is a management strategy.

Theory X assumes that human nature is basically evil. Employees therefore are indifferent, irresponsible, lazy, untrustworthy and incapable of self-direction and self-control. The manager who subscribes to this theory persuades, rewards, punishes and controls subordinates. McGregor (1960), the originator of the concept, argues that this is the philosophy of most American managers.

Theory Y is a very different philosophy (but not the opposite to Theory X). The assumption is that human nature is basically good. This means that if employees are provided with the right type of opportunities, they will respond in positive and constructive ways and will blend their personal goals with those of the organization.[12]

Basic to Theory Z are three concepts: the collective work ethic, trust and loyalty. At the organizational level, this translates into teamwork, the merging of individual and organizational goals, collective decision making, group sacrifice in times of adversity, and implicit group control of each employee (see Figures 3–5 and 3–6). Theory Z philosophy can be and is practised in North American companies, namely IBM, Intel, Procter and Gamble, and Hewlett-Packard.[13]

To implement Theory Z philosophy throughout a company requires money, executive time and executive interest. If the program is important at the executive level, it will be important down the hierarchy. If it is not, that message also is transmitted quickly. One of the best methods of transmitting the message is by the assignment of funds—for training, for materials, for learning to use the process, for release time and perhaps to make some mistakes.

Last, but most important, patience is required. An individual must learn to crawl, walk and run before becoming an award-winning athlete. So, too, circle members need time—to absorb the techniques and skills, to learn to work together, to decide on a problem to study, to analyze the issues, to reach a satisfactory consensus, to implement the decision, for the "bugs to be ironed out" and for visible results. This process may take two or three years. If the groundwork is properly laid, subsequent projects will show results after a short time.

What about a pilot project? Pilot projects either do not work, or work too well for all the wrong reasons. When a company begins with a pilot project, it is communicating that it doesn't feel this activity is going to be successful. Such lack of confidence generally is the kiss of death. Sometimes employees, enjoying the attention and limelight which they are receiving, ensure that the experiment

FIGURE 3–5
Douglas McGregor's Theory X and Theory Y Assumptions

Two Sets of Assumptions or Propositions Concerning Management's Task of Harnessing Human Energy to Organizational Requirements

Conventional View: Theory X   *A New View: Theory Y*

1. *A Proposition Common to Theories X and Y.* Management is responsible for organizing the elements of productive enterprises—money, materials, equipment, people—in the interest of economic ends.

2. With respect to people, this is a process of directing their actions, modifying their behavior to fit the needs of the organization.

2. People are *not* by nature passive, or resistant to organizational needs. They have become so as a result of experience in organizations.

3. Without this active intervention by management, people would be passive—even resistant—to organizational needs. They must therefore be persuaded, rewarded, punished, controlled—their activities must be directed. This is management's task. We often sum it up by saying that management consists of getting things done through people.

3. The motivation, the potential for development, the capacity for assuming responsibility, the readiness to direct behavior toward organizational goals are all present in people. Management does not put them there. It is a responsibility of management to make it possible for people to recognize and develop these human characteristics for themselves.

4. The average man is by nature indolent—he works as little as possible.

4. The essential task of management is to arrange organizational conditions and methods of operation so that people can achieve their own goals best by directing *their own* efforts toward organizational objectives.

5. He lacks ambition, dislikes responsibility, prefers to be led.
6. He is inherently self-centered, indifferent to organizational needs.
7. He is by nature resistant to change.
8. He is gullible, not very bright, the ready dupe of the charlatan and the demagogue.

Source: Douglas McGregor, *The Human Side of Enterprise* (New York: McGraw-Hill, 1960).

FIGURE 3–6
Theory Z Management

Comparison of American-Style Management and Japanese Management Using Theory-Z Philosophy

Japanese Organization	*American Organization*
1. Lifetime employment	1. Short-term employment
2. Slow evaluation and promotion	2. Rapid evaluation and promotion
3. Non-specialized career paths	3. Specialized career paths
4. Implicit control mechanisms	4. Explicit control mechanisms
5. Collective decision making	5. Individual decision making
6. Collective responsibility	6. Individual responsibility
7. Holistic concerns	7. Segmented concerns

Making Theory Z Work

1. Managers should understand Theory-Z organization and individual roles.
2. Periodic audits of company philosophy should be made.
3. The desired philosophy should be defined clearly.
4. The desired philosophy should be implemented by creating both structures and incentives.
5. Employees must be encouraged to develop interpersonal skills. Managers must also develop interpersonal skills.
6. The union should be encouraged to become involved.
7. Stabilize employment through the use of temporary employees. The majority of the work force should be permanent employees.
8. Evaluate employees over a lengthy period of time. No one can perform at a one hundred percent level all of the time.
9. Employees should be encouraged to have broad career paths.
10. Managers should seek out areas to implement employee participation.
11. Managers should permit the development of a holistic relationship.

Source: Based on William Ouchi, *Theory Z: How American Business Can Meet the Japanese Challenge* (Reading, MA: Addison-Wesley, 1981).

---

is perceived by senior management as a success. That, after all, is what management wants!

What is needed, of course, is the opportunity, every hour of every day, for employees to collaborate in problem-solving situations with the knowledge that they will succeed. What then is in doubt is not whether success will occur but the extent of that success.

Lack of Middle Management Support

For most American managers, the quality circle concept involves an extensive delegation of authority to rank-and-file employees. This delegation means that there is a diffusion of the prerogatives to which management has clung tenaciously in the past. Middle management and industrial engineers especially dislike the idea because they fear a loss of job security. Other managers believe that they have the responsibility, that they are in control, and that the contribution of workers is marginal. As one manager who was interviewed stated: "I've worked my ass off for fifteen years to get where I am. Why should I give it up? Why should I help some guy who hasn't known the tough times I have to do my job and make me look bad?" As a consequence, they tend to resist introduction of any participatory management.

What can be done to overcome this? A number of ideas come to mind:

1. Fear occurs because of misunderstanding. Thorough training in the philosophy and the process will remove some of the insecurity.

2. Thorough training in quality circle skills needs to be provided for these managers. This will mean that they will be as qualified as are the circle members.

Presently, in most factories, rank-and-file workers learn basic technical skills which assist them in performing their production tasks. They are not trained in problem solving or statistical analysis. This training is reserved (if done at all) for members of the specialized quality control department and for managers.

When circles begin to function, "quality control disciplines" are required. As a consequence, plant workers have the opportunity to learn these techniques. Supervisors, however, are often ignored. The superior knowledge of the workers often adds to the insecurity of the supervisory group.

3. Middle management and engineering staff can be trained for and assume new challenges, jobs and responsibilities. Numerous researchers have shown that power within an organization is not finite.[14] In fact, executives have discovered that the more responsibility they ask subordinates to assume and the more authority they give them, the more powerful and respected they themselves become.[15] The process, of course, must start at the top.

4. Middle management should be encouraged to form its own quality circles.

5. Senior management can make a commitment that no one will be terminated because of quality circle improvements.

Adversarial Relationship Between Management and Union

Management maintains that it is using quality circles in order to humanize the workplace. Unions, however, are nervous and skeptical of this claim. At least four factors, in the past, have impeded labour–management cooperation. First, most older union executive members remember the broken promises of the past. They also are committed to familiar ways and dislike change which threatens their power. Second, they believe managing the company is management's business. In this sense, leaders feel it best to remain aloof from management because unions have no real control over final decisions. Third, in the fear that they will be seen as being "in management's pocket" and fail to win re-election, union leaders are discouraged from establishing too close or too compatible a relationship with management. Fourth, most unions feel that improving productivity implies line "speed-up" and hence layoffs and decreased union membership. Finally, the popularity of quality of working life (QWL) programs with many non-union corporations has reinforced the feeling that keeping unions out is the real "hidden agenda" of QWL and QC programs. Typically, most American managers have shown little concern for their employees. As observers of labour–management issues often note: "The two sides of the American industrial equation are workers to be exploited by managers and managers to be sabotaged by workers." In this atmosphere, it is extremely difficult, but necessary, to promote a harmonious relationship and a feeling of trust. Management, because company well-being is its responsibility, has the onus of establishing open communications between management, workers and the worker representatives.

Implementation Process

Other reasons why quality circles experience problems have to do with the implementation process:
1. The training of members in analytical skills and, more importantly, in interpersonal skills, is superficial. Sometimes, an organization makes the mistake of training only leaders. It then expects the leaders to train circle members. The ability to train and to prepare educational materials are specialized skills. This, for the majority of individuals, requires many years to develop. Confidence is difficult to attain. Circle leaders generally do not have these skills. The leader must also know when to provide training. If the leader provides it at a time when it is not needed, he or she is "hogging the show"; if, on the other hand, it is to be provided at the exact time that it is required, the leader must be infinitely ready—a task which is viewed with misgivings by even professional trainers!
2. Training of management is at the orientation level, and these members do not understand the process or the difficulties. If management is truly committed, it can show this by being willing to participate in the full training program. It must be remembered that, in Japan, presidents and rank-and-file employees, even of large corporations, study the same topics. This suggestion is not as unreasonable or time-consuming as it might seem. Members of management, because they are more experienced and better educated, require a much shorter time to learn the same skills.
3. A poor choice of facilitator is made. The facilitator must be the type of person who is capable of training and developing people. The preferred individual is one who can assist in the "processes" and leave "content" to those who are more closely associated with the problem. Also, facilitators may become over-

extended. There may be too many circles within the organization for one facilitator to coordinate. To make matters worse, because of their skills, these people are invited to become external consultants to suppliers and consumers of the organization.

The conflict-of-interest issue may be one problem. A second one is that the overextended facilitator is not available when required and is unable, physically and emotionally, to provide the type of assistance and support that a circle leader and members may require.

4. A poor choice of members for the steering committee is made. As pointed out previously, the steering committee is key to the success of the program. It follows therefore that the members must be committed to its philosophy and concepts and that all major interested parties must be represented. If the union and the shop-floor workers participate in top-level decisions that affect them, they will feel more committed to the process.[16]

An interesting and novel approach to this problem has been adopted by Cumis Insurance Company, of Burlington, Ontario. Ernie Long, the company's former facilitator, reports:

We have provided some flexibility in the membership of the steering committee. Each circle elects one representative to sit on the committee. With five permanent members, this may appear cumbersome. In reality, it works well; the actual size of the committee rarely exceeds ten. Circle members tend to go to a committee meeting only when they have a vested interest in the agenda. The advantage, however, is that each circle knows that it can influence decisions insofar as they could be affected by the decisions.[17]

Lack of Readiness

Some external consultants, particularly those who have been trained in quality of working life methodology, insist that an organization must be "ready"—that an atmosphere of trust and willingness to cooperate must exist before a quality circle program is started. Of course, the probability that a program will succeed is enhanced when these preconditions exist. As the study, reported later in this book, of Ford Motor Co. of Canada indicates, improvement in relationships and cost-saving benefits can occur even if the organizational climate is not ideal.[18] Key management, union personnel and circle participants must be willing, however, to expend the time and effort required to make quality circles work. Without either climate or commitment, the circle program will be in difficulty.

Objectives and Roles

A frequently heard complaint of circle members is that the organization has not implemented problem solutions that have been suggested. Generally, however, there is another side to the story. The quality circle has extended itself beyond its authority and boundaries and has made decisions regarding work and practices which were not directly within its control and of which it had little first-hand knowledge. The issue is further complicated by the fact that those who were not only most knowledgeable but also most affected by the decision were not consulted. Such a solution can lead only to disappointment and disillusionment with the process; it cannot be implemented.

To avoid problems of this type, it should not be assumed that circle members can set objectives and roles that are compatible with quality circle principles. Of course, they can be taught to do so. At the beginning, however, circle objectives and roles, together with guidelines, should be clarified and clearly communicated prior to the inauguration of the first circle. If these are broad in scope, they will not be stifling or overly restrictive and will permit the circles to learn and grow on their own. Generally, this is the role of the steering committee. The facilitator may be required to explain tactfully why a circle cannot "solve" a particular problem or to ensure that appropriate steps are taken to include those who will be affected by the decision. In the long run, each circle should be permitted to determine its own roles and objectives within the broader organizational framework which has been determined by the steering committee.

Feedback

A recent study of a large Michigan heavy equipment firm[19] indicates that a quality circle program within the company can be extremely successful but may not be perceived as successful. In this company, substantial cost savings were occurring, quality was improving, and attitudes toward the organization of those who were participating in quality circles had improved. Suggestions were also being implemented. Of course QC members knew about the success of their own limited improvements. Since they did not hear otherwise, they assumed that the activities of their circle were the only benefit to the company and that the program was not a company-wide success. Unfortunately, because of a lack of recognition and because the program did not appear to be important to the company, a number of participants became discouraged and stopped attending meetings.

Management, in this case, made a deliberate decision not to publicize QC improvements. The company wanted to play down the quantitative aspects of the success and preferred that attitudinal changes evolve slowly. Of course, there is merit in this viewpoint. In this case, however, employees within the firm, other than those who were involved in quality circles, were not aware that a quality circles program existed.

What has been described is a frequent problem. The steering committee and the facilitator are so busy making the program function satisfactorily that they forget that feedback and recognition also are important to the success of their efforts.

FACTORS WHICH CONTRIBUTE TO PROBLEMS

Lack of senior management commitment. For success:
- Management must believe employees want to do and can do a responsible job.
- Money is required.
- Executive time is required.
- Patience is required.

Lack of middle management support. To overcome this:
- Thorough training is needed.
- New challenges should be assigned to this group.
- A promise should be made that there will be no terminations because of quality circle improvements.
- Management should receive training similar to that which quality circle members receive.
- Management should be encouraged to form its own quality circles.

Management has responsibility to improve the adversarial relationship which exists between management and union. Reasons for distrust on the part of the union include:
- Past trickery.
- Old habits.
- Role differences.
- Fear of not being re-elected.
- Feeling that quality circles are just another method for obtaining increased productivity without benefit to workers.

Implementation process is poor. Present practices should be improved. These include:
- Training of circle participants is minimal.
- Training of management is at orientation level.
- Poor choice of facilitator is made.
- Poor choice of members for steering committee is made.
- Lack of readiness.
- Feedback inadequate.
- Objectives and roles are unspecified.

4 A Comparison of Japan and North America

Differences and Similarities

Before a system that works in one culture can be transferred and translated into a second culture, it is important to understand the differences and similarities between the two cultures. The Japanese culture is fundamentally a paternalistic one; the American culture is based on middle-class entrepreneurial values. The dominant goal of the key elite in Japan is the preservation of the traditional society; in America, it is individual self-advancement.

It must be remembered also that, for the most part, the Japanese people are racially homogeneous. This contrasts with the American melting pot of nations. Many Americans retain the national cultures and values of their immigrant ancestors. Superimposed on this are dominant racial groups. In the United States, people of black and of Spanish ancestry have distinct cultures. In particular geographical areas, these cultures are the majority. Canada has its French and native cultures. Heterogeneity means that there exists a large variety, not only of different cultures and values, but of very different methods and argots. Even communication can be a problem.

Values and Human Relations

There are important value differences between the American and Japanese cultures. Japanese firms are people centered, not task centered. This does not mean that production is unimportant. On the contrary: the paternalism, the group values and the company dependency of employees ensures that the company and its productivity are uppermost in the minds of employees (See Table 4–1).

Also, Japan is a small nation with a large population. People live in relatively crowded quarters. Because of this, group and community interests are paramount, and cooperation and harmony are stressed. In addition, the extended family and the traditional benevolence of Japanese firms provides greater security and less necessity for a keenly competitive individual work orientation. As one writer explains:

46

TABLE 4–1

A Comparison of Japanese and American Systems

Values and Human Relations

Japanese

Basic value and strategy of key people is preservation of traditional society.

Homogeneous race of people.

Extended family system.

Education system is very specialist oriented and geared to life's work; education is key to access of prestige and initial position.

Closed social system; class structure is rigid.

Social and economic status are dependent on traditional organization standards. Organization for which one works and "school ties" are extremely important. Little job mobility.

Company interests supersede family interests.

Groupism, i.e., the group comes first; the individual is devoted and loyal to the group. Mutual dependence and *schicksalgemeinschaft* consciousness.

Blending of the firm's goals and the individual's life goals. Sense of being, prestige, security and morale tied to company and to company's prestige and prosperity.

Stress on harmony in human relations (emphasis on warm human relations, mutual consent of all members, and community relationships).

American

Basic value and strategy of key people is individual self-advancement.

Heterogeneous peoples.

Nuclear family system.

Education system is liberal in nature; education is key to vertical mobility.

Open social system; class structure is fluid.

Social and economic status are dependent on size of organization and on hierarchical level attained. "School ties" of some importance. Through ability and entrepreneurship can attain wealth and prestige; therefore intense individual competition.

Purpose of life resides in the family and in leisure.

Individualism, i.e., ultimate value is on the individual; devotion and loyalty to the group are weak.

To the individual, the firm is nothing more than a means to obtain wages. To the firm, the individual is a resource similar to machinery or raw materials..

Human relations are artifical relations for work purposes; cease outside the company.

| Egalitarianism in substance (little chance for class discrimination; small earnings differentials). | Egalitarianism in theory (strong class consciousness; competition for equal opportunity). |

Patriarchial management in Japan retains the socially responsible characteristic of the traditional kinship system. Although it gives little encouragement to individualists and indeed individualism is frowned upon if not actually punished, each member of the organization is regarded as an integral and important cog in the functioning of the whole enterprise. Conformity to the purpose of the unit rests upon fostering and structuring the situation to achieve complete identification between superior and subordinate.[1]

Japanese people accept their role within society. The social system is closed, and the class structure is rigid. Education, therefore, is important in assisting an individual to obtain a managerial position with the most prestigious government organizations, banks and companies.[2] This keen competitiveness begins with kindergarten. If one goes to the best kindergarten and is successful, one can go to the best primary school, to the best junior high school, the best high school, and the high-status universities such as Tokyo Imperial University. The high suicide rate among the young has been directly attributed to the competitiveness of the educational system and of family expectations.[3]

In North America, by contrast, the nuclear family is important and life is directed toward the family. An open social system exists and, except in the minds of the "old families," is extremely fluid. Instant status and prestige can be achieved by becoming "nouveau riche" through ability and through entrepreneurship. Also, America is a relatively new nation which was built on the rugged individualism of its pioneers. Individual accomplishment has always been glorified and rewarded. There is little incentive for group-mindedness. Equal opportunity, at least in theory, is available to each person within the North American system.

The wage system also rewards individualism. Unions have ensured that the worker is paid relatively well and that the work is not too difficult. Incentive and bonus systems, except at upper echelons of an organization, are not common. Group incentives are seldom paid. As a consequence, no reason exists for employees to cooperate and to work together.

The education system prepares people, in the English tradition, not to be workers, but, through its general approach, to be leaders and managers. The education system itself is not highly competitive; instead, the self-fulfillment and development of the individual is stressed. Funding, through loans and grants, is available to help all who have demonstrated minimal qualifications to attend a university or a college.

Company management also has a different value orientation regarding employees—they are considered a replaceable and dispensable resource, just one cog in a multi-cog production process. It is not surprising therefore that relationships established between employees within the company are work related and not social in nature. The company is a place to obtain wages to purchase more valued commodities.

In summary, the Japanese system tries to preserve the existing society. Groupism and stress on harmony in human relations is important. The mutual dependence and the group-value consciousness means that individual goals and organizational goals blend. In North America, acceptance of the firm's goals by employees is rare. There is a stress on the individual, and on improving one's own well-being. The social system is fluid, and "school ties" are of only minor importance.

VALUE SYSTEMS

	Japan	*North America*
Key strategy	Paternalism	Entrepreneurship
People	Homogeneous	Heterogeneous
Basic concern	People	Tasks
Orientation	Group and harmony	Individual
Social system	Closed and rigid	Open and fluid
Family	Extended	Nuclear
Education	Specialized	Liberal
Employees' feelings about firm	Oneness with firm	Place to earn money

Labour–Management Relations and Personnel Systems

What do these values and human relations practices mean in terms of labour–management relations and the personnel systems that exist?

Labour–Management Relations. In Japan, unions are company unions (Table 4–2). For the most part, there is cooperation between the executive members and management. Conflict is abhorred, and the union assumes the role of keeping workers in line. The union also organizes social functions. Wage negotiations do not cause problems at the workplace; negotiations occur on a national basis during the *Shunto* (spring wage offensive). Strikes are political in nature and of short duration, and occur during employees' lunch hours or in their own time after work. Few work rules are written into the "collective agreement"; because management has all the rights, only general rules exist. Trust between union executive members and management and between management and workers is nurtured. This means that there is a desire to experiment, to innovate and to learn together. In short, in the majority of manufacturing companies, Japanese unions do not impose a constraint on management.

For North American managers, this approach on the part of unions would be akin to paradise. North American unions are organized by craft, industry or discipline, and generally there is more than one union (or at least more than one local branch of a union) in each company. Each union or local protects its own members and its own work territory. Strikes, when they occur, are directed against the management of the organization and tend to close the plant. After a strike begins, the union–management relationship tends to deteriorate, and bargaining positions become more rigid. As a consequence, strikes in North America tend to be of long duration. Some have lasted six months, eight months or even a year.

The union may organize social functions; its primary purpose, however, is to attain a reasonable portion of the gains in productivity and to protect individual rights. Since conflict between union and management is expected, a set of ground rules has been established by which both parties agree to abide. Negotiations are conducted at a national or local level—if the company is large, at both levels. To protect the rights of workers, a grievance and arbitration process exists. To ensure equity at the workplace, a detailed set of rules has been established. Most of these are negotiated, but management, through the "residual rights of management," can specify additional regulations. If the union believes these regulations are unjust, it can grieve them. Bargaining power, game playing, and "fishmarket haggling" strategies create an adversarial relationship where suspicion and distrust abound. Unions do impose a constraint on management (Table 4–2).

TABLE 4–2

A Comparison of Japanese and American Systems

Personnel Systems and Labour–Management Relations

Japanese	*American*
In the large firms, there is lifelong employment, i.e., there are no layoffs. Flexibility is gained through part-time and temporary employees.	Employment of people only at times when needed; layoffs in recessionary times.
Seniority-based promotion system. Evaluations for promotions are comprehensive and stress not only work results but incentive, effort and perceived capability.	Seniority system at times of promotion and layoffs at lower levels. Political system in promotion at upper management levels.
Career progress is slow.	Career progress rapid in early years.

Wage system is based on seniority and age. About one-third of wages are based on bonus system which depends on profitability of the company.

Wages are based on classification, position, negotiating ability and power. Incentive systems are rare.

Enterprise assumes obligation for welfare and benefits.

Pension and welfare plans regulated by government and subject to negotiation.

Extensive mobility within organization. Little mobility to different organizations; individual is dependent on company.

Extensive mobility; individual is independent of company.

Extensive employee training and education; training is work directed.

Training and education is primarily responsibility of the individual; reimbursement of expenditures often possible.

Employees are generalists.

Employees are specialists.

Acceptance of robots, innovation and decreases in number of employees.

Resistance to robotics, innovation and decrease in number of employees.

Labour unions are organized by company; cooperation between labour and management.

Labour unions are organized by craft and job type; unions safeguard the rights of the individual.

Role of unions—social functions, keeping workers in line; little constraint on management.

Role of unions—political in nature, keeps management honest at the local level; protects rights of individual worker; considerable constraint on management.

Nature of conflict—political strikes, of short duration, on worker's own time.

Nature of conflict—strikes against enterprise to gain concessions; could be lengthy in nature.

Conflict abhorred; unions participate in management through labour–management councils, etc.

Conflict accepted within rules of game; much tension in labour–management relationships.

Spring wage offensive (*Shunto*) at a national level.

Negotiations every 1 to 3 years at national and local level.

General rules at workplace.

Detailed rules at workplace mostly specified in the collective agreement.

Trust nurtured

Adversarial relationship nurtured.

Desire to experiment and learn together.

Games of one-upmanship.

Personnel Systems. In large companies in Japan, there is lifelong employment; that is, permanent employees are not laid off or terminated. Incompetent employees are given less desirable and less challenging tasks or assigned to smaller firms. Flexibility is gained through the use of part-time and temporary workers. Usually, workers over the age of fifty-five (fifty-seven in some firms) and women are temporary workers.

Large Japanese industries practice a just-in-time inventory policy, that is, they minimize the

time from initial entry of parts and raw materials to their actual use. As much as possible, in-process stocks [are] eliminated or reduced to the absolute minimum. Both inventory costs and labor time on materials handling are considered as surplus and thus waste.[4]

This means that fewer people are hired in materials management, and that employees in small or supplier firms could be subject to greater employment variability depending on the needs of the large firm.

Career progress is slow. Evaluation of employees is lifelong and promotion is based on work results, employee incentive and effort, perceived capability and seniority. Older workers are given preference over younger workers for promotion. This leads to some dissatisfaction among the younger men. In spite of this, there is no mobility of managerial employees to competitive organizations and little from one large firm to another large firm. The mobility that does occur is among younger employees who transfer from the large enterprise to smaller firms—usually subsidiaries of the parent company.

This does not mean that employees become narrowly specialized. There are extensive training and education programs within the enterprise. Transfers from one functional area to another functional area within the company are frequent. Employees therefore become generalists, knowing a great amount about the entire organization, rather than specialists, who know almost everything about a particular aspect of operations. When jobs are eliminated, workers are retrained and placed in new positions.

Japan is also unique in its approach to compensation. The employees' welfare and benefits are the responsibility of the enterprise. Wages are based on seniority, position, age and need. About one-third of the wages are dependent on the company bonus system. The bonus system depends, in turn, on the profitability of the firm. This means that the financial well-being of the employee's family, its self-esteem and its prestige depend upon the success of the firm.

It is not surprising in this environment that employees should accept organizational goals, robotics and innovation and not resist the elimination of jobs and the retraining of employees.

In contrast, in North America the Protestant work ethic is important. Workers are given the opportunity to work and to receive wages that will provide them with a life of dignity and comfort. They are, however, engaged on a contractual basis and are retained on the payroll only as long as the company is profitable and their services are required.

Career progress is relatively rapid in the early years. Promotion is on the basis of seniority at lower levels, and on a political basis at the upper levels. While performance appraisals exist, these are subjective in nature and often lack validity and reliability. Their usefulness is therefore limited. As a result, selection for promotion is based on the key organizations which the individual has joined, the activities which have been performed and a variety of personal characteristics such as the ability to enhance the career of some senior official.

Dissatisfied employees join competitor firms and other allied companies. Training and education are the responsibility of the individual. Companies do have some internal training programs, and unions have negotiated for reimbursement of educational expenditures. Generally, specialized training is important and employees tend to remain in one, perhaps two, specialized disciplines during their career with an organization.

Wages are based on classification, on position within the hierarchy and on the individual's or union's negotiating ability and power. Benefits and pension plans are regulated by governments and are subject to negotiation between management and the union.

Unions make the argument that a resistance to innovation and change (for example, the use of robotics) is built into this "dog-eat-dog" system. Productivity increases through technology or innovation generally come at the expense of jobs. As one manager so aptly put it, "Oh, we don't want the [products] to be defect free. If there aren't enough repairs, we'll lose employees. Already we have lost two this year."

Summary. Japanese unions cooperate with enterprise management. Trust is nurtured. The relationship between North American unions and management is more likely to be adversarial in nature.

The personnel systems of the two countries are also very different. Career progress is slow in Japan, rapid in North America. Promotions in Japan are based on a lifelong evaluation system; in North America, they are based on political considerations. Wages in Japan are a combination of salary (based on seniority, age, need and position) and bonus. In North America, salary is based on discipline, level within the organization, seniority and negotiating ability and power. Japanese enterprises train their workers; in North America, training is each person's own responsibility. While Japanese employees accept innovations, robotics and retraining, North American employees, perceiving that their jobs will be threatened, resist them.

LABOUR–MANAGEMENT RELATIONS

	Japan	*North America*
Union	Company	Craft, industrial, by discipline
Conflict	Abhorred	Expected within rules of game
Role	Keep workers in line	Protect work of members
	Plan social functions	Protect rights of individuals
		Obtain gains of productivity
Wage negotiations	National	National and local
Strikes	Limited	Prolonged
	Political	Against management
	On workers' own time	Close plant
Rules at workplace	General	Detailed
Trust	Extended and nurtured	At times and in certain organizations, non-existent
Strategy	Build trust	Power and game playing
Constraint on management	No	Yes

PERSONNEL SYSTEMS

	Japan	*North America*
Employment	Lifelong for permanent employees	Contractual
	Temporary work force	
Career progress	Slow	Fast
Mobility to other firms	Minimal	Considerable
Mobility between functions	Considerable	Limited
Orientation	Generalist	Specialist
Wages	Salary and bonus	Salary; based on negotiating power
Training	Extensive programs	Responsibility of individual

Organizational Structure and Managerial Practices

The organizational structure and the managerial philosophy in Japan are different from those of North America (see Table 4–3).

TABLE 4–3

A Comparison of Japanese and American Systems (Organizational Structure and Managerial Principles)

Japanese	American
Organizational Structure	
Organization is people centered, not functionalism centered.	Organization is production oriented. People are a dispensable commodity.
Firm is a partnership among shareholders, managers and workers. Stress is on cooperative teamwork.	Work system is based upon individual input. Jobs are specialized through design, and each individual does only own job.
Indeterminate and fluid job descriptions; a generalist orientation.	Clearly defined job descriptions, authority and responsibility; specialist orientation.
Every worker is an inspector.	Inspection teams are built into the work staff.
Japanese-style adaptation of modern bureaucracy. Few staff resources which are isolated from line functions. "Desk" jobs integrated fully into line management. First-line supervisors report directly to plant managers.	Pyramid-shaped bureaucracy. Many staff departments and "desk" jobs. Supervisors never report directly to plant managers.
Key managerial positions are preserved for family members or "the school" graduates.	Key managerial positions are political in nature.
Managerial Practices	
Management has long time horizons.	Management has short time horizons.
Long-range planning. Labour is a fixed cost, therefore production and marketing strategy must be carefully determined.	Many fire-fighting and crisis-coping techniques.
Harmony and stability emphasized.	Creativity and environmental coping emphasized.
At workplace, worker is treated as an equal. Kept informed of prices, technological advances, competition.	Management feels that shop-floor worker lacks intelligence, is incapable of contributing and is unwilling to do so.
Paternalistic concern for welfare of subordinates and ensuring that individuals can "save face."	Concern for self-preservation (colloquially known as "covering your ass").

Emphasis on production—cost economy, quality control and product simplicity.	Emphasis on marketing and creating a changing consumer need.
Experience curves and product cycles are linked.	Experience curves are a marketing tool.
Quantity of suggestions is important. Training assists employees to improve suggestions. Ninety percent are usable.	Quality of suggestions is important. Few suggestions are used.
"Work smarter, not harder" philosophy.	Work hard and be consistently perfect.

The Japanese firm is a partnership among shareholders, managers and workers. People are important. They in turn ensure that productivity occurs. Few employees work in a purely staff function; the "desk" jobs have been integrated fully into line management. Job descriptions are very fluid; every worker shares responsibility for all the jobs that must be done. A good example of this is the fact that every worker is an inspector. Also the formal organizational hierarchy is much flatter; the first level supervisor reports directly to the plant manager.

North American firms, by contrast, are production oriented. Employees are dispensable. The structure is tall and pyramid-shaped. This bureaucracy has many staff positions and "desk" jobs. Responsibility, authority and jobs are clearly defined. Too, jobs are highly specialized. Each employee therefore feels responsible only for his or her own task. Inspection teams and quality control units try to ensure that standards are maintained.

Managerial principles under which companies in the two countries function are in many ways bipolar. In Japan, harmony and stability in operations are emphasized. The Japanese also have a longer-term outlook. Because labour is a fixed cost, a production and marketing strategy that maximizes this resource over the long run must be determined. At the workplace, workers are treated as partners. They are kept informed of technological advances, competitors' strategies, prices and other marketing and production matters which concern "their" product.

The suggestion system is vital to productivity goals. Quantity, not importance, of suggestions is stressed. As a consequence, the number of suggestions received is high. Toyota, for example, received 17.9 suggestions per employee in 1980 and adopted close to 90 percent of these. This compares to a meagre 0.84 suggestions per employee per year and an adoption rate of 23 percent for General Motors Corporation. In Japan, financial incentives for suggestions are small (ranging from a few dollars to less than five hundred dollars). In 1980, for example, for 25 million suggestions worth 10 billion dollars annually, companies paid only four billion dollars.[5]

At Nissan Chemical, for the first five years in which an *Ai* (all members' ideas) movement has been in operation, the return on investment has been considerable. For the first three years, the movement produced 928 suggestions for a total cost savings of 600 million yen ($2,400,000 U.S.). The implementation cost was only 125 million yen ($500,000 U.S.)—an ROI of 5:1. In 1981, 987 proposals realized a cost savings of 630 million yen ($2,520,000 U.S.) on an expenditure of 160 million yen ($640,000 U.S.). This ROI was better than 4:1. At the time of writing, management's target cost savings for 1982 was the equivalent of $4 million on an investment of $800,000. It appears that suggestion systems are good business in Japan.[6]

Production, with its corresponding emphasis on cost economy, quality control, and product simplicity, is more important than marketing. One of the techniques used for this purpose links product life cycle and economies of scale. McMillan explains this concept (experience curves) thus:

. . . indicates that not only do total average costs per unit decline logarithmically with each doubling of output, but also that fast growth produces a learning effect . . . there is more widespread understanding . . . [that] aggressive marketing in foreign markets can improve productivity and unit cost structures.[7]

The Japanese management philosophy can be summed up in two mottos, "be prepared for the future" and "work smarter, not harder."

North American management normally has short time horizons and emphasizes creativity and coping. A large amount of managerial time is spent fire fighting and managing crises. Because responsibility lies with one individual, in some companies considerable time is spent in self-preservation (i.e., in ensuring that if something goes wrong, the manager cannot be blamed for it).

The marketing department is key in any consumer-oriented organization. An emphasis is placed on creating consumer demand for a current product and ensuring that this preference changes as the product changes.

Since management frequently believes that shop-floor workers lack intelligence, are incapable of contributing to improving the company, and, in any event, are unwilling to do so, the idea is that workers should work mechanically—hard, consistently and accurately. The following statement by a young training director is typical of this attitude: "Those dumb girls can't be taught anything; they do nothing right." Many of those "dumb girls" were thirty-five to fifty-five years old, ran successful households, managed investment portfolios, had responsible positions within community clubs and projects, had worked with the company for many years and probably knew more about the company than the young training director did. It did not occur to the company that employees at all levels require an opportunity to express an opinion and have a decision-making role in the work they do.

So, the prince found Cinderella (well, quality circles) and everyone lived happily ever after? No. Unfortunately, the management of that large, successful, well-known company, whose net profits are dropping, and the management of many other companies are still convinced that their management people have all the answers and that their shop-floor people do not understand the problem and could not and would not contribute to its solution if they did.

Perhaps a more receptive suggestion system might help. In North America, substantial compensation (e.g., a new car; up to $20,000) can be received for a quality suggestion. In spite of this, most companies receive relatively few usable suggestions. The organizational structure and process often hinder suggestion submission. One young man expressed the feelings of many North American employees with this story:

My suggestion was accepted. I received $5,000 in company shares or in a bond—my choice. Wow, was I happy—until the end of the month. I had chosen a bond but discovered that I could not cash it for six months. In the meantime, income tax deductions for the additional $5,000 of income were being taken from my paycheque. I'll never write another suggestion!

The stories and the reasons differ but the conclusion is the same: No more suggestions!

It is unlikely that the Japanese have more intelligent and conscientious employees than can be found in North America. It is more likely that the Japanese have a structure and managerial practices that encourage employees to be concerned and contribute to the company. North American systems appear to encourage the opposite—apathy and a lack of commitment.

Decision Making

In Japan, collective, bottom-up consensus decision making occurs. Everyone who is affected by the decision studies the problem and the implications. There is a shared search for information and optimal solutions. A great deal of behind-the-scenes manoeuvring occurs. Since harmony is valued, compromises are made. This is most visible in the collusive type of relationship that exists between government, business and labour. Although the study of a problem takes a considerable length of time, once the decision has been made, implementation occurs quickly.

In North America, strategy, policies and goals are determined at the upper echelons of the organization. The goals of the more senior levels are then accomplished in an end–means chain: the end (assignment) of the senior level becomes the means (tasks to be accomplished) of the lower level.

Power, nature and scope of decision making increase as position within the hierarchy becomes more senior. At the shop-floor and first supervisory levels, the individuals are responsible only for their specific tasks. Design engineers, who may or may not be familiar with the work tasks, have simplified these jobs so that there is a need to perform and not make decisions. The decision to implement an innovation is relatively rapid; the change process itself often meets with considerable resistance. Greater detail regarding decision making is given in Table 4–4.

TABLE 4–4

A Comparison of Japanese and American Systems (Decision Making and Communication)

Japanese	*American*
Collective decision making (bottom-up consensus-type decision making as seen in the *ringi* system, proposal system, etc.).	Top-down decision making and one-way orders. Little consideration given to opinions at the lower echelons; end–means chain.
Verbal and nonverbal communication (*nemawashi* or behind-the-scenes manoeuvres; information transmitted by implicit understanding, gut decisions, etc.).	Autocratic authority of the top; expanded power of the bureaucracy.
Collective work performance systems (common room system; total membership participation and planning).	Individual work performance.
Exemption from responsibility (seat of authority is obscure; no one and everyone takes responsibility).	Individual responsibility and scapegoating.
Separation of ownership and management. Real power lies with operatives.	Strong owner pressure. The company president is a hired hand who can be terminated.
Shared search for information and optimal solutions.	Segregated responsibility for information search and optimal solutions.
"Japan, Inc." (collusive relationship of government, business and labour).	Insistence on and protection of individual rights through all means, including legal.

MANAGEMENT AND THE ORGANIZATION

	Japan	*North America*
Job descriptions	Fluid	Rigid
	Worker responsible for all jobs	Worker responsible for one job

Structure	Flat bureaucracy	Tall pyramidal bureaucracy
	Few desk jobs	Desk jobs often exceed production jobs
Outlook	Long term	Fire fighting
	Production stressed	Marketing stressed
Worker	Partner in production	Poor substitute for a machine
Suggestions	Quantity encouraged	Quality stressed
	Little financial incentive	Large financial incentives
	Many received	Few received
	Majority implemented	Few implemented

DECISION MAKING

	Japan	*North America*
Process of deciding	Bottom-up	Top-down
	All who are affected are involved	
	Slow	Rapid
Implementation	Rapid	Difficult

Deming's Principles

No discussion of what American industry can learn from the Japanese would be complete without reference to the fourteen principles established by the father of the quality control movement, Dr. W. Edwards Deming (see Table 4–5).

Deming feels that managers must learn to plan for the future. The company must know where it wishes to be in ten, twenty or more years and must be willing to reallocate resources and to be innovative in using these resources. Part of the reallocation involves a new philosophy regarding what is acceptable. No company, to be competitive, can function with the level of mistakes, defects, unsuitable materials, untrained employees, incompetent management and antiquated training methods that have been acceptable in the past. A second part of this reallocation involves the elimination of quality control offices. Instead, Deming suggests, every employee should be trained in statistical process control. A third part of this reallocation involves suppliers. The number of companies which provide the same part or material to the company must be minimized. Only those suppliers who have accepted the new philosophy and who apply statistical process control should be retained.

The reallocation cannot occur without recognizing certain fundamentals. First, two sources of problems exist. The system contributes 85 percent of these and

TABLE 4–5
Fourteen Obligations of Top Management (Dr. W. Edwards Deming)

1. Innovate and allocate resources to fulfill the long-range needs of the company and customer rather than short-term profitability.

2. Discard the old philosophy of accepting defective products.

3. Eliminate dependence on mass inspection for quality control; instead depend on process control, through statistical techniques.

4. Reduce the number of multiple source suppliers. Price has no meaning without an integral consideration for quality. Encourage suppliers to use statistical process control.

5. Use statistical techniques to identify the two sources of waste—the system (85 percent) and local faults (15 percent); strive to constantly reduce this waste.

6. Institute more thorough, better job-related training.

7. Provide supervision with knowledge of statistical methods; encourage use of these methods to identify which defects should be investigated for solution.

8. Reduce fear throughout the organization by encouraging open, two-way, non-punitive communication. The economic loss resulting from fear to ask questions or report trouble is appalling.

9. Help reduce waste by encouraging design, research and sales people to learn more about the problems of production.

10. Eliminate the use of goals and slogans to encourage productivity, unless training and management support is also provided.

11. Closely examine the impact of work standards. Do they consider quality or help anyone do a better job? They often act as an impediment to productivity improvement.

12. Institute rudimentary statistical training on a broad scale.

13. Institute a vigorous program for retraining people in new skills, to keep up with changes in materials, methods, product designs, and machinery.

14. Make maximum use of statistical knowledge and talent in your company.

Summarized by Ford Product Quality Office Manufacturing Staff, April 28, 1981.

employees contribute 15 percent. It makes sense, therefore, to concentrate on the "important many instead of the trivial few." Second, a new emphasis on thorough job-related training and on modern training techniques is required. This massive training of all employees must be general in nature and must emphasize statistical techniques and good supervision. And retraining must ensure that employees do not become obsolete and that they can keep up with changes in materials, methods, styles, models and new equipment.

As a consequence of the new emphasis on training, statistics can be used to determine whether the fault lies with the system or the worker, and supervisors can have time to help employees to do the job for which they were hired. People must also be made to feel secure rather than afraid. Deming maintains that in American industry at the present time, employees, even those in management, do not understand what their job is, how to do it correctly, or who to ask. Many, in fact, are afraid to ask questions or to report trouble. The training of generalists, rather than specialists, is important because employees need to understand the problems of other departments and of the organization as a whole rather than just the problems of one department.

A third fundamental which management must recognize is that the work standards within the organization must be examined carefully to ensure that quality has top emphasis. Numerical goals, slogans and posters do not accomplish this and should be eliminated. In fact, states Deming, these are just indications of managerial incompetence.

In summary, Deming feels that management must create the type of work environment that ensures that employees who have the statistical and work skills that are needed are permitted and assisted in doing the work for which they are employed.

Summary

In summary, what can be learned from the Japanese and what role can quality circles play in bringing about changes to assist North American industries, if not to re-establish market supremacy, at least to be competitive?

First, Japanese methods cannot and must not be accepted without adapting them to North American culture and circumstances.

Second, managerial attitudes toward quality control and shop-floor and other blue- and white-collar workers must change. Management must recognize that each worker, even if only in some small way, can contribute to solving problems that affect the company and him or her directly. The quality circle approach is a good beginning.

Third, large companies must accept the responsibility of better training their employees and the challenge of assisting educational institutions in the education of graduates in workplace human relations and human resource management.

Fourth, a careful examination must be made of the collective bargaining process. The old adversarial methods may have been adequate in the days when workers were uneducated and the issues were simple. It does not appear to be the answer today. This is not to suggest that unions must make the concessions. That would not work; owners and managers of many companies have a history of dishonest manipulations. The alternative is that companies should make concessions. That is a possibility, but short-term gains may mean long-term losses. The failure to remain competitive may mean that the company will fail and all jobs will be lost. The key, then, is for the parties to develop trust and to search for solutions that are in both their best interests.

But developing trust is no easy chore. Perhaps it may be accomplished only by changing attitudes, values, and philosophies and by changing structures. On the other hand, perhaps trust can be accomplished more simply—by getting to know each other and by setting aside the stereotypes that are held. By working together, by solving problems together, by helping one another, opportunities arise to understand each other. Quality circles can assist this process.

Unfortunately, there is no cookbook formula and no right answers. The direction is one which each organization and its employees must choose. For many companies and their workers, however, there is a wrong answer—to continue in the present manner. Continuation will bring the inevitable—the inability to remain competitive and to keep jobs.[8]

PART II

THE IMPLEMENTATION PROCESS

5 *Implementation*

In Chapter 3 some of the problems that can be experienced because of poor implementation were addressed. This chapter outlines additional steps in a successful implementation. Before circles are initiated, commitment should be secured, existing threats alleviated, and the establishment of the groups set in motion. The first step, however, is to decide whether to employ an external consultant.

The External Consultant

The employment of an external consultant to assist in the implementation of the program is optional. All the work is done internally by employees. There are advantages and disadvantages to using an external person.

First, external consultants generally have a broader theoretical and practical background, either because they have observed a greater variety of circles in operation or because they have had a greater opportunity to study the available research. For this reason, they are able to present a greater variety of options, alternatives and ideas. This also means that they will be more conscious of inconsistencies between practice and the goals and objectives of the organization.

Second, because they are external to the organization, they are relatively immune to the power structure and can view the organization and the quality circle program more objectively. Because of this, they are in a better position than the internal consultant to challenge the established behavioural patterns of senior and middle management, and the information and insights which they present are viewed as being more neutral and more credible.

Third, generally they can gain access to key people within the organization more readily—after all, consultants do cost money. They also can be influential in behind-the-scenes manoeuvring should this become necessary.

Fourth, a good external quality circles consultant can aid in changing the climate of the organization. Individuals generally are afraid to try new techniques and behaviours. Consultants can encourage experimentation and can assist individuals in successful personal adaptations. They can also nurture positive changes in attitudes and, through feedback, can discourage negative ones. Consultants can aid the process even more by modelling constructive communications. In one instance, for example, middle managers, during a training seminar, were helped in perceiving the existing attitudes and viewpoints within the organization by making a collage (a series of posters) about the climate of the organization.

Sometimes middle and senior managers require a "support system"—particularly one that is external to the organization—or just someone on whom they can try ideas. Consultants can perform that function and be that sounding board.

Perhaps one of the most important purposes of external agents is to retain the momentum. As circles continue to function, the initial excitement, attention and glamour tend to diminish. Furthermore, it is not always possible for the organization to implement the solutions which have been suggested. The circle members may begin to feel disappointed, frustrated, resentful and manipulated. Consultants can provide support, encouragement and counsel. They can coach and educate members. But more important, they can be good listeners and can assure the circle members they are on the right track and that the problems which they are experiencing are expected or are the usual type of difficulties. To overcome some of the unanticipated or negative outcomes which cause disillusionment, external consultants can lead the steering committee and others through "anticipatory planning" and in periodic re-evaluations of the circle processes. Again, external consultants can be a source of new ideas and alternatives.

Consultants, however, are expensive and generally do not, and cannot, do the detailed planning and required work. They also can be insensitive to the organization and its needs, the unofficial power structures and the organizational chart. Often, they are too busy and, at least in Canada, located too far away for frequent and easy consultation. Consequently, there are many large organizations that do not utilize externals.

If the organization decides to hire an external consultant, the choice of individual or company should be made before any work is done. He or she then can assume some responsibility for obtaining commitment, providing initial explanations, seeing that training programs are developed, and ensuring that adequate training occurs. This individual is extremely important to the success of the program, and care must be taken to select a person who is mature, sensitive to people's feelings, supportive and approachable. If the company is unionized, an individual who is perceived to be sympathetic, or at least neutral, to the union movement can give credibility to the program and help union executive and rank-and-file members to feel greater trust regarding management personnel with whom they must work.

There are other traits which the consultant should possess. The organization will want a generalist—someone who understands the structure and purposes of the organization, as well as the external environment in which, and the constraints under which, the organization operates. Certainly, too, a specialist is required—

someone who understands quality circles and has the necessary interpersonal, process and statistical skills.

Of course, the consultant should not have a vested interest in improving the status of a particular group–management, labour, or any other. He or she should be open and be willing to confront conflict, even when senior management is involved. The person should have an awareness of practice, research and theory and be experienced in a variety of consulting situations instead of having worked in the same type of situation over and over again.

Other characteristics of good consultants include flexibility, the willingness to listen and to tailor existing informational and training materials to the needs of the organization, the ability and desire to train others, the willingness to work themselves out of a job, and last, but most important, to be available when required.

Not all external consultants are trained in interpersonal skills, basic statistical techniques and group processes. Different consultants have different expertise. With the popularity of quality circles, many management consulting firms, both large and small, have embraced the concept by purchasing one of the commercial packages which are readily available. In evaluating the credentials of external people, organizations should be leery of a smooth polished approach which is based on ''have canned package, will implement'' and assure themselves that the consulting firm or individuals have the requisite skills needed to advise about and implement quality circles.

EXTERNAL CONSULTANTS

Advantages
- more ideas, options and alternatives
- immune to power structure
- better access to key people
- help employees experiment with new behaviour
- provide support system
- retain momentum

Disadvantages
- expensive
- do not do the work
- sometimes insensitive
- busy

Required characteristics
- mature
- sensitive to people's feelings
- supportive
- approachable

- credibility with union
- generalist
- specialist in quality circles
- willing to confront conflict
- flexible

Preliminary Commitment and Planning

Five issues must be addressed before quality circles are instituted:
1. Senior management should be committed to the endeavour.
2. Union involvement and commitment should be assured.
3. Threats felt by middle management should be anticipated and programs developed to neutralize them.
4. Plans should be established to overcome the threat of empire building by quality circle leaders or facilitators.
5. An analysis of the organizational climate should be made.

Senior Management Involvement

Often in the implementation of a change program, it seems sensible to start small and build to bigger and better things. This is not appropriate for quality circles; the commitment that is required from senior management is crucial to the success of the program. First, either release time from duties or payment for time spent working on quality circles (if one of these methods is chosen) must be approved. Resources must be redeployed, not for the next month or the next year, but for many years to come. The results of the deliberations of each of the circles must be presented not only to appropriate technical and middle management groups but also to affected senior management personnel. The reception which these presentations receive will influence the enthusiasm and willingness which the circles show for continued problem solving. And finally, changes suggested by quality circles must be implemented. This often requires an unanticipated utilization of resources. Because of these involvements, upper management commitment is mandatory.

It is important too to have the commitment of more than one individual of the senior management group. Where only one person is committed to the concept, that person's promotion, illness or other fortune or misfortune may adversely affect the circles.

Union Involvement

Mentioned earlier was the fact that union executives are often very suspicious of management and feel that quality circles are one more in a long series of methods to extract greater productivity from the workers. Furthermore, there is considerable fear that this concept, if successful, will lead to the dismissal of great numbers of employees and make the union unnecessary in the representation of workers' interests. To assist in overcoming these feelings, it is necessary to:

1. Contact the members of the union executive in the very early stages of discussion.
2. Consult with union representatives at every step.
3. Place influential union members on the steering committee.
4. Refuse to consider issues which properly belong in the collective agreement and within the grievance procedure.
5. Not permit the union to make gains as the price of members' participation. Because of the nature of the union and its legitimate activities, it is not unusual for the union executive to place conditions or to make demands in exchange for the promise of members' participation. Such demands generally do not improve the relationship and should not be a condition of participation.

Middle Management

In the traditional system of management, a hierarchical structure exists. Individuals who, after many years, have "made it" to middle management have subordinates who report to them and over whom they exercise a certain degree of legitimate reward and coercive power. Issues and problems are reported, after screening, through the hierarchy to more senior management; line people seldom meet or formally express their concerns directly to anyone except their supervisor.

Quality circles change this relationship and structure. First, members of senior management who are concerned with the particular improvement are included in presentations. Second, middle management often perceives that circles have assumed a substantial portion of their unique problem-solving role. In the eyes of the first-level supervisors, circles also appear to be doing work which rightfully belongs to the supervisor. Additionally, line people may use the direct link with senior administration as a lever over their bosses.

To assist these two groups, the new role expectations which the organization has should be clarified. But more is needed. It should be demonstrated, through explicit actions, that quality circles do not threaten, but do enhance, these individuals' roles and positions. One of the best methods to overcome the insecurity which the supervisor may feel is to make that person the quality circle leader. But before this occurs, extensive training is required to teach this person to behave as a leader rather than as a boss. In short, if these managers are educated in the new management system and in the philosophy of managing human resources and taught how to function in their new roles, there should be little resistance to the perceived encroachment on their power.

No matter how adequately the pre-planning has been done, and how carefully the changes have been implemented, some managers will oppose quality circles either vocally or surreptitiously. There must be an office or official (perhaps the steering committee) which can detect and respond to opposition and any acts of sabotage that may occur.

Empire Building

Because facilitators and leaders are organizational members, there could be a tendency on their part to use their positions to further their visibility and career. Consequently, facilitators may establish circles, not because they are desired or necessary, but because they increase their own prestige and status. Leaders have been known to build empires too—particularly when the leader is a line person and the members wish to discredit a supervisor.

The story is told of a quality circle that was extremely successful and was the pride of senior management. Through threats and bullying, the circle members made life miserable for supervisors and middle management. Tremendous hostility was created within the shop. Needless to say, at the first opportunity, middle management made it impossible for the circle to function; it died a premature death.

The problem of empire building must be foreseen and a contingency plan developed to deal with it.

The Organizational Climate

If the organization is committed to the implementation of quality circles, it is wise to organize these in the most advantageous area first. For this reason, it is better that an organizational climate analysis be conducted. But climate surveys have other advantages too. They indicate the attitudes and perceptions which employees have regarding such organizational processes as motivation, communication, decision making, goal setting, leadership, control and the level of trust and interaction which exists within the various units. The initial climate survey also serves as a basis of comparison when improvements occur in the future. Lastly, it provides busy managers with feedback regarding their own interpersonal skills.

In reality, however, it may be necessary to begin "where the system is," that is, to proceed with the implementation of quality circles in a particular designated area rather than beginning with a climate diagnosis. Facilitators, for example, do not have a choice; their instructions often are top-down. Additionally, organizational units do not necessarily like being "diagnosed"; the budget will not permit it; senior management does not believe it is necessary; and members are intimidated by the expected results. There are many reasons. Even if it is impossible to do a survey, it is necessary for those charged with quality circle implementation to understand the organization and the people who function within it. To do this, rapport has to be established so that employees at all levels can be questioned frequently, in an empathetic manner, to elicit their responses and attitudes.

Initiating the Circles

A five-step process will help quality circles to get off on the right foot. The five steps are:

1. An explanation of quality circles to all levels of the organization.
2. Participation in training programs by management, supervisors, leaders, facilitators, coordinators and union personnel.
3. The development of a procedure for implementing circle suggestions.
4. The development of evaluation programs for measuring the impact of the suggestions which are implemented.
5. The establishment of required structures.

A discussion of these five steps follows.

Explanation About Quality Circles

After approval has been obtained, the next step is to explain the quality circle concept to all those who are interested and may be participating. The purpose of this explanation is to provide facts about the circles and how they operate. More importantly, however, the explanation illustrates to prospective participants that the concept has merit and that it will help the organization and its members to grow without threatening the job or position of any person. This means that the fears and apprehensions which employees have must be anticipated and dispelled.

As noted previously, the idea of worker contribution frequently poses a threat to middle management and first-level supervisory staff, who feel that quality circles will be doing their work, making them look incompetent and rendering their positions unnecessary. In dealing with this perceived threat, a number of issues can be addressed. First, members at all levels within the organization should understand that collective thinking is better than that of the individual or the sum of the individuals. Second, most operations are extremely complex; even the simplest of actions can affect many other departments and people. This system of interrelationships can be better visualized if the organization is compared to a labyrinth in which all the units are connected by elastic bands (see Figure 5–1). When the slightest pressure is placed on the maze—by changing the shape or size of the units or by pulling on any one of the elastic bands—the entire system changes. Employees should have an input into those changes that affect them. Third, the new role of first-level and middle management, as true leaders and managers, should be not only communicated, but also carefully planned and taught. Furthermore, opportunitites should be provided to practise

FIGURE 5–1

Change in Organizational Relationships When Pressure Applied at Any
Position

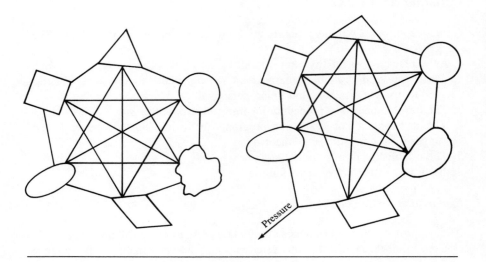

this new role in non-threatening circumstances and suitable positive reinforcement
should be offered when these new behaviours are displayed. Lastly, fears should
be alleviated if policies are determined, strategies are developed and promises
are kept which ensure that no person is laid off as a result of any circle implementation but is assisted in growing to full potential within the organization.

Both management and union should be aware that the success of quality circles
will change employees and management. By experiencing an opportunity to
work together, each group is better able to understand and empathize with the
attitudes and requirements of the other. Because of this, employees are able to
cooperate to preserve customers and markets and hence jobs and positions within
the company.

Financial success, however, is seldom immediate. It is not unusual for very
few tangible results to occur for the first two or three years of a program. A
more realistic time frame is three to five years.

Finally, the explanation must include the fact that quality circles are not a
means by which union or management can make gains that they have not achieved
at the bargaining table. Bargaining continues as usual; those issues that belong
at the bargaining table or within the grievance process do not belong in a quality
circle meeting. Also, participants should be aware that quality circles are not a
panacea or a cure for one or more ills of the company. Indeed, they will not be

given a fair trial if they are perceived only in terms of being the cure to a specific ailment.

In addition to the explanation, participants could be allowed to visit another company and have an opportunity to observe a successful circle in operation. Alternately, external employees, who perform the same type of work and have participated in a successful quality circle in another organization, could explain the benefits and what quality circles have accomplished within the organization for which they work.

In summary, the quality circle should be so well explained, with free and open discussion permitted, that there are no surprises for any of the participating groups. All participants, particularly those in management, should be aware that their philosophy of management may have to change. For one thing, quality circles can be successful only if management believes that workers can and want to make a contribution. Secondly, it follows that as a result of quality circles, an improvement in things like quality, productivity and scrap loss may occur. These gains, however, are not the primary purpose of a circle; the primary purpose is to provide employees with an opportunity to contribute in the decision-making process in those fields or areas of knowledge where they have the expertise. Management will be required not only to encourage these contributions but to seek active ways to elicit them.

Training Programs

Seven groups of people require training or orientation. These are:
1. Senior and middle management.
2. Union executive members.
3. First-line supervisors.
4. Steering committee.
5. Facilitators.
6. Leaders.
7. Members of the circles.

Comments have been made throughout this book regarding the training and orientation that is required for the first three groups. This final section addresses the training of those in the last four categories, that is, the people involved in the actual operation of the circle. Sample training programs are shown in Appendix 1.

Steering Committee. The immediate training of the members of the steering committee is general in nature. Certainly they need to understand the quality circle concept, how management philosophy must be adapted, the benefits that can be attained as a result of employee participation, the activities and techniques used by the circles, as well as their role as policy makers (and not circle participants). They also require interpersonal skills. Although information is always advantageous, because of time and money constraints, much of the practical day-to-day information which will not be immediately useful to members can be postponed.

Facilitators. The most vital person in the quality circle program is the facilitator. This individual is the liaison among the various groups. It follows that his or her ability and the education provided determines the direction and success of the program. The exact training, however, is difficult to specify; personal qualities are more important than factual information.

Perhaps the only way in which the magnitude and intensity of the training can be understood is by examining the role which these individuals play. They:
1. Sit and advise the steering committee.
2. Develop or assist in developing training materials.
3. Train or assist in training the other six groups.
4. Attend some meetings or portions of meetings for each circle that operates.
5. Actively promote circles.
6. Arrange for visits to other plants and for visitors to speak to quality circles at their home base.
7. Coordinate activities of all circles.
8. Help circles to prepare reports and presentations.
9. Provide support and assistance as required.

From this description it should be obvious that facilitators are not developed through a few days of training. Instead, they have been educated in the required skills over a long period of time—generally at a university, with another company, or in another function in the same organization. Graduates who might have these skills could come from extremely diverse fields such as business administration, education, industrial engineering, or the social sciences.

Leaders. Just as the coordinator is the key person in the quality circle movement within the company, leaders are the key people to the individual circles. Leaders generally are first-line supervisors. In that role, they have learned how to be bosses and how to get production out. Quality circles require a very different role, and considerable time must be spent teaching leaders the new role and providing an opportunity for them to practice it. The training that occurs will be in five main categories:
1. Human resource management.
2. Team building models and techniques.
3. Organizational climate.
4. Statistical procedures.
5. Conducting meetings.

As pointed out previously, quality circles are built on the philosophy of the worth of the human being and on the assumptions that employees can and wish to participate in decisions that affect them and that they have needs and motives which they want to satisfy in the workplace. Leaders need skills that will enable them to assist employees who wish to contribute to do so.

Many organizations have found that teams which work together well have better productivity and quality records. Increased effectiveness in brainstorming, offering suggestions, feedback, criticism, group decision making and negotiating increases team cohesiveness. Leaders need the ability to build these skills in others. Also, an ability to interpret and react to nonverbal communication assists them in sensing covert deviations.

Leaders, even when they function as first-line supervisors, have a responsibility to members of the group to ensure that the environment is conducive to excellent work. The key to this is the degree of trust that exists and the system, methods and philosophy of work, including that regarding the chain of command, information requirements and access, idea receptiveness, promotional opportunities, flexibility, planning, decision making and control. Some methods are better for improving the climate of the workplace than are others. Because of this, leaders should examine key ideas that have been developed. At the minimum, they should understand the processes, structures, philosophies and power bases within the company.

The statistical procedures which leaders require and need to reteach to circle members include cause and effect diagrams, sampling, control charts and a wide variety of graphing techniques including histograms, scattergrams and Pareto diagrams. (These are explained in Chapter 9.) Leaders need to be able to explain the techniques and to know why, when and how each should be utilized.

One of a leader's most important skills is the ability to chair meetings. Chairing, in the broad sense, involves more than conducting the circle meeting. Part of the responsibilities include budgeting time, starting and stopping on time, ensuring that each member is provided with agendas well in advance of the meeting, ensuring that each member participates, ensuring that records are kept and pre-planning for a successful meeting.

To top it off, leaders must jog memories, ensure that work is completed on time, promote the quality circle concept, recruit new members, train, and be pleasant and enthusiastic through it all. The training of leaders therefore must be a continuous process; the preliminary few days are a beginning. At that time only the philosophy and some of the basic skills can be imparted.

Members of the Circles. Work must be done in a cooperative manner, and all members should participate in problem solving. For this reason, members need interpersonal and technical skills (brainstorming, statistics, graphing, etc.) and a sense of responsibility (attending meetings on time, keeping within rules and procedures, completing work assigned to them, etc.). Because members promote the circle and recruit new members, they should also have promotional and public relations skills.

Quality circle members also require training in group team work, new roles and behaviour, and in interpersonal skills. Many books are available which address the best approaches; reference librarians can assist interested members in locating one or two of these. Generally, personnel within the company, particularly the training and development department and the quality circle facilitator, can develop or assist in developing programs to accomplish these aims. Various commercial companies also sell pre-packaged materials.

Suggestions

Very early in the initiation process, guidelines should be established to determine some methods and techniques by which suggestions can be brought before the appropriate quality circles and implemented. Since this involves policy, the steering committee is probably in the best position to formulate these guidelines.

Measuring the Impact

Methods, too, must be established for deciding whether a circle has been successful. This usually means that some *a priori* measures and standards must exist and some measurement must occur at varying intervals after circles have been established. Generally, in a manufacturing firm, these types of measures are fairly easy to obtain—a job is done more easily, in less time, with less waste. In service institutions, such as libraries and educational institutions, the impact of the change is more difficult to observe and to measure. At times the only available means of measurement are attitude surveys at varying points in time. One such survey is shown in Chapter 11.

Establishing the Structure

After commitment has been secured and quality circles have been explained to those who are concerned or interested, quality circle structures are required. These involve:
1. The establishment of a steering committee.
2. The naming or hiring of a facilitator.
3. Staffing the circle.
4. Arranging for meeting rooms and times of meeting.
5. Setting up operating rules and procedures.

The Steering Committee

Members of the steering committee are selected from a cross-section of levels and departments. At the minimum, senior management, middle management, each of the unions, first-level supervisory staff, the operating core, support staff and technostructure personnel such as design engineers and quality control are represented. This is the policy-making group; it does not become involved in day-to-day activities but determines general guidelines. Responsibilities of the steering committee include:

1. Establishing general policies regarding the structures and processes of the circles.

2. Determining the channels for reporting. Some examples include guidelines concerning minutes of meetings, publicity and opportunities to report findings and recommendations to functional areas and to concerned senior management.

3. Determining the number of circles that is appropriate for the company. If only one circle operates, a considerable amount of pressure for success is placed on the members of that circle. Furthermore, if it should fail, the whole concept fails. If the circle is perceived to be too successful, members may feel they are entitled to special treatment. Resentment tends to arise because of this, and an underground movement could develop to sabotage the circle concept. The steering committee therefore should think in terms of numerous circles. Costs, of course, are a constraint.

4. Determining the selection methods and the final membership of the circles. Sometimes there are too many volunteers for one circle; other times there are too few, and other individuals must be encouraged to volunteer. There have even been occasions when only a buddy group has come forward and used strong-arm tactics to keep others from doing so. Policies should exist that facilitate easy access to a circle for all employees who are interested.

5. Determining whether circles will meet on company time or on individuals' free time. Is one method better than the other? Perhaps, but evidence is sparse. Some evidence indicates that both methods of participation can exist side by side. In the Ford Motor Company, for example, depending on the plant, employees meet either on company time or on their own time. Both types of circles have met with equal success. If the decision is made to meet on company time, the steering committee should facilitate the release from work for employees who are participating. In most companies it is customary for the meetings to occur during work hours.

6. Determining how suggestions from the general work force might be solicited and implemented.

7. Establishing guidelines governing the reward system that is appropriate for improvements which result from the efforts of the circles.

The steering committee is a standing committee that meets once every one or two months. As new problems arise, new policies are formulated.

Facilitators

When more than one quality circle exists, an individual is required to coordinate and facilitate the activities of the circles and to perform those roles which have been outlined earlier in the chapter. Depending on the number of circles, this responsibility is delegated to one or more persons. As the circles increase in number, a coordinator of the facilitators may be necessary.

The facilitator attends at least one meeting of each circle. While at the meeting, he or she does not interfere with the circle activities, but listens and provides assistance if requested. In addition, the facilitator assists and trains leaders when this assistance is requested or when the need to offer guidance becomes evident. Generally the facilitator is not a volunteer, but should be someone who is interested in this type of work, who is willing to work hard and who has been trained in the required skills.

In a unionized company, the choice of a facilitator can be a thorny issue. Management typically feels this person should be someone from managerial ranks. If the choice is made arbitrarily, the union may use the appointment to argue that the program is "another management effort to gain greater productivity from employees." To overcome this, some organizations have decided on two facilitators—a union person and a management person. But this avoids the real issue and forces a difficult role upon the two facilitators—particularly if the union uses its appointee to undermine the program. It is probably better to resolve the situation through discussion and compromise. The union can assist in selecting a person who has been a respected union official or who has the necessary personal characteristics and high credibility with union members.

Staffing

Quality circles are staffed by volunteers. Membership can range from three to twenty persons. Usually seven to ten is an ideal number. If the membership is too small, an insufficient number of ideas are advanced; if the membership is too large, some people feel intimidated and do not contribute to their fullest potential.

One member of the circle is usually the leader. A leader can be any member. Generally it is the first-line supervisor, who has been trained in the techniques of conducting a meeting, in encouraging others to participate, and in brainstorming techniques and the new non-authoritarian role that this position requires.

There are a number of reasons why the first-line supervisor should be chosen as leader:

1. If this person is not chosen, she or he may feel threatened.
2. If the circle is successful, employees, because they have direct access to management, may intimidate and blackmail the supervisor.
3. The most thankless and difficult job is that of the first-line supervisor. This individual is a buffer. Being a successful leader generally enhances the self-image of the supervisor and the respect that the workers feel toward this person.

The Meeting

Quality circles usually meet once a week in a conference room away from the work area. Meeting times are always pre-determined, and the agenda for the coming week and reminders of the responsibilities undertaken are sent well in advance of the meeting to all members. Minutes are kept and are circulated to the members, the facilitator and the steering committee.

Shift work presents a problem for circles. To cope with the different times when members are available, two methods have been used successfully for scheduling meetings: (1) A quality circle for each shift can function with a linking pin (one or two people who attend all meetings) being the coordinating mechanism. (2) The second method involves scheduling. For one week, the circle meets one hour before quitting time for the first shift; the next week the circle meets for the first hour of the second shift. If three shifts exist, the same type of rotation pattern can occur. There is a fourth alternative: each shift can form its own circle which is independent of other circles in the unit.

Operating Rules and Procedures

The circle determines its own operating rules and procedures. Decisions are made through consensus rather than by a majority vote or by a dominant member forcing his or her opinion on the group.

Circle members should be pre-trained in consensus decision making. The process involves assuming that every suggestion that is offered, until proven inadequate, will help to solve the problem. In other words, better decisions are made when members:
1. Listen carefully to what others are saying without judging the statement.
2. Examine each proposal in detail.
3. Ask for clarification of unclear and hazy details.
4. Avoid dominating or forcing their opinions on other members of the group.
5. Provide support and acknowledgement to others and their ideas.
6. Build on others' ideas by adding to them.
7. Originate new ideas and approaches when the time is appropriate. So that members do not spend group discussion time determining the best method to present their own ideas, a thinking and organization break can occur—two or three minutes when members can, without interruption, think through ideas and jot these down for later presentation.
8. Confront differences that occur by: (a) Specifying where the differences lie. Sometimes issues become clarified through a restatement of the problem or the tangential issues. (b) Questioning the assumptions underlying the solutions or alternatives given. (c) Pointing out details and facts that may have been forgotten or overlooked. Personal attacks or evaluative judgments generally detract from a consensual solution.

Summary

In summary, what are the actual steps in the process of implementing quality circles?

External Consultant

1. A decision is made whether to use only the internal organizational development department or specialist, if the company is large enough to have one, or an external consultant to assist in the implementation.

Obtaining Commitment

The next step in the process is obtaining the commitment of the major parties who are concerned. To do this:

2. An off-site seminar is held at which members of senior management are introduced to the concept of quality circles. Usually a short review of motivational and leadership issues, the advantages of circles, the need for their commitment, the required new role and management philosophy, and similar topics are discussed. Appendix 1 gives a sample program.

Seminars can be held on company premises, but the proximity of offices and work distractions may hinder the training.

3. Senior management evaluates the approach and makes a decision as to whether or not the concept should be introduced to middle management. Senior management may decide at this stage to proceed with implementation or to establish a study group to investigate and report. There are advantages, however, to waiting until input is received from middle management.

Although a decision made by the more senior group can be implemented quickly, the involvement of middle management provides an opportunity for clarification of organizational goals and contingencies and for feedback and information exchange. The information disseminated is more accurate, therefore there are fewer speculative rumours. But input by middle management provides these individuals not only with greater input, but also with greater control over the process. As a consequence, they are more committed and ensure that implementation proceeds more quickly and with minimal disruption. Researchers argue that another advantage exists. By allowing participation in the decision-making process, senior management gains the acceptance of middle management and, through group norms and group influence, attains a greater control over their actions.

4. Off-site seminars are held for middle management and union executive members.

5. Both middle management and the union executive make independent analyses of the program, its advantages and disadvantages, their new roles and whether or not to actively support the first steps in the implementation process.

Setting Up the Circle Structure

6. Senior management announces to the employees within the organization that it intends to proceed with the implementation of the quality circle program, the reasons for the decision and the perceived future benefits to the company and to the employees.

Depending on the management style of key personnel, the number of unions involved, and the existing union–management relationships, this communication could originate with both senior management and the union executive.

7. A steering committee is established.

8. A facilitator is selected by the steering committee. This person becomes an additional member of that committee.

Getting the Program off on the Right Foot

9. The steering committee, together with the consultant, if there is one, establish guidelines and principles. At the minimum, this must include such items as release time, the incorporation of the present suggestion plan into the quality circle program, the evaluation of the impact which circles have, and the remuneration system to be used.

10. The facilitator holds informational meetings and training seminars on quality circles and QC processes for members of the human resources department and other supervisory staff. An example of the content that can be included is given in Appendix 1.

11. The facilitator holds informational meetings for rank-and-file workers. Among the issues which are explained are the concept of quality circles itself, what advantages it has for the company and for the employees, the broad framework and guidelines within which circles are to function, the structure, the reporting relationships and the process and activities of the circle.

12. The facilitator, steering committee and external consultant, if there is one, develop an ''anticipatory planning'' program. The idea is to anticipate the problems, negative behaviours and attitudes that may occur, and the consequences of these for participants and for the organization. Response patterns are developed that can be utilized; this avoids fire fighting if the problems do materialize.

13. A request is made for volunteers by sending each member of the organization a pre-printed form to complete. To ensure the success of the initial program, managers in some companies, on an informal basis, may ask specific rank-and-file workers to volunteer. If there are more members than required, the selection is made by drawing names.

14. The facilitator, together with the supervisory committee, select team leaders from first-level supervisory ranks.

15. The facilitator develops training programs for team leaders and trains them.

16. Team members are trained.

17. Each circle begins to function.

18. The facilitator develops training programs and assists team leaders in developing mini-training sessions which address the circles' needs for the coming week. For example, when circles have begun to function, a mini-session may concentrate on the process of setting goals and objectives. During the first weeks, a review of brainstorming and the Ishikawa diagram may be appropriate. Later each circle needs to learn about statistical techniques and evaluation. Examples of all these are given in this book and may be used as a guide. It is best, however, if each circle develops its own criteria and those forms it wishes to use well in advance of the time that they are needed. In this way it can feel ownership, a pride in the creativity and a greater commitment to the decisions which are reached.

IMPLEMENTATION

External consultant?
Commitment
- senior management
- middle management
- union

Setting up the structure
- announcement made
- steering committee established
- facilitator named

Off on the best foot
- guidelines, principles and objectives established
- managerial informational meeting held
- rank-and-file informational meeting held
- anticipatory planning programs developed
- volunteers requested and circles established
- team leaders selected
- leaders trained
- other training programs developed
- circle members trained
- circles begin to function
- leaders continue training of circle members

6 *The Circle Begins to Function*

Identifying and Solving a Problem

Beginning circles often have difficulty knowing where and how to begin. The procedure, however, is common sense: the completed activity suggests the subsequent requirement. As a guide, suggested procedures for identifying and solving problems used by one quality circle follow.

Extensive informational search has been included in the procedure. In many cases, these (observation of the work situation for potential problems and for sub-causes of a problem) will be unnecessary. Because employees are extremely familiar with their work situations, they will be able to recall irregularities or dysfunctional aspects quite readily.

Before a step-by-step procedure can be explored, five terms, because they are used in a somewhat different context than usual, should be understood: "problem" or "effect," "cause," "sub-cause," "verify the sub-cause" and "solution." Also, certain processes and techniques—brainstorming, consensus decision making, delphi technique, fishbone diagram, action plan, checklist and sheets— are basic to the process of identifying and explaining a problem. These also are defined and an explanation is given regarding their use.

The Terms Defined

The terms "problem to be solved" and "effect to be solved" are used interchangeably to indicate a broad area of difficulty or activity or inactivity that exists. Problems or effects in the hotel industry could be complaints about quality and price of food, customer theft, late deliveries, damage to parked cars, noise and rowdy guests.

A *cause* contributes to a problem. In quality circles, the cause-and-effect diagram (commonly known as the fishbone diagram) is always used, and the word "cause" refers to the names that are given to the fishbones protruding from the main skeletal structure (backbone). For convenience, most people think in terms of four causes that contribute to the effect—materials, equipment, meth-

85

ods and personnel. Other names for these fishbones can be used; the names are not important to the process.

Sub-causes are the specific issues, difficulties and activities that have been identified as contributing to the problem. For example, in the hotel industry, if the selected objective of a particular circle is to increase the number of hotel dining room customers, and one of the problems or effects that must be solved is "poor service," some of the sub-causes could be:

Regarding Materials:
- frozen food—poor quality, unappetizing appearance, discoloration
- food types—inadequate selection
- table service—chipped, faded
- liquor—poor selection
- uniforms—unattractive colours, need repair, unattractive style, improper fit

Regarding Methods:
- cleanliness of utensils
- reservations
- payment procedure for food bill
- problems with tips

When a circle member *verifies* the sub-causes of the problem (does an analysis of the sub-causes), that individual examines the various facets of the sub-cause through methods such as observation, surveys, time studies, frequency studies and motion studies. The process includes graphing (particularly with Pareto diagrams) and charting the activities. For example, if "reservations" was one identified sub-cause, a member might want to determine and graph:

- the number of times that the telephone was not answered promptly compared to the number of times the telephone rang
- the reasons for the unanswered telephone
- the length of time that parties who had a reservation were kept waiting
- the number of patrons who could not be accommodated satisfactorily (together with the reasons, the day of the week and the hour)
- the extent of use of alternate arrangements or facilities (e.g., bar)
- the manner in which the telephone was answered
- the occurrence of the many additional service activities that affect whether or not the system of reservations works to the advantage of the hotel dining room

The *solution* goes beyond improvement in the reservation system and other sub-causes and addresses the initial problem. In the example given, solutions are suggested for "poor service."

Brainstorming is used at any time that the circle feels that many new ideas are needed. At the minimum, brainstorming is needed at the time the circle is beginning to function and is attempting to find problems within the organization that should be solved. The technique also is used in generating sub-causes and in generating solutions to sub-causes which have been verified as contributing to the problem. The brainstorming procedure is extremely simple—circle members spend a few minutes suggesting ideas as quickly as they can think of them or when their turn occurs.

Consensus decision making is another way of saying that everyone agrees (or at least does not disagree too strongly) with the option that has been selected. Generally this occurs after the advantages and disadvantages of all options have been discussed. Circles always attempt to arrive at decisions and options through consensus.

The Delphi technique is a procedure that assists in the evaluation of two or more alternatives (if members were not successful, through the process of consensus decision making, in selecting the best alternative).

Generally each person rates the importance of an evaluative factor (e.g., cost) on a specified scale. The ratings of all members on each factor are averaged and this becomes the new "weight" for the importance of that specific item or factor. Each member then rates how well, in his or her opinion, the particular sub-cause satisfies the evaluative factor (e.g., cost—a high cost would score low; a reasonable cost would score high). Again all ratings for each item are averaged. Finally the two averages for each item are multiplied together. The highest (or lowest) total score determines the most acceptable alternative.

Three terms—"cause and effect diagram," "fishbone diagram" and "Ishikawa diagram"—are used interchangeably. The fishbone diagram is a structured method to list the sub-causes of a problem or the solutions to a sub-cause and to organize the ideas so that relationships that exist are perceived more quickly. Circle members concentrate, through brainstorming, on one cause or solution (e.g., methods). When no member has any further suggestions about the first cause or solution, the circle does the same thing for the second cause or solution (e.g., materials) until all ideas have been written on the diagram.

Action plans and *checklists* are usually used together and specify work that must be done to verify a sub-cause or to determine a solution to a subcause or to a problem. An action plan outlines the necessary activities in broad terms, their order, and specifies the person who has responsibility for the action. A checklist or checksheet lists the specific items for each action that must be examined to verify if a sub-cause is contributing to the problem or if a suggested solution eliminates or improves a sub-cause or problem.

The Steps in the Process

The steps in the process, which are shown schematically in Figures 6–1a to 6–1f, and the suggested time intervals are:
1. *The initial meeting* is held (Week 1). At this meeting, eight activities occur:
(*a*) Members introduce themselves and talk about their specific tasks, their work and external interests, and their expertise. This is generally beneficial even if all individuals of the circle are members of the same unit; employees know surprisingly little about their co-workers.
(*b*) A team leader is elected (if one has not been appointed previously).

FIGURE 6–1a
Flow Chart Showing Overview of Process for Identifying and Solving a
Problem

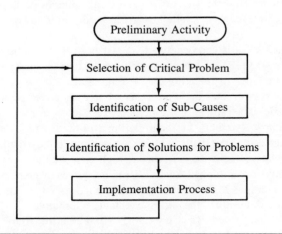

FIGURE 6–1b
Flow Chart Outlining Preliminary Activity

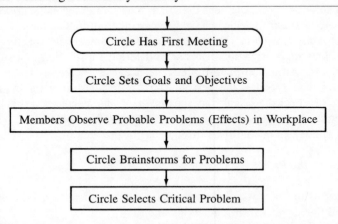

(*c*) The circle members give their circle a name.

(*d*) A secretary is elected. This person keeps the minutes, looks after circulation
of agendas and does other necessary paper work.

(*e*) The necessary supplies or a working kit are given to all members.

FIGURE 6–1c
Flow Chart Outlining Selection of Critical Problem

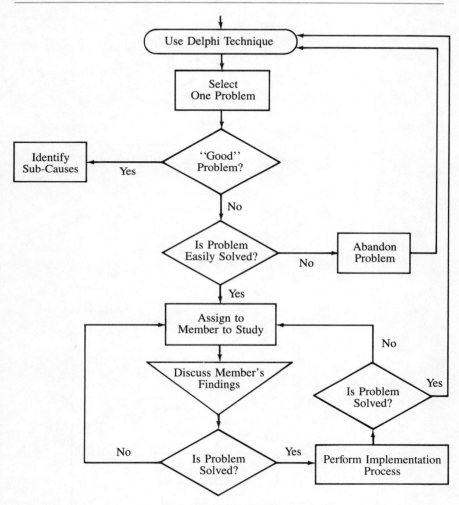

What is in the "kit" depends on the unit itself. When supplies are freely available within the unit (an engineering circle), the dispensing of supplies is unnecessary. For a shop-floor group this is more important; these employees do not have the same access to supplies and equipment.

One firm gave each member who had joined a plant circle his or her own briefcase (personalized), complete with QC logo, pens, pencils, ruler, coloured

FIGURE 6–1d
Flow Chart Showing Process for Identifying Sub-Causes

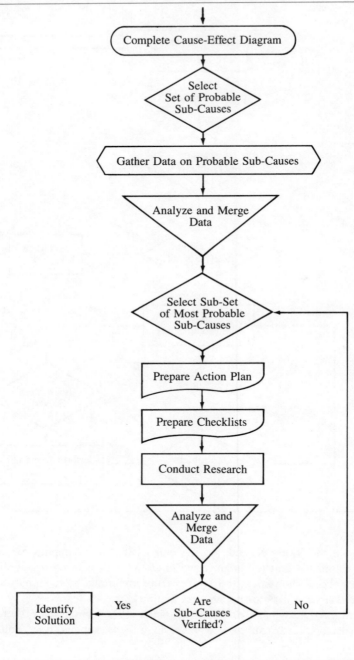

FIGURE 6–1e
Flow Chart for Process of Identifying Solutions to Selected Problem

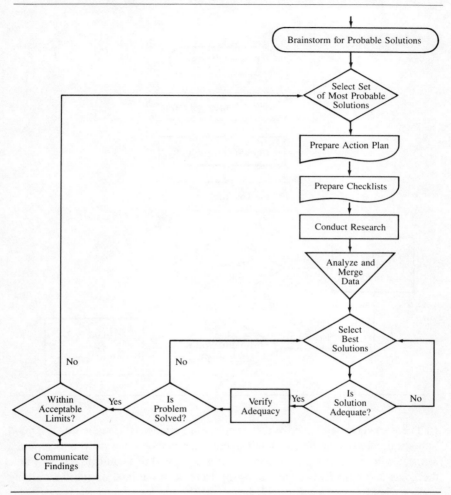

pencils, transparency materials, three-ring binder, looseleaf paper, graph paper, notebook, writing pad, appropriate readings and "how to" reminders, calendar, file folders and carrying folders. Although relatively minimal, some cost was involved. The benefit obtained, however, far exceeded the cost. Members showed considerable pride in their briefcases; the boost in morale and commitment was significant; and the gesture was a catalyst for a larger number of volunteers and more circles.

FIGURE 6–1f
Flow Chart Showing Implementation Process

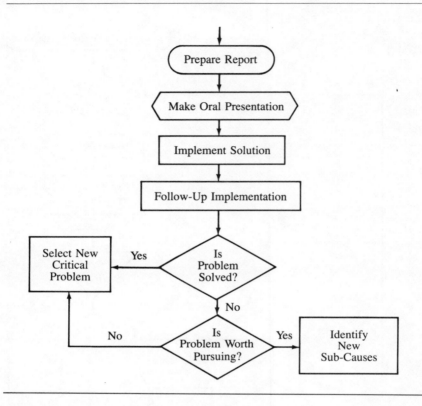

(f) The goals and objectives of the company are reviewed. Usually this is a good opportunity for one of the senior managers or a member of the steering committee to meet with the circle, to show personal interest and to establish rapport. Since the goals and objectives of the company have been outlined during the training sessions held prior to the establishment of the circles, only a short review is necessary.

g) The unit or department supervisor (and others) share with circle members those problem areas within the unit or department which are affecting productivity adversely, such as quality and down-time. This is an excellent opportunity to review such things as production, sales figures, trends, environmental constraints, gross margin, unit expenses and overhead.

h) Before the meeting breaks up, circle members are asked to think about goals and objectives for the circle itself. These will be established at the next meeting.

2. *The next meeting* (Weeks 2-3). Through consensus decision making, the circle

sets specific goals and objectives for itself (e.g., decrease waste by 5 percent; improve quality so that there are 20 percent fewer rejects; decrease costs by 5 percent). To keep members on the right track, leaders sometimes review the problem areas within the unit which were outlined during the previous week. Important goals and objectives include not only quantitative measures but also qualitative ones—circle recognition and an opportunity for members to learn new skills and improve their working conditions.

3. *During the following week* (Week 4), the circle members brainstorm for possible problems. Circle members may find it advantageous to observe and jot down specific problem areas within the unit during the week prior to the brainstorming session. The process of brainstorming should be reviewed at the beginning of the meeting.

4. *The analyses of the advantages*, disadvantages and problems in implementing each of the suggestions is usually left for the next meeting (Week 5). This has several advantages: circle members will have forgotten who offered the initial suggestions, new problems may have surfaced during the week, and members also can use the delay to study each of the problems.

5. *Difficult problems are eliminated.* These include those which do not assist in fulfilling circle goals and objectives, those for which the circle will not receive credit, those for which information is not available and those which other organizational groups are studying. Also, each problem that can be easily analyzed and rectified is assigned to one group member for study. The member is asked to report within a specified time period.

6. If no agreement on a problem occurs as a result of the discussion, the group decides on a *method to select the best problem* (Week 6). The Delphi method is a useful tool for this purpose and should be reviewed by the team prior to or during this session.

7. In the next step of the process, members first search within their work setting for *sub-causes of the problem*. To do this, they examine the materials, equipment, methods and personnel. After reviewing the Ishikawa principles, this diagram is constructed showing all sub-causes (Week 7).

8. Usually members have similar *perceptions* of the important sub-causes at this point. The circle, however, may wish to do more data gathering (on how sub-causes contribute to the problem) before making a decision regarding their perception of the few that account for most of the variation in the problem and which should be examined more thoroughly.

9. The group is finally ready to *use the seven basic tools of statistics* (Week 9). After these are reviewed and a plan of action is developed by the circle (e.g., observe scrap, rejects, rework), each member accepts an assignment and agrees to complete it within a specified time period. This assignment will verify whether or not the sub-causes which have been identified are critical to the elimination of the problem.

Generally, a checklist or checksheet for each sub-cause, procedure or technique that must be observed and charted is also developed.

10. Each member of the circle *performs the assigned work* and prepares charts, graphs and Pareto diagrams (in subsequent weeks). Each week while the research is continuing, members make progress reports to the circle.

11. Also, during the time period when members are conducting their research on an individual basis, the *circle determines the criteria* that are to be utilized, if necessary, to determine if a problem (effect) can be "solved" by eliminating or improving the specified sub-causes. Such factors as cost, availability of materials and political considerations are specified.

12. The results of the individual analyses, together with the Pareto diagrams, are *presented to the circle meeting* and the findings are discussed.

13. Often sub-causes that must be improved, eliminated or adapted will be obvious after this presentation. If not, the circle members, using the criteria previously developed and the modified Delphi technique, *select* these.

14. At this point, the circle has only identified certain sub-causes that are contributing to the problem. *Solutions to the sub-causes* are suggested by use of brainstorming. (Some circles, however, like to use the fishbone diagram).

15. *An action plan and checklists* are developed specifying the activities and procedures that must be examined.

16. *The results* of the individual analyses, together with charts and graphs, are presented to the circle meeting and the findings are discussed.

17. *The circle selects* the "best" solutions.

18. *Solutions are implemented*, if possible at this stage, on a small trial basis and the effects of the implementation are observed.

19. *Observations are discussed* by the circle.

20. When the circle feels it has information that should be shared with management and technical staff, or when it cannot proceed without approval or funding of its plans, it *prepares a report* outlining its research and its conclusions. In the process of preparing the report, data gathering again occurs. At this stage, this information search should provide confirmation of the previous conclusions.

21. Circle members make an *oral presentation* to appropriate technical and managerial personnel.

22. *Members participate in the implementation* of the recommended solutions and in analyzing and solving unforeseen events that occur.

23. A check is made that the problem has been eliminated or resolved. If it has, the circle begins again with a new problem.

The Process in Detail

Considerably greater detail is given in this and the following chapters. Brainstorming and the Delphi technique are described in the latter portion of this chapter. In Chapter 7, the Ishikawa diagram, the use of statistical tools and the selection of criteria for analyzing solutions are explained. In Chapter 8, suggestions for preparing professional reports and oral presentations are given.

REQUIRED DEFINITIONS

Problem

Cause

Sub-cause

Verifying the sub-causes

Solutions

Brainstorming

Delphi technique

Ishikawa/fishbone/cause-and-effect diagram

Action plans

Checklists and checksheets

THE STEPS IN THE PROCESS

Initial meeting
- Introductions
- Team leader selected
- Circle named
- Secretary elected
- Working kit provided
- Goals of company reviewed
- Productivity record reviewed

Circle goals and objectives established

Brainstorming for problems to be solved

Discussion of problem suggestions

Selection of one problem

Completion of fishbone diagram

Selection of sub-causes *perceived* to be most crucial to problem elimination

Development of action plans, checksheets and checklists to assist in sub-cause analyses

Assignment of activities to individual members for purpose of verifying sub-causes

Presentation to circle of verification (results of analyses, Pareto charts, etc.)

Selection of sub-causes *shown* to be most crucial to problem elimination or improvement

Brainstorming for solutions to identified sub-causes

Selection of most probable solutions

Development of action plans, checksheets and checklists to assist in analyses of solution

Assignment of activities to individual members for purposes of investigating and verifying solutions.

Selection of best solutions

Preparation of report

Oral presentation to members of technical and managerial staff

Implementation follow-through

New problem selected

Selecting a Problem

Brainstorming

The first task of the circle is to generate problems; the second is to choose one problem from the many alternatives that have been generated. One method by which problem ideas can be produced is through brainstorming.

Brainstorming is a thought-generating session. The aim is to provoke as many ideas as possible in the time available. No thought is given to the practicality of the suggestions or the changes that may be required to implement them. All ideas are simply jotted down without appraisal. Appraisal as to advantages, disadvantages and problems in implementing occurs only after all ideas have been generated. Two examples of a problem list generated through brainstorming are given in Figures 6–2 and 6–3. Five other variations can also be used. These are: (1) the Gordon approach,[1] (2) the black box technique,[2] (3) the synetics system,[3] (4) the collective notebook method,[4] and (5) the Phillips 66 buzz session.[5]

The Gordon Approach. The Gordon approach is very similar to brainstorming, but there is one difference: the specific reason for the brainstorming is not revealed

---

FIGURE 6–2
Results of Brainstorming in a Medical Laboratory

Brainstorming for Problems: Medical Laboratory
 1. Excessive removal of supplies by non-lab personnel
 2. Stat abuse, especially on holidays
 3. Lack of orientation for doctors
 4. Broken drawers
 5. Holiday weekend scheduling
 6. Improperly filled-out requisitions
 7. Mislabelled specimens
 8. Getting admission results on charts
 9. Specimens dumped en masse on the lab by nurses at the end of their shift
10. Excessive phone calls for results
11. Slick floors outside histology
12. Inadequate directions to help patients find the lab
13. Time wasted on multiple trips to the copying machine
14. Bad connections on phone calls from reference lab
15. Unnecessary ordering of tests
16. Coverage of clerk's phone when clerk is out
17. Insufficient recognition for jobs well done
18. Excessive memoranda
19. Too much noise made by maintenance workers
20. Abuse of beeper paging

Source: Sybil A. Wellstood and Linda Wright, "Using Quality Circles to Solve Lab Problems," *Medical Laboratory Observer*, February 1983: 34.

---

to the members. Members participate in suggesting problems or issues which they have observed.

Gordon, who originated this concept, felt that brainstorming had certain drawbacks. Often, when members feel that they have suggested the correct answer (problem idea, in this case), they lose interest in the process and concentrate instead on how to sell their idea at the evaluation stage.

The Black Box Technique. The black box technique solves problems through graphic presentations. Generally two situations are presented and the question that is asked is "What common problems could be causing this situation?" or "How can these two situations (machines, designs, structures) be made more compatible?" or "How can they function more harmoniously?"

The Synetics System. The synetics system is mentioned here even though it may

FIGURE 6–3
Results of Brainstorming for Problems Within a Prestigious Hotel*

Brainstorming for Problems: Hotel Industry

Complaints about staff

Linens

Poor-quality food

Leaky faucets

Bad supplies

Customer theft (towels, jewelry, pictures, ash trays, keys)

Dirty windows

Deliveries late and incomplete

High-priced food

Damage to vehicles in parking lot

Theft of contents of vehicles in parking lot

Valet abuse

Poor air conditioning and heating

Poor sales of desserts in dining room

Tea badly made

Poor elevator service

Slow or poor room service

Excessive noise and rowdy guests

Slow busboys

Lack of pest control

Lack of timely snow removal

Overbooking

Shortage of accommodation, couches, cribs

Complaints about child care

Inadequate advertising and promotion

Pool water too cold

TV reception inadequate

Insufficient use of conference rooms

Poor information desk and tour guides

Music in bars

Weak drinks

Inadequate security and safety

Bookings and reservations

Poor service in dining room

Inconvenient parking facilities

* This brainstorming problem list is a composite of lists developed by Central Michigan University students in the MSA 620 course (Organizational Behavior and Human Effectiveness) during October 1983.

be more useful in generating solutions than in problem ideas. There are three basic steps which involve an analysis of PAG (problem as given by the leader) and PAU (problem as understood by each of the members of the circle). When this analysis is completed, certain generalizations are reached. On the basis of the generalizations, model building occurs. The last phase involves extensive research and exchanges of thoughts and ideas, not only by members of the circle, but also by outside experts who may have expertise to help in the solution of the problem.

Collective Notebook. For the collective notebook technique, each member is provided with a pocket-sized notebook. Participants record in the notebook all problem ideas as they observe them during a one- or two-week period and present them at the circle meeting. All ideas are subsequently discussed and evaluated.

More frequently, notebooks are collected by the leader or the facilitator and are summarized for the next meeting.

Brainstorming is an excellent idea, but there is a tendency for members to evaluate the source of the idea rather than the suggestion itself. Under the collective notebook system, ownership of an idea is ambiguous; the responsibility of presenting and arguing for the concept is that of the leader or facilitator. This individual can clarify ambiguities prior to the meeting. To enhance participation and make threatened members feel more effective, she or he can obtain support for ideas from more dominant members of the circle.

Phillips 66 Buzz Session. The Phillips 66 buzz session uses a sub-group of six people who generate problem ideas for six minutes (6,6). Each group selects a recording secretary who reports the ideas to the larger group.

BRAINSTORMING

Thought-generating session.

Ideas flow freely.

No appraisal occurs.

Variations:
- Gordon approach
- black box technique
- synetics system
- collective notebook method
- Phillips 66 buzz session

Choosing One Problem

Many problem ideas will be generated at the brainstorming session. Many of them can be solved within a week or two because the causes are readily identifiable, because the information needed is readily available or can be obtained by the group and because the resources to complete the solution are within the control of the group. These types of problems are categorized as "immediate action," and one person is given the responsibility for seeking the additional information that is needed to resolve each issue and for implementing the solution.

This type of problem is illustrated by the following: An employee tried for many years to have the stool on which he sat moved eight inches to the right so that he could more easily reach his work area without standing. All requests failed; the man finally gave up. When he joined the quality circle, this was a top priority item. The circle designated it for immediate action, ascertained through research that the move had no additional consequences, and had the stool shifted immediately. The man was sold on circles!

The group problem which is chosen should be a more complex one, that is, one which appears to have no apparent or discernible solution. These require further analysis. If more than one problem idea of this type has been generated through brainstorming, the group must choose the most appropriate and acceptable one. This choice may be difficult because members sometimes feel committed to their own suggestions. A process of eliminating less desirable problem ideas is required. Generally, a three-pronged approach is useful. This includes:

1. Elimination of all problems which do not relate to or complement the established objectives of the unit.
2. Elimination of additional problems which do not meet pre-established operational criteria which the circle has set for itself.
3. The application of a modified Delphi technique to determine the one best problem.

On the Basis of Goals and Objectives. Prior to brainstorming for problem ideas, the circle usually sets some general objectives for improving the unit, that is, goals that the members feel should be attained. Generally, objectives that are set are very general in nature and can be such things as less machine down-time, lower scrap costs, better quality, improved cleanliness, better scheduling, etc.

Before selecting the objectives or goals, the circle can ask the production superintendent or quality control department to review the performance data for the unit and the objectives of the department and the company with them. The circle also may wish to set additional criteria by which the problem can be judged. Some of these criteria might be:

1. Is the implementation of the problem within the control of the unit? A problem suggesting that the company should be reorganized might be desirable, but the unit cannot control the implementation of this.
2. Is a solution attainable by the circle?
3. Does the problem provide sufficient challenge to the team and is it reasonably difficult?
4. When it is accomplished, can the results be measured?
5. Is the problem acceptable to each member of the team (or at least not objectionable)?
6. Is it within the unit work area?
7. Is it congruent with goals and objectives which the circle has established?
8. Is the opportunity cost that will be incurred to achieve success reasonable? Opportunity cost may include finding information, spending time in doing analyses, or giving up other opportunities.

These criteria, of course, are suggestive. The circle may feel that they do not need criteria for judging problems, that a different set are needed, or that they want to modify some existing set. Sometimes, it is better for the facilitator or leader to establish a set of criteria independently for himself or herself and call attention to particular ones that may cause the circle difficulty.

What purpose do these criteria have? The first, and the one of immediate interest, is that problem ideas can be eliminated from further discussion if they do not tie in with or complement the circle's established objectives.

On the Basis of Operational Criteria. A number of complex problems will be eliminated because they do not fit the goals which the circle has determined for the unit. Additional practical issues must be addressed, however, to eliminate other problem ideas. Of importance are:

1. Whether the problem lies within the area or unit. If the answer is no, the problem, at least for beginning circles, should be postponed. Circles, when they first begin to function, are extremely eager and feel that they would like to solve problems of considerable significance to the organization—that is, problems that are created for them in other units within the organization or external to the organization. There are some dangers in this approach.

First, external problems require a considerably longer time to solve. It is important that the circle experience early success. If the project takes too long, some members might become discouraged.

Second, the circle may be accused of meddling in other units' affairs. This may result in a lack of cooperation from those units. Considerable pressure may be placed on middle and senior management to disband the circle or to "clip its wings." External hostility always makes it difficult, if not impossible, for a circle to solve the problems that it has set for itself.

Third, because the problem lies elsewhere, the circle will lose control of methods to implement the solution. If that happens, other departments receive credit for the solutions determined by the circle.

2. The information requirements. An evaluation is made of how much outside help is needed, from whom, if each of these people or units are willing to cooperate, and if not, whether other sources of information or methods of getting this information are available. Obviously, if the information cannot be procured easily, that problem should be abandoned.

3. Timing. An estimate is made regarding the time that will be required to complete an analysis and to implement it. An ideal time span for a beginning circle to solve its first problem is approximately three months.

4. Effectiveness. Some thought is given to the benefits that can accrue to the organization and to individuals and how these improvements can be measured.

The group discusses each of these issues and generally is able to come to a consensus that certain problems should not be investigated because they are too difficult in terms of the benefits attained.

Using The Modified Delphi Technique. If more than one problem suggestion remains after discussion of the relationship to goals and the practicality of each, the modified Delphi technique can be used to reach a final decision.

In using this technique, members first discuss the merits and the importance of each of the outstanding problem ideas. After everyone has provided input, each member of the group ranks each of the remaining problems according to his or her preference (from 1 to the number of problems which remain) and assigns it a rating according to his or her perception of the importance of the problem to the organization (on a scale of 1 for most important to 10 for least important). The two rankings are multiplied together. Members' rankings for each problem idea are totalled. The one with the lowest score is chosen. Figures 6–4 and 6–5 illustrate the use of the modified Delphi technique. Figure 6–4 shows that the chosen problem is C—to try to eliminate the noise level; in Figure 6–5, Computer A is selected.

FIGURE 6–4

Use of the Modified Delphi Technique to Choose Among Problems Generated Through Brainstorming

Circle	A			B			C			D			E			F		
Members	P	I	T	P	I	T	P	I	T	P	I	T	P	I	T	P	I	T
Mary	6	1	6	3	10	30	1	1	1	2	1	2	5	6	30	4	3	12
	(6 × 1 = 6) (3 × 10 = 30)																	
John	4	4	16	2	2	4	1	6	6	3	1	3	5	2	10	6	3	18
Peter	1	3	3	2	6	12	3	7	21	4	1	4	5	5	25	6	5	30
Louise	2	3	6	1	9	9	3	1	3	4	7	28	5	6	30	6	5	30
Hilda	5	6	30	2	8	16	1	1	1	3	8	24	4	6	24	6	4	24
Brenda	4	8	32	1	6	6	2	5	10	3	4	12	6	6	36	5	8	40
Irene	6	1	6	5	7	35	4	1	4	3	1	3	2	4	8	1	2	2
Will	2	7	14	1	8	8	3	4	12	6	10	60	5	8	40	4	9	36
Total for problem idea			113			120			58			136			203			192

Problems which remain (lettered for convenience):
A Slick floors outside histology
B Coverage of clerk's phone when clerk is out
C Too much noise
D Mislabelled specimens
E Specimens dumped
F Excessive phone calls

P = Preference on a scale of 1–6 (there are 6 items); 1 signifies high preference for solving this problem; 6 indicates a low preference.

I = Importance on a scale of 1–10; 1 indicates that its solution would be highly important to the unit; 10 indicates that the solution would have a low effect.

T = Total (Rank multiplied by Importance).

FIGURE 6–5

Computer Comparison Worksheet* Used in Modified Delphi Technique Decision Making

	Average Weight (Importance of Factor)	Perception of "Goodness" of Each Computer on Given Factor					
		Average Raw Score			Average Weighted Score**		
		A	B	C	A	B	C
Cost	7						
Initial	4	8.0	6.7	7.3	32.0	26.8	29.2
Add on	1	0.0	0.0	0.5	0.0	0.0	0.5
Maintenance	2	8.0	7.0	6.0	16.0	14.0	12.0
Performance	7						
CAD	4	7.3	7.7	7.5	29.2	30.8	30.0
Other Academic	3	6.0	7.5	7.3	18.0	22.5	21.9
Function	10						
CAD Workstations CAD Analysis CAM Interface	5	9.0	6.0	7.5	45.0	30.0	37.5
Academic • Cobol • Fortran • Basic • PL1 • RPG II • IBM Assembler	3.5	7.2	7.1	7.0	25.2	24.9	24.5
Applications Software Micro Communications Alternate Operating Systems Networking Capability	1.5	7.0	5.7	5.0	10.5	8.6	7.5
Operating System	3	8.5	6.0	7.0	25.5	18.0	21.0
Resource Control Facilities	0.75						
Conversion	0.5						
Ease of Maintenance	0.75						
Ease of Use	1.0						

(cont'd)

Growth Capability		3	5.3	7.2	5.0	15.9	21.6	15.0
CAD CAM ·	1							
Interactive Terminals	1							
Processing	1							
Product Growth *Capability*	4	4	7.0	6.8	5.9	28.0	27.2	23.6
Vendor Support	3	3	2.0	6.8	9.0	6.0	20.4	27.0
Compatibility with *current equipment*		2						
Backup	1		4.0	0.0	0.0	4.0	0.0	0.0
Peripheral Mass Storage Sharing	1		4.0	0.0	0.0	4.0	0.0	0.0
						259.3	244.8	249.7

*This Delphi worksheet for the comparison of computers was developed at St. Clair College of Applied Arts and Technology under the guidance of Mr. Bruce McAusland, President, and Mr. Tom McCarthy, Executive Director of Educational Planning.

**Each member of the computer evaluation team would make two sets of evaluations. The first set weights the importance of the factor (cost, performance, etc.) to the purchaser/user. The second set describes the perception of the committee member of how adequately each computer would satisfy the criteria specified. The *average* response for the importance of the factor appears in columns 1 and 2; the *average* response of the adequacy of each factor for each computer appears in columns 3, 4, and 5. Columns 6, 7, and 8 are the product of the first two sets of columns, i.e., the average weighted score is obtained by multiplying the average factor weight by the average raw score. Numbers given are hypothetical. In this case, the highest number signifies the highest importance or the highest adequacy.

Should a number of problems receive almost identical scores, the group may wish to discuss the issues again and to rank and rate once more those which remain.

By Decree. A problem can also be selected by decree of the steering committee, the production superintendent or another party. The big advantages to this method are that circle members can begin work on a problem immediately and that the problem is pertinent to the organization. The main disadvantages are that the problem may not be important to the circle, that the circle members may feel used and manipulated, and that they will not approach the analysis and solution with the same dedication as they would for a problem selected by the circle. Nevertheless, it is probably the method that is most widely used with beginning groups.

There are many reasons for this. Members of the steering committee feel that they know the problems of the organization better, that the process is too complicated for rank-and-file workers, that it wastes too much time, that circle members cannot be trusted to choose suitable problems, that they do not know the problems, or that it is necessary to go slowly. Each of these beliefs violates the basic management philosophy and concept on which quality circles are based.

On the other hand, there can be considerable advantage to the circle in having the facilitator or steering committee assign a problem that is vital to the organization. First, when circles start out, the process can be extremely confusing; there are many new ideas and concepts and a new role is expected of members. Some of the confusion can be eliminated by having a ready-made problem. Second, problem delineation can be an extremely difficult and frustrating experience. The circle members, at the beginning, have not tested the problem selection skills which they have learned and have not yet established successful work-team relationships. Third, a problem selected by a senior group is one that is important to the organization. When the problem is resolved, greater recognition results. Fourth, senior groups, because they have more decision-making experience, are more likely to select a problem that can be analyzed and resolved within a relatively short period of time. Fast progress will hold the member's interest. The circle therefore should think seriously about requesting that the first problem be assigned.

CHOOSING THE ONE PROBLEM

Criteria
It is congruent with unit objectives.

It is practical.
- Lies within the unit.
- Has obtainable information requirements.
- Can be completed within a reasonable time.
- Will benefit organization or individuals.

Procedure
By decree.

By modified Delphi technique.
- Discussion.
- Each member ranks problem ideas according to preference.
- Each member rates problem ideas according to importance to organization.
- Rank score is multiplied by importance score for each person and each item.
- Scores of all members for each problem area are added together.
- The idea with the lowest score is chosen.

7 Problem (Effect) Analysis

After the problem (effect that will be analyzed) has been selected, the activities of the circle centre around four main activities:
1. Suggesting possible sub-causes of the effect (problem) by analyzing the situation from a materials, equipment, methods and personnel perspective.
2. Investigating or verifying each probable sub-cause. This is generally accomplished by gathering and analyzing information and by obtaining input from experts who have the necessary knowledge.
3. Deciding on a course of action to eliminate or improve the most crucial sub-cause deficiency.
4. Preparing a report and making a presentation to senior and functional management who can authorize implementation of the ideas.

Three of these activities are discussed in this chapter; the last is discussed in the next chapter.

Analysis of the Problem

After there is agreement on one problem, there is a need to define that problem more precisely and to verify it. This is done by:
1. Determining how it is affecting the operations of the unit or company.
2. Determining what is the sub-cause of the problem through cause and effect analysis.
3. Verifying the diagnosis through checksheets, sampling, graphs and Pareto analysis.

The details of sampling, preparing graphs, and doing Pareto analysis are described in Chapter 9. The other two issues are discussed here.

How Is the Problem Affecting Operations?

The first issue that must be decided is how and to what extent the problem that has been selected is affecting the operation of the unit and company. This information is generally easily available from such sources as the rejects and repair sheets. If the problem selected has no significant impact on the company, it probably should not be tackled no matter how interesting it sounds or how interested individual members are in pursuing it. It will be extremely difficult to justify later and will give the circle little opportunity for interacting with technical people and middle and senior management, or for gaining credibility.

The Cause of the Problem

Two main methods exist by which an analysis of the causes of the effect can be made: cause-and-effect diagrams and process analysis or flow diagrams. Both types are similar and differ only in the method of construction.

A cause-and-effect diagram is a sequence of lines and symbols which illustrate the relationship between an effect (the problem that has been selected) and its causes. The flow diagram achieves the same purpose through a series of steps or boxes.

The cause-and-effect diagram is also known as a fishbone analysis or Ishikawa diagram (after Professor Kaoru Ishikawa of the University of Tokyo, who first used this method at the Fukiai iron works in 1953). It starts with a skeleton such as that shown in Figure 7–1. The head of the fish is the problem that the circle is attempting to solve (i.e., the effect that has been observed).

FIGURE 7–1
Fishbone Diagram

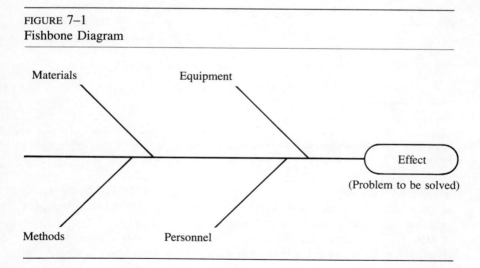

Four main areas in which the deficiency could occur are the *Materials*, the *Equipment*, the *Methods* or the *Personnel*. Circle members, through brainstorming, examine each of these four areas one at a time. At the same time, they suggest possible sub-causes. As each person makes a suggestion in turn (or

FIGURE 7–2
Completed Fishbone

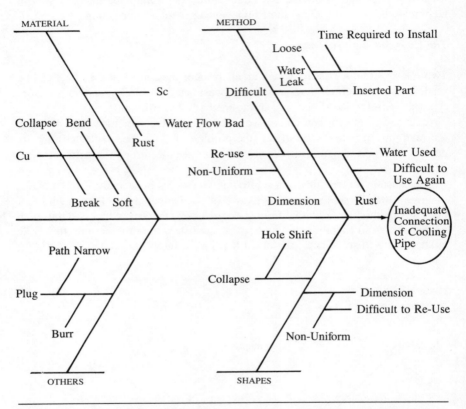

Source: Ford Casting Division Japanese Productivity Study Group, *Report on the Japanese Automotive Foundry Industry*, December 1980, unpaginated.

passes), the idea is placed on the fishbone (see Figure 7–2). Finally the group as a whole decides on the most likely sub-causes—those that will be investigated further—and these are circled (see Figure 7–3).

After the sub-causes are discussed, if a consensus decision has not been reached, the group can either vote on those which are most likely or decide that additional analysis needs to be done. Additional analysis answers such questions as: Does the same sub-cause occur under more than one classification? Are there deviations? Is there consistency or does it change? Does it occur all the time? Some of the time? At the end, an action plan is developed for the purpose of determining whether each of the identified sub-causes is at fault and as a written

FIGURE 7–3

Completed Fishbone With Most Likely Causes Circled

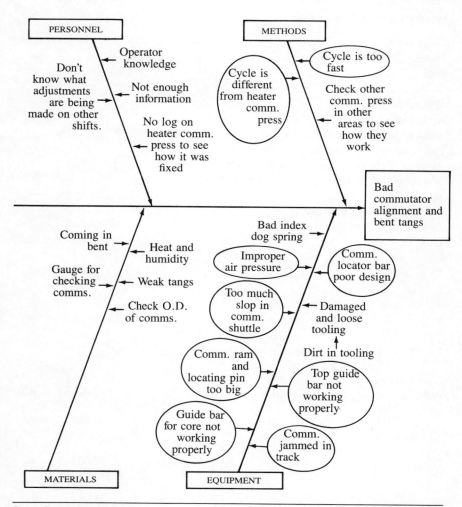

Source: R.A. Ball and S.P. Barney, *Quality Circle Project Manual* (Dearborn, MI: Ford Motor Co.): 23.
"Comm." = commutator.

record of who is to do the work. Figures 7–4 and 7–5 are two different types of action plans.

Process analysis is very much like fishbone analysis. At the beginning of the process is the effect we have noticed (that is, the problem we have chosen to analyze). Each of the activities or steps in the process is retraced, beginning

FIGURE 7–4
Action Register

Quality Circle Action Register

Circle Name _____   Circle Area _____

Problem Selected _____

Date _____

Meeting Agenda
Review of previous meeting—Leader
Status update on projects—Leader
Follow-up report of implementation of projects—Facilitator
Analysis of current problem(s)—Circle members
Assignment of action items—Leader and members

Action Items (Immediate problems):
Assignment or problem to be investigated   Responsible member
1.
2.
3.
4.
5.
6.
7.
8.

Long-Term Items:
Problems currently being analyzed   Responsible member
1.
2.
3.
4.
5.
6.
7.

with the most recent and working backwards (Figure 7–6). Each of the steps or activities is then examined for possible sub-causes. Again, all ideas are jotted down, interrelationships are indicated, and sub-causes are analyzed to determine the ones that are most probable.

FIGURE 7–5
Action Plan

Action Plan (to tie objectives with established timetable)

Target Area: _____   Date: _____
Shop: _____   Facilitator: _____
Section: _____   Circle Leader: _____

| | | Scheduled Completion |
Tactics	Assigned To	Date
1.		
2.		
3.		
4.		
5.		
6.		
7.		
8.		

Prepared by: _____
Date: _____

Constructing the Cause-and-Effect Diagram

Cause-and-effect diagrams are the key method of problem analysis. As a consequence, every circle member needs to be able to construct the fishbone without hesitation. To review the process again:

1. Goals, measurement criteria and time limits are established.

2. The problem to be solved is identified (effect). Steps 1 and 2 have been discussed in some detail earlier.

3. The cause-and-effect diagram starts with a basic fishbone in which the specific effect is indicated with an arrow. An arrow leads to the effect or the "head of the fish" (Figure 7–7).

4. The four words "materials," "equipment," "methods," and "personnel" are placed on the bones of the fish. These are the causes of the effect (see Figure 7–8). Other items such as "shapes" and "design" also may be used.

5. The circle starts with one of the causes, such as "Equipment." Each member, in turn, suggests a sub-cause. These are written on the fishbone. No evaluation, comment or criticism occurs at this stage. Also, there are no "bad" ideas; even

FIGURE 7–6
Process Analysis or Flow Diagram with Verifications

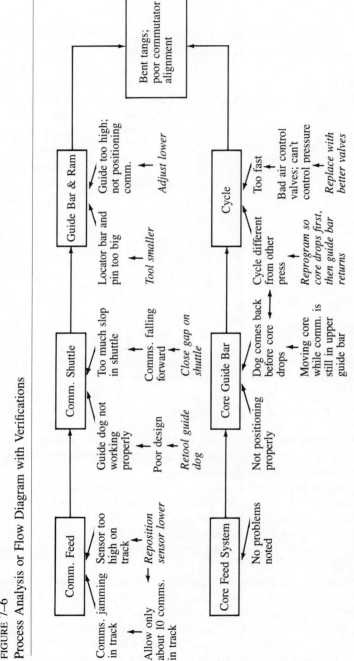

*Corrective actions are italicized.

Source: R. A. Ball and S. P. Barney, *Quality Circles Project Manual* (Dearborn, MI: Ford Motor Co.): 23.

FIGURE 7–7
Fishbone Diagram

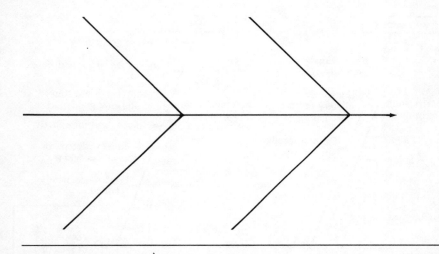

FIGURE 7–8
Fishbone Diagram

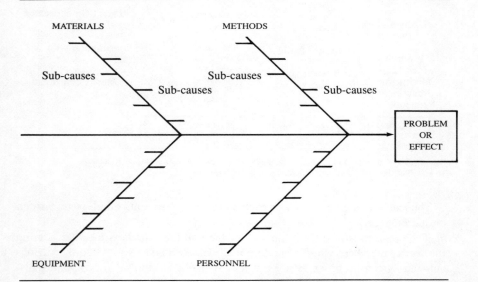

false or ''dumb'' ideas can inspire other circle members to identify the true sub-cause.

FIGURE 7–9

A Completed Fishbone Diagram for In-House Cafeteria

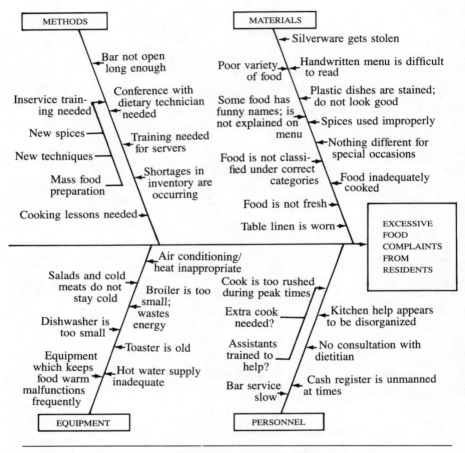

Source: This cause-and-effect diagram was contributed by Central Michigan University students Jane McGlauflin, John Kern, V. Joyce Milton, and Jim Young.

6. The leader continues to call on each member, in turn, until all ideas are written on the diagram (Figure 7–9).

7. The diagram is posted on the wall of the unit until the next meeting. During the week, members who have additional ideas can add these. Also the various sub-causes can be observed for a week. A major advantage of postponing discussion is that members will forget who originated the idea. As a consequence, they will be more comfortable criticizing the idea and will not feel they are criticizing the person who suggested the idea.

8. Members analyze each of the sub-causes in an attempt to find the most likely or "true" causes. As these are identified, they are circled.

9. The diagram is left on the wall. It may be necessary to determine new "true" causes if analysis indicates that those which have been selected contribute to the effect in only a limited way.

10. Each of the circled sub-causes is analyzed by the circle group to determine how investigation and verification can be conducted.

11. Members select or the leader assigns each of the sub-causes to one or more members of the group for investigation.

12. Members conduct research on each sub-cause and report, presenting charts and graphs, at the next meeting.

Verifying the Sub-Causes of the Problem Through Data Collection

When suspected sub-causes have been identified, a follow-up of each is required to determine if it is contributing to the problem. This is the data-gathering and analysis part of the diagnosis. Four techniques can assist in the gathering of data:

1. using checklists or sheets
2. drawing graphs—line, bar or circle graphs, histograms or scatter diagrams
3. doing Pareto analysis
4. carrying out sampling and statistical analyses

   The use of all techniques is discussed here; the introduction to the construction of graphs and to sampling is left to Chapters 9 and 10.

Checklists and Checksheets

Everyone uses checklists. For example, a checklist shows the groceries that must be purchased at the store or the activities that must be completed during a specified time period. As each item is purchased or as each activity is completed, it is checked off or crossed off the list (see Figure 7–10). In the same way, the circle members use the checklist as a guide to the processes and activities which they must observe and analyze.

A checksheet is just a checklist that is a bit more complicated. It specifies what action is to be taken, when it is to be done, by whom, the tools that will be used, and the specific standards or cautions (Figure 7–11).

The items that go on a checklist or sheet are agreed to by circle members. Frequently the responsibility for constructing the checklist or sheet is given to an individual member; in that case, additional items are added later by the group. After the members have agreed to the items on the checklist or sheet, the responsibility for carrying out the actions specified is assigned to individual team members.

FIGURE 7–10
Checklist Regarding Situation Which Exists in a Shop

Checklist—Situation Analysis

Circle _____ Date _____
Shop and Section _____ Circle Leader _____
Target Area _____ Facilitator _____
Circle Members _____ _____
_____ _____
_____ _____
_____ _____
_____ _____

Repair Method
☐ Appropriate shop tools and machinery
☐ Availability of unrepaired product
☐ Capital alignment
☐ Excessive wait time
☐ Junking of material
☐ Line balance
☐ Material availability to operator
☐ Material flow
☐ Repetitive motions
☐ Shop inventory of material
☐ Use of modern technology
☐ Appropriate use of floor space
☐ Wasted motions
☐ Working conditions and environment

Utilization of Human Resources
☐ Employee application
☐ Employees have proper skills and training
☐ Labour relations
☐ Safety
☐ Supervisory management

Other Items (Write these out)
☐
☐

FIGURE 7–11
Checksheet

Maintenance Check Sheet

Systems: Cupola
Maintenance ranking: A

Checking Items	Checking Cycles	Checkpoints and Standards	Checked By	Tools	Reference
1. Outer shell of melting zone	Every 3 months	• Thin spots on outer shell • When a thin spot is found, the thickness is checked with a small run through hole. • Minimum limit: 3 mm	Melt Foreman	Hammer	Melting one is replaced every 2 years.
2. Pre-heat zone	"	"	"	"	Pre-heat zone is replaced every 2 years
3. Tuyere	Every day	• Thin spots, hollows, water leaks • Hollows are filled by welding	"		
4. Cooling condition in melting zone and tuyere	More than 3 times a day	• Checking and cleaning of cooling water nozzle holes • No foreign body allowed	"		In case of many foreign bodies, checking cycle is shortened to every 3 hours
	Every Month	• Foreign body in tuyere cooling water box • No foreign body allowed.	"	Specified tool	

(cont'd)

Checking Items	Checking Cycles	Checkpoints and Standards	Checked By	Tools	Reference
5. Recuperator	Every 5 shifts	• Dust removing • Checking outer shell • Checking and mending of lining	"	Wire brush Broom	Replace interval • Secondary recuperator Upper part—2 years Lower part—4 years • Primary recuperator—6 years
6. Corrosion on chimney	Every 3 months	• Tapping test	"	Hammer	
7. Air leak	"	• Duct joints, recuperators • No air leak at all	"		

Systems: Dust Collector
Maintenance ranking: A

Checking Items	Checking Cycles	Checkpoints and Standards	Checked By	Tools	Reference
1. Filter	Every month	• All damaged filters are replaced	Foreman	"CONEX 5055U" by "Nakao Filter"	
2. Dust bag	Every 3–4 hrs.	• Replace bag when full	"		

Problem (Effect) Analysis 119

3. Duct fan motor	Every year	• Grease	"	
4. Duct fan	Every 3-4 hrs.	• Thermo color tape on bearings "White"	"	When the temperature rises over 70°C, the color tape turns from white to red
	Every year	• Grease the bearings	"	
	Every 3 months	• Impelor —Endusting —No deposit is allowed	Specified tool	
5. Rotary valves	Every 6 months	• Motor oil replacement	Maintenance people	
	Every year	• Grease the bearings	Foreman	
	Every month	• Chain tension check and oiling	"	
6. Dust remover	Every month	• V-belt tension check	"	Wear in V-belts and pulleys are also checked
	"	• Grease the worm speed reducer	"	
	"	• Oil pan cleaning	"	

Source: Ford Casting Division Japanese Productivity Study Group, *A Report on the Japanese Automotive Foundry Industry* (Windsor, Ont., unpaginated).

Graphs

Someone once said that a picture is worth a thousand words. Graphs are visual representations of what is occurring. Their purpose is to illustrate connections or interrelationships among two or more elements (such as variables and causes). Also, well-constructed graphs save time and make explanations easier. For these reasons, circle members should graph as many of their observations and analyses as possible.

There are many types of graphs. Among the simplest are bar graphs, line graphs, circle graphs and pie graphs. Often these four are all that are necessary. If more sophisticated graphs are desired, then histograms, scattergrams and the widely publicized Pareto diagram can be used.

As circle members become more experienced in graph construction, they may wish to show comparisons and relationships through cumulative frequency polygons, geometric line charts, ogive curves and Lorenz curves, and through the use of various types of logarithmic graph paper.

Graphs are extremely easy to construct, and members of circles should not hesitate to use even the most complex-sounding of these. Generally, the most awesome part of a graph is the name that has been given to it. Usually graphs are easier to read if they are drawn on graph paper or on grids. Colour coding and labels may be used if desired. Instructions are given in Chapter 9 for the most commonly used types of graphs.

Pareto Diagrams

The Pareto diagram is named after the Italian economist and sociologist Vilfredo Pareto (1848-1923). Pareto first used the illustration to show the number of people in various income classes and added the numbers in these groups from poorest to richest. Today, Pareto diagrams are used to identify sub-causes which contribute to a particular effect. The most important sub-causes are shown first on the graph so that the greatest amount of attention and resources can be directed to correcting these first.

While this section refers to showing sub-causes using the Pareto diagram, causes and effects can be shown just as well. In fact, these diagrams are usually constructed on the basis of many variables, including defect, shift, machine and operation.

Pareto diagrams are used to indicate how one particular element or sub-cause contributes to the entire problem. These diagrams are particularly useful in showing improvement. When a particular sub-cause is identified and corrected, its occurrence and contribution to the total number of defects should decrease. It is not unusual for circle members to start their problem diagnosis with Pareto diagrams, then brainstorm, construct cause-and-effect diagrams and finally construct additional Pareto diagrams.

This graph combines bar graphs and a line graph. The bar graph illustrates the amount which each sub-cause contributes to the whole, and the line graph illustrates the whole or total problem.

Sampling

Probably the most difficult decisions that circle members make are those concerning sampling. Sampling involves a process where a small number or proportion of items (or people) is selected from the entire population for detailed examination and analysis in order that decisions (estimates) can be made about the quality or the nature of the whole population or the entire product being produced.

In the factory or plant, sampling is relatively easy. The quality control centre is already engaged in this activity. Individuals from this centre, therefore, can be most helpful in explaining the methods which they use.

The two simplest methods of sampling are to choose a specified number of items at random (without concern for time, machine, operator, etc.; in other words, in the same way that numbers are chosen from a hat) or at varying intervals. When varying interval sampling is utilized, a few items are selected every half-hour, or at some specified interval, and are analyzed or compared to predetermined standards. On the basis of the chosen sample, conclusions are made about the entire production process.

"How big should the sample be?" is a question that is often asked. For beginning circles, a good common-sense rule is to take as large a sample as is needed to feel reasonably comfortable with the decision that has to be made. Sampling, however, is costly, and caution must be exercised. Frequently the quality control department can assist in this decision. The question also is discussed in Chapter 10.

Completing the Process: Eliminating Sub-Causes

After the sub-causes of the effect have been analyzed and it has been determined with some reasonable certainty that some sub-causes are more important than others, some type of closure is necessary. In other words, because of the expense, a decision must be made to seek solutions for only one or two of the most important sub-causes. To do this, the verified sub-causes are listed and the available data, complete with observations, charts and graphs, are reviewed. Finally, following a team discussion, solutions to the selected sub-causes are suggested and a selection of the one or two most suitable solutions is made (after additional observations and analyses) using criteria which are developed by the circle.

Examples of such common-sense criteria include:
1. Does it solve the problem?
2. Is implementation possible?

FIGURE 7–12
Analysis Sheet: Does Solution Meet Established Criteria?

Circle _____   Department _____
The Problem _____   Cause No. _____

To What Extent Does/Is Solution

Possible Solution and Causes	Solve Problem?	Implemen- tation Possible?	Effective?	Acceptable?	Require Resources? Available?	Provide Credit for Our QC?

3. Is it the cheapest and most effective method?
4. Is the solution acceptable to the main parties?
5. Are the resources available or could they be made available without upsetting the organization?
6. Will the quality circle receive credit for it? If not, is there an equally good solution that can solve the problem and for which the quality circle will get credit?

Criteria can be developed if desired through brainstorming; generally this is unnecessary. Circles which do prefer to formalize their evaluation process can develop a useful device similar to the matrix that is shown in Figure 7–12 for analyzing whether the solution meets the established criteria.

Finally, the solutions that receive the highest rating, that is, those which will contribute most to the elimination of the problem and which best satisfy the established criteria, are selected and, after approval, are implemented. Implementation requires that an action plan be developed. This plan specifies what will be done, who will do the work, by what deadline, how they will do it, what assistance or resources are needed, and the standards that must be met.

FIGURE 7–13
Control Chart

Circle _____   Department _____
Target Selection Area _____

General Objectives

1. _____   3. _____
2. _____   4. _____

Actions

1. _____   4. _____
2. _____   5. _____
3. _____   6. _____

Progress on Objectives/Actions

Date	Monitored By	Results	Additional Problems/Actions

Monitoring Results

Solutions that have been implemented are monitored. There are five reasons for this:

1. To ensure that the problem really has been solved.
2. To measure improvement.
3. To modify any ancillary effects that might not have been anticipated in the implementation which could detract from the solution.
4. To assist employees in accepting the change.
5. For quality circle prestige and recognition.

Two instruments are required for monitoring results—a checklist of activities that are required and observations that are to be made and control charts. The checklist information is already available on the action sheet and can be transferred easily. Control sheets show the progress on a daily or weekly basis. An example is shown in Figure 7–13.

FIGURE 7–14
Reminder Sheet Regarding Goals and Objectives

Circle Name _____   Department _____

Goals which the group has selected

1. _____
2. _____
3. _____
4. _____

Current Performance	Desired Standard	Benefits to be Realized
1.		
2.		
3.		
4.		

Progress on goals (activity and information about progress)

To conclude the project, new graphs may have to be drawn, a new sample selected, and additional statistical calculations may have to be done.

The circle also will wish to record the progress that has been made toward the goals and objectives that have been set. A large wall chart, similar to the one shown in Figure 7–14, can be used.

A final word of caution is in order. Many techniques and forms have been provided in this chapter. They are suggestive in nature. *It is always better for the circle to develop its own criteria, its own methods and its own forms, if and when they are required.* The illustrations indicate the type of format and the terms that can be used.

PROBLEM ANALYSIS AND SOLUTION

Problem (effect) defined.

Causes of the problem are MEMP:
- materials
- equipment
- methods
- personnel

All probable sub-causes identified by use of fishbone or process analysis.

Sub-causes investigated through use of:
- checklists and checksheets
- graphs
- Pareto analysis
- sampling

Preferred sub-causes identified.

Possible solutions to identified sub-causes investigated.

Preferred solutions identified.

Actions required to implement preferred solution identified.

Action plan and checklist developed.

Action implemented.

Implementation monitored to:
- ensure problem solved
- measure improvement
- modify unexpected effects
- explain the change
- for prestige and recognition

Report written and oral presentation made.

CONSTRUCTING AND USING CAUSE-AND-EFFECT DIAGRAMS

Goals Set
Use of Ishikawa (fishbone) diagram.
- problem identified
- basic fishbone drawn
- fishbone labelled
- sub-causes identified, written on fishbone

Members conduct research and report.
- "true" causes identified and circled
- circle determines *how* investigation of sub-causes can be done
- members select sub-causes to investigate
- final sub-cause selected

8 The Final Details: The Report and the Presentation

Writing the Formal Report

When the circle has completed its investigation and made some decisions, it writes a formal report presenting its findings to the technical experts and senior management. This report serves at least five purposes:
1. It assists readers in understanding the problem and the facts.
2. It convinces readers that the information is trustworthy.
3. It assists readers in reaching a decision.
4. It assists readers in evaluating the competence and ability of those who wrote the report.
5. It provides a permanent record of the work and the recommendations.
To accomplish these objectives, it is necessary to:
1. Follow a conventional style in organizing the report.
2. Answer specific questions that the reader may have.
3. Know the audience who will be reading the report.
4. Prepare the report in a technical format that will be psychologically appealing and easy for the reader to follow.
5. Distribute the document.
   A further analysis is made of each of these details.

Organization

By convention, reports have at least four sections. The first section explains the problem, why it was undertaken and the possible benefits that improvements were perceived to have. The second portion explains the methodology—what the circle members did and how they gathered information. A third part includes a presentation of the findings, that is, the cause-and-effect relationships. These generally are in both text and quantitative data format. The fourth section includes the conclusions, the recommendations, the cost-benefit analyses and/or the results of the monitoring process. Recommendations address *what, who, where, when* and *why*: issues of what is to be done, who is to do it, where it should be done, at what time or within what duration it should be done and why it is recommended.

Findings in Text Format. The text describes, in words, the results of the investigation that circle members conducted. It should be written in short simple sentences, without the unnecessary use of technical or difficult words. It is better to impress others with the thoroughness and high quality of the analyses than by the use of long complicated-sounding words. Indeed, these may make it more difficult for others to understand the substance of the problem and the recommendations. Care should be taken to arrange topics and facts in logical order.

Headings and subheadings are important in the organization of the data. The most important heading is usually in capital letters and centered. The lesser heading is centered, in normal typing and underlined. A more subordinate heading is in normal typing, appears at the left-hand side and is underlined. Each company, however, has its own style, and circle members should consult other reports which have been prepared by executives (and their staffs) within the organization. It goes without saying that the report focuses on the practical, is complete, is honest and is highly readable. Readability can be accomplished by attention to grammatical style and technical detail.

Presenting Quantitative Data. Bosses usually want the facts (numbers) together with what these numbers mean (conclusions) and what should be done about them (recommendations). This means that special care must be taken to make statistical sections not only accurate and precise, but also interesting. Certain guidelines are generally followed:

1. All numbers are checked for accuracy.

2. A generous number of *useful* charts, graphs and tables are included, particularly small or "spot" tables (these highlight parts of larger tables). The use of spot tables avoids cluttering the writing with too many figures.

Because most readers find it annoying to have to flip back and forth, supporting information is placed as close to the discussion as possible. It also can be placed at the end of the report or in the appendices. If the table or illustration is large and only marginally relevant, or if only certain parts of it are relevant to the topic under discussion, it is common for the table to appear in the appendices. Of course, the text must report that the figure or table exists and its function. Furthermore, the figure or table, if placed in the text, appears after (not before) it is mentioned.

3. Each table and figure should be so well labelled that it can stand alone, without the text. At any time in the future, it should be possible to determine what it represents and the point in time at which the study was done. Headings therefore must be very complete.

4. Many readers find it difficult to interpret charts, graphs and tables. It therefore is necessary to talk, within the text, about the contents of supporting information.

5. The use of too many or too large numbers can intimidate readers. Figures can be made more meaningful if they are related to the whole or to another variable, by the use of percentages, ratios, ranges, averages and trends, or if

very large numbers are rounded off. (For example, $2,556,789.34 is more easily understood if, in the text, it is given as two and one-half million dollars).

6. Each table, illustration and appendix begins on a new page.

Questions

Readers generally want the following seven questions answered:

1. What is the problem?
2. What is the best or necessary way for the problem to be resolved?
3. On what basis has this decision been made?
4. Is the implementation feasible? How?
5. What pitfalls exist as a result of implementation?
6. What alternate actions are available and what are the costs and benefits of each of these?
7. What costs and benefits (both financial and personal) result because of the implementation?

The report attempts to answer these questions. In doing so, it considers the temperaments and personalities of the key readers. Some readers prefer extensive quantitative data, while others want none at all. The circle members should determine who the key readers will be and what those readers' preferences are.

Generally, most readers expect the report to be accurate, reliable, unprejudiced and clear. They also expect conclusions to be objective (based on fact) rather than emotional. That is not to say that subjective judgments (feelings and impressions of the circle members) cannot be used. They can, but they must be clearly identified as such.

In answering the questions, documentation is provided to back up what is said. Here the observations, charts and graphs play a major part.

Technical Details

A good report has a cover, title page, table of contents, table of illustrations, list of tables and executive summary. All start on a new page. If other authors' work has been used in preparing the report, or if such information is paraphrased, a bibliography is also necessary. Other preliminary material that is included within a specific organization can be observed by examining reports which are on file.

The cover merely protects the remainder of the report. Most organizations have guidelines regarding the type of cover page or cover that should be used. The title page specifies the name of the study and its nature and purpose, to whom the study is being presented, who has prepared the report, and the date. Tables of contents and lists of tables and illustrations enumerate the respective items and the page on which each item is located. The executive summary is a one- or two-page abstract of the report. It is necessary because it gives a quick view of what the report is about, because executives are busy people and generally will not read a full report, and because an executive summary is cheaper to distribute—especially if a large number of people must know the essence of the report but do not need the entire copy. The executive summary is placed after the title page.

Finally, nothing makes a report look shabbier and less credible than a bad typing job. Unless circle members have considerable report-typing skills, this task should be delegated to a competent secretary. The facilitator has the responsibility of ensuring that support services of this type are available.

Distribution

One last question remains. To whom should the project report be sent? First, all circle members, the facilitator and the members of the steering committee receive a copy. Second, it is distributed at the oral presentation to all those who are present. Unless participants are required to examine the report during the presentation itself (this should be unnecessary), it is given out following the oral session. In this way, participants are not distracted and can concentrate on the oral presentation itself.

Following this (and not before), the document may be distributed to all others who are interested or concerned. Most circles seek as wide a distribution as possible—keeping in mind the formal hierarchical structure of the organization and the fact that reporting channels do exist.

A Different Type of Report

A report that was prepared by a Japanese quality control circle is illustrated in Figure 8–1. Interesting to note are the details:
1. Signatures of the members.
2. Details regarding the membership and the history of the circle.
3. Reasons for the selection of the project.
4. Analysis of the present situation.
5. Details of countermeasures (causes and improvements).
6. Details of the follow-up.
7. Results and impression of the improvements.

This particular report was reduced to one $8^1/_2''$ × 11'' page—a very handy format. (Perhaps U.S. and Canadian organizations should ask quality circles to suggest ways in which organizational reports here could be reduced to similar size!)

Has the work of the circle concerning the project been completed at this point? No. Circle members also should make one or more presentations. The next section assists members in preparing for this.

FIGURE 8–1
A Japanese Quality Circle Report

Report on "MQ" Circle Activity Results

Date _____

Signatures

Chief   Q.C.   Foreman   C. Leader

Dept. Name: 2nd Casting Group, 1st Sect

Circle Name: Kin (plane) Circle

Circle Leader: Susumu Kaneichi

Content of Project: Transfer from molding to cleaning operations

Activity Theme: Improve the rate of operation by counter-measure or planning

Goal of Project: Number of trouble should be reduced by 70%

Project duration: March to August 1980

Members

Members: 6

Average Age: 43 Yr.

Oldest Age: 50 Yr.

Youngest Age: 33 Yr.

Circle Formation: Oct. 1975

Meeting Time: Approx. 5 Hr.

No. of Meeting: 4 Times

Project History: Eleventh

Reasons for Selecting Project

1. In order to challenge on the model line, this theme should be tackled.
2. It makes operations easier.
3. Do not block molding line process.

Analysis of Present Situation

Equipment and Number of Breakdowns at Product Transfer

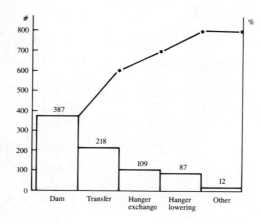

(cont'd)

(Figure 8–1 cont'd)

Project Planning Table (1980/83)

Execution Item	*Person in Charge*
Selection of theme	All member
Analysis of present condition	
Pickup of problem points	
Study of counter-measure	
Implement counter-measure	
Certification of results	
Drag or brake	All member

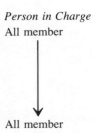

Analysis of Main Causes

Problem Points	*Main Causes*			
Trouble of dam breakdown equipment	No breakdown	No dag under impact	Position cannot be determined	Position of product is shifted sideways
Trouble on transfer equipment	Does not catch products	No product under clamp	Position determination is poor	Product is shifted when dam is broken
Hanger exchange equipment	Hanger of S.M.B. cannot be in position	Not at the center of receiver	Product moves	The receiving stage is not stable
Hanger lowering equipment	Casting does not slide from a slide	Product is stuck	Metal overflows at pouring cup	Too much metal flow

Details of Counter-measures (Itemize all and please write in detail the following):
Who was in charge.
Designation of responsibility to members.
Date of meetings and schedules.

Major Cause	**Counter-measure and Improvement**
Trouble of dam rupture equipment	*Counter-measure 1*—Install Y-shaped receiver on the surface plate

Position of product shifted
sideway on plate

Result—The products bump into the receiver
　　Failure

Counter-measure 2—Install stopper on slide
Result—There was a slippage depending on the
type of machine

Counter-measure 3—Installation of guide—A guide
was installed along the sides of the support on
the surface place
Result—The problem of side sliding was eliminated
397 cases → 33 cases
　　　　　　　　Big Success

Trouble in transfer equipment

When broken, the product
position is shifted

Counter-measure 4—Installation of guide plate
against pusher to determine position
Result—Very effective for small slide
218 cases → 173 cases

Counter-measure 5—Installed thick rubber sheet of
10mm in thickness to hold products when dam
was broken
Result—No effect

Counter-measure 6—Installed an additional metal
piece to hold product in addition to the counter-
measure 5
Result—Position shifts by the reaction of the dam
rupture was decreased
173 cases → 47 cases

Trouble in hanger change
equipment

*All type of machine is not
stable on the receiving
stage uniformly

Counter-measure 7—Manufactured a larger size
receiving stage, which include crank for all types of
machine with different shapes
Result—Most of them are stable on the receiving
stage
109 cases → 42 cases

Trouble in hanger lowering
equipment

*Overflow hot metal stays
some part of slide

Counter-measure 8—Present situations were
reported and cooperation was requested to man in
charge of melt
Result: 67 cases → 11 cases

(cont'd)

(Figure 8–1 cont'd)

Follow-Up

3 check items were added to daily "PM check list" and the items were checked and confirmed before operation.
1. Adjustment of guide plate.
2. Adjust and wear of rubber sheet and support metal piece.
3. Adjust the receiving stage.

Results (as specific as possible)
—Amount of money (yen/mo.)
—Amount of labour (EH/mo.)
—Number of technical suggestions
—If possible, amount of money and amount of labour should be recorded to obtain the results

1. 658 case out of 803 case of (choko-tei) cases are obtained and thus the result of 82% was successful, which is far above our goal of 70%.
(803 cases/mo. − 145 cases/mo.) × 0.5 min./case × 9 men/line = 49 H/mo.; Labor Cost Reduction By this improvement, the rate of operation of the total line was increased by 1.5%.

2. Number of suggestions → 120 cases applied (Ward 4 cases) Amount of money and labor to obtain the above result:
Money—about 50,000 yen
Labor—48H

Impression of the Result: (Section chief or foreman should describe it)

The results are reflected on the reduction of standard time.

Impression of the foreman (Must be written)

There have been a large number of problems in the old equipment, which had to be improved by means of schedule change and decrease in slags. This is the result that all members of the circle understood the operation of equipment and worked hard to solve the problems.

Impression of section chief (Must be written)

The results obtained here are exceptionally great by implementing each counter-measure, by analyzing in detail on the cases and details of (choko-tei). I would like to evaluate the results very highly, because the result is directly related to the reduction of manpower on the [in Japanese].

Source: Ford Casting Division Japanese Productivity Study Group. *A Report on the Japanese Automotive Foundry Industry* (Windsor, Ont., December 1980), unpaginated; diagrams and Japanese script have been omitted.

THE WRITTEN REPORT

Purposes
• Helps in understanding.
• Documents that information is trustworthy.
• Helps in decision making.
• Used in performance evaluation.
• Is a permanent record.

Organization
• Part I: The Problem
• Part II: How Solved and the Difficulties
• Part III: Findings
• Part IV: Conclusions and Recommendations

Questions that are answered
• What is the problem?
• Best way to resolve?
• Why?
• Is it feasible?
• Pitfalls?
• Alternate actions?
• Costs and benefits?

Distribution
• Members, facilitator, members of steering committee.
• All those who attend oral presentation.
• Others who are interested through formal channels.

Making the Oral Presentation[1]

Presentations by quality circle members to functional areas and to middle and senior management who are affected by the improvement are used to:
1. Persuade these groups that the recommended solution should be implemented.
2. Report the results of a successful implementation.
3. Show management that quality circles are successful and money allocated to the program is being well spent.

A good presentation is a show-and-tell. It has many of the features of a good report, namely:
1. Facts are presented—why the problem was selected, the methods that were utilized in analyzing and solving the problem, the solution, the monitoring pro-

cess, the improvements and benefits that have been or will be attained, the costs involved, problems in implementation and how these have been or will be overcome and the recommendations.

The report should not be overloaded with facts. There should be enough to cover the subject but not so many that the reader will lose interest.

2. A variety of audio-visual materials can be used, including graphs, charts, diagrams, overhead transparencies, slides, flip charts and the blackboard. Visual aids increase audience interest and result in greater learning.

Visual aids can, however, be used badly. Some steps to make the presentation more professional include:

a) For maximum visibility, print on audio-visual materials should be large, clear and legible. A very limited amount of material should be presented on each "aid."

b) Diagrams are more visible when large and heavy lines in black, red, blue or green are used. Colours such as brown, pink, orange and yellow are good for highlighting but are more difficult to see. A variety of coloured backgrounds helps to break the monotony of one colour.

c) Materials should be prepared so clearly and legibly that turning out lights is unnecessary.

d) If possible, materials should be tested ahead of time in the room where the presentation is to be held.

e) "Aids" should be checked to ensure that they are in the correct sequence. They then should be numbered and the same number written in the appropriate position in the notes.

f) To ensure that the audience's view of the material is not blocked, a pointer should be used.

g) One problem experienced by most beginning presenters is the tendency to speak to the visual aid rather than to the audience. To overcome this, a deliberate effort must be made to "look the audience in the eye" throughout the presentation.

3. The talk should be given from an outline or from notes and should *never* be read verbatim. The presentation has to sound spontaneous and exciting. To achieve this, circle members should maintain eye contact with the audience.

4. Appropriate humour should be used. A technical presentation can be extremely boring—particularly if it goes on for a long time. Appropriate jokes or cartoons help the audience to relax and to participate in the presentation.

5. Time should be set aside for questions. The question period is an important time for gaining audience rapport and for convincing reluctant members. It helps to:

a) Look directly at the person who is asking the question but answer to the entire audience. In this way, everyone is included in the answer. Otherwise, some feel left out and lose interest.

b) If one person asks two or three questions, jot them down as a reminder and answer each question separately, stating the question prior to the answer. This keeps the audience from becoming confused.

c) If a question is unclear, the presenter or circle leader should request clarification. The question then is answered, as are all questions, briefly and with specifics. If the answer is not known, circle members offer to find the answer.

d) The voice and body gestures of audience members often reveal the content and the intent of their questions. Good speakers learn to watch for these messages.

e) Finally, and most important, questions that could be asked are anticipated prior to the presentation, and suitable answers are prepared.

6. The presentation begins with interesting opening comments. These are given in such a way as to arouse interest in spite of the fact that they tell the audience the purpose of the presentation and what will be covered.

7. Equally interesting closing remarks are made. The closing leaves a final thought—a summary of ideas, a restatement of the main points, a poem, a quotation, a story or a joke. The closing is probably the part of the presentation that will be remembered longest.

8. Finally, circle members acknowledge all those who participated in solving the problem and all those who have attended the presentation.

Prior to the presentation, considerable preparation and planning occurs. First, circle members decide who should attend and which circle members are to be involved in the presentation and to what extent. A detailed agenda is prepared, including a suggested time schedule and key speakers. This and an invitation to attend are circulated to all expected participants. Generally circle members enjoy the opportunity of presenting the details of their work to members of the technical staff and to management. Each member who wishes to do so should be given an opportunity to participate at some point in the presentation.

Participation, however, requires preparation. Part of this preparation includes writing out what is going to be said, having it typed with double or triple spacing and then highlighting it with a red pen. Highlights mark the statements that have to be emphasized and the places where extra-long pauses should occur, the various visual aids are to be introduced and the jokes are to be told. Practising out loud and trying to make the presentation sound spontaneous and interesting is important. This practice, in front of the mirror and using a tape recorder, or before other circle members, should continue until the material is known so well that it can be "read" while looking at the audience, that is, presented using the manuscript as a guide only.

Some reluctant circle members hesitate to volunteer for presentations because they are "too nervous in front of a group." Nervousness is very natural; most good speakers are nervous before a presentation. In fact, some nervousness is needed to do a good job. There are, however, techniques that can be used to control excessive nervousness. These include:

a) Acting natural. The presentation is being made to a group of friends. After all, each person has the same interests—the best for the company.

b) Practising before colleagues and in front of a mirror with a tape recorder until the results are pleasing.

c) A few deep breaths just prior to beginning the presentation help the speaker to relax. A sip or two of water keeps the throat and mouth moist so coughing or choking does not occur.

d) Most important, of course, is the pep talk to oneself—the positive thinking that states, "Of course I can do an excellent job."

The final step in the presentation is to arrange for a follow-up meeting so that a response by management can be provided, particularly if recommendations and not a completed project are being presented.

In summary, the presentation is a SPEECH:

Subject
Point
Enthusiasm
Exhibits
Conciseness
Humour

That is, the *s*ubject chosen is delivered in a manner that is to the *p*oint, with *e*nthusiasm and *e*xhibits, *c*oncisely and *h*umorously.

A sample of the written portion of a quality circle presentation is given in Figure 8–2.

FIGURE 8–2
Japanese Quality Control Circle Presentation and Agenda

15th Improvement Activity Presentation Within Company
Outline of Presentation Content
December 1, 1980

1. *Presentation title*: "Improvement of Gauge Supervision Method"
2. *Name of speaker*: Kensaku Kawazoe, Metal Mold Plant, Metal Mold Section
Name of circle: Asai Group Circle *Number of members*: 4 persons.
3. *Present situation and reasons to select this theme*:
Up-to-date supervision of all gauges has been done locally in the east side of the Metal Mold Building. Thus, in order to take out a gauge, traffic of employees has been increased. And when we take out a particular gauge, it has been very difficult to find the gauge because of the tremendous increase of number of gauges.

Thus, this circle decided to select this situation to eliminate the problem to make it more efficient.
4. *Goal*:
a) When to complete: end of November b) What problem: checkout of gauge c) How to improve: to be able to check out within 5 minutes.
5. *Approach*:
"Why," "what," "when," "who," "what method"—these are passwords for our

group to ask and find answers by ourselves. Based on the QC method, at the meetings we repeated to collect our ideas to make progress in this theme.

6. *Counter-measure* (solution):

We have had several meetings together and discussed how to make gauge checkout and walking distance to be simpler and shorter. We did not have any good ideas for a while. Then our suggestion was "The best way is to have gauges closest to where they are needed." If we can condense our idea, the essence was that the gauges should be controlled where the gauges are used most frequently by local control (eliminate central control). Thus, we may reduce employee traffic. We are agreed on the idea. By the result of the above study, we planned to find a method of localized control.

7. *Results*:

The following results are obtained

a) Re-arrangement of gauges: unnecessary gauges were discarded and number and types of gauges were reduced from 434 to 317.

b) Local Control: Walking distances were shortened by spreading the control to locations, such as finishing process, lathe, electrode, outside request, etc.

c) Color Coded: All gauges were color coded to make checkout easier.

8. *Effect*:

a) (Items which cannot be indicated by number of money)
  i. Cooperative structure was enforced among the circle members
  ii. We recognized once again the importance of positive action by the members and
     this result helped to make us more positive in our daily activity
b) (Money and Number)
  i. Now the gauge checkout time was reduced to within 3 minutes
     Before improvement: 15 minutes
     $(15 - 3) \times 13$ persons $\times$ 23 days $= 59.8$ hours per month thus reduction of 209,300 yen.

9. *Problems*:

Location of gauges, changes in installation, supervision of accuracy—how did we decide?

a) Location of gauge—map will be distributed to all workers

b) Change in installation—once a drawing is made, it should be decided by a route from section chief [to] foreman [to] circle leader.

c) Supervision of accuracy—accuracy should be checked twice a month by man in charge.

10. *Future Plan*:

We have to obtain confidence for future circle activity by this experience to solve problems of gauge administration. There are many problems left for further improvement. We would like to utilize this valuable experience and to make further improvements.

Source: Ford Casting Division Japanese Productivity Study Group, *A Report on the Japanese Automotive Foundry Industry* (Windsor, Ont., December 1980), unpaginated.

Audio-visual materials:
- large, clear, legible
- better if lights do not have to be turned off
- black, red, blue and green diagrams are seen more clearly
- pre-tested in presentation room

- in correct sequence
- pointer used so view is not blocked

Presentation is *never* read word for word.

Humour helps.

Time is set aside for questions. Presenter
- looks at person asking question
- answers to the audience
- answers one question at a time
- gives specific but brief answer

Circle anticipates questions prior to presentation.

Interesting opening statement.

Interesting closing statement.

Acknowledgment.

Pre-preparation:
- full talk typed and highlighted
- talk practised

Overcome nervousness by:
- acting natural
- practising
- taking deep breaths
- taking sips of water
- positive thinking: ''I can do an excellent job''

Follow-up meeting arranged.

SPEECH:
- *S*ubject
- *P*oint
- *E*nthusiasm
- *E*xhibits
- *C*onciseness
- *H*umour

PART III

STATISTICAL ANALYSIS AND EVALUATION

Analyzing Problem Causes Using Graphs and Statistics

This chapter outlines the use and construction of the remaining most important tools needed for the analysis of causes. This includes line, bar, circle and pie graphs, histograms, scattergrams and Pareto diagrams.

Graphs[1]

Line Graphs

A line graph shows an event that has occurred. If the following data regarding defects were plotted as line graphs, they would appear as shown in Figure 9–1c.

Cause of defect	No. of defects previous week	No. of defects this week
Porosity	21	15
Opening too narrow	9	4
Opening too wide	6	6
Calibration	12	3
Leakage	15	6
Off centre	12	2

By convention, the Y-axis of a graph is the vertical one and the X-axis is horizontal. Appropriate scales or labelling are placed on the two axes. In this illustration, the scale representing the number of defects (from 0 to 30; where possible, graphs always begin at 0) is placed on the Y-axis and the sub-cause or defect is placed on the X-axis.

A dot is placed at 21 for porosity, at 9 for opening too narrow, at 6 for opening too wide, etc. (see Figure 9–1a). When dots have been placed which correspond to the number of defects for all sub-causes, the dots are joined (see Figure 9–1b). This line represents the number of defects for a particular time period. The title on the graph is so complete that it will be identifiable many years in the future.

FIGURE 9–1a
First Step in Drawing a Line Graph

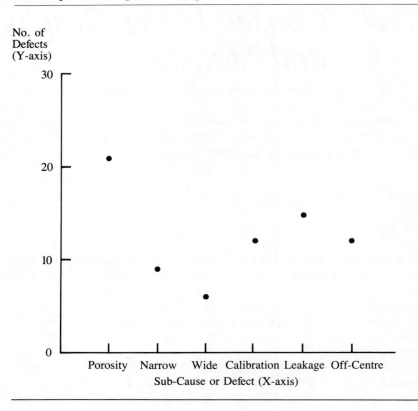

No. of
Defects
(Y-axis)

Sub-Cause or Defect (X-axis)

Line graphs are extremely useful for comparisons. Figure 9–1c compares the defects made before and after the implementation of a quality circle suggestion. Figure 9–2 illustrates a different type of line graph comparison—warehouse productivity (as an index) compared to total productivity (on the same index).

Bar Graphs

A bar graph is very similar to and is used for the same purposes as a line graph (see Figures 9–3 and 9–4). The only difference is that bars are drawn instead of lines.

FIGURE 9–1b

Line Graph Showing Defects in Widget Department (L) by Sub-Cause During Week of April 8, 198X to April 12, 198X

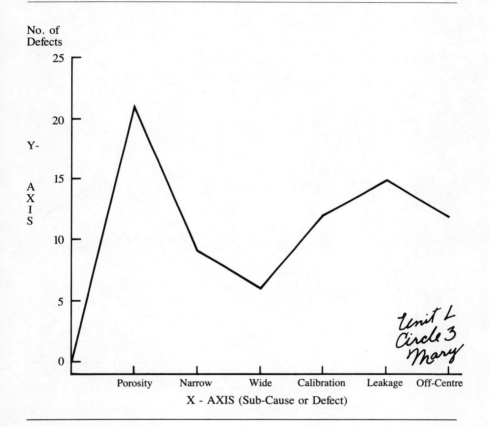

No. of Defects

X - AXIS (Sub-Cause or Defect)

Circle Graphs

Circle graphs show the percentage of one item as a percentage of the whole. They are more difficult to construct because measurements must be exact. A protractor and a compass are required.

The procedure for constructing a circle graph is as follows:

1. Observations are made on the sub-causes of the effect in question. For example, a quality circle member observes that of seventy-five defects that occurred on a particular machine, twenty-one were attributable to porosity, nine to a too-narrow opening, six to a too-wide opening, twelve to improper calibration and fifteen to leakages. Twelve were off-centre.

FIGURE 9–1c

Line Graph Comparing Defects in Widget Department (L) for the Week of April 8, 198X and the Week of April 15, 198X

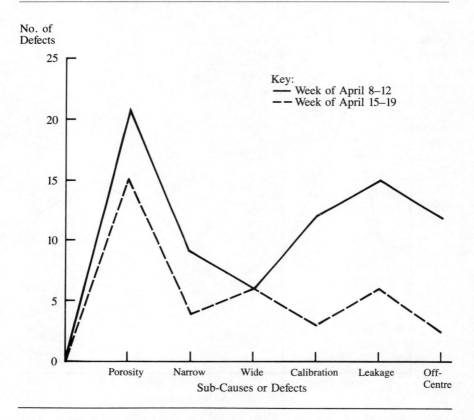

2. The actual number of occurrences are translated into percentage form by dividing the actual number of occurrences that are attributable to the problem in question (21 for porosity) by the total number of defects (75) and multiplying by 100 (percent). In the above example, this would mean that 28 percent of the defects were attributable to porosity, 12 percent to a too-narrow opening, 8 percent to an opening that was too wide, 16 percent to improper calibration and 20 percent to leakage. The remaining 16 percent were off-centre.

3. To find the number of degrees (out of 360, the number of degrees in a circle) which each percentage represents, each percentage is multiplied by 3.6. (Divide by 100 (percent) and multiply by 360 degrees). The figure that is obtained is the proportion of 360 which each cause (defect) represents.

To illustrate:

Sub-cause	No. of Defects	Percentage	Degrees (Angle)
Porosity	21	28*	100.8*
Opening too narrow	9	12	43.2
Opening too wide	6	8	28.8
Calibration	12	16	57.6
Leakage	15	20	72.0
Off centre	12	16	57.6
	75	100	360.0

*21 divided by 75 multiplied by 100 = 28; 28 divided by 100 and multiplied by 360 or 28 times 3.6 = 100.8.

In other words, when defects are shown on the circle graph, an angle is drawn that shows porosity as 100.8 degrees of the 360 degrees that are available; the too-narrow opening is an angle of 43.2 degrees, and so on.

4. A circle of desired size is drawn using a compass (see Figure 9–5a). This usually is sufficiently large to make the majority of labels and numbers visible and readable. The size usually does not exceed half a page unless a large graph is required for a group presentation.

5. A straight line is drawn from the centre point of the circle to the edge of the circle, usually horizontally (see Figure 9–5b).

6. Using the midpoint of the circle and the straight line as a base, the required angle is measured with a protractor.

7. A line is drawn from the midpoint to the edge of the circle to represent the required angle (see Figure 9–5c).

8. For each of the other defects, using the midpoint of the circle and any straight line as a base, the required angle is measured and a straight line is drawn to enclose the angle. The completed circle graph is shown in Figure 9–5d.

By this means, a visual diagram is constructed which shows each part (cause of the defect, etc.) as a proportion of the whole.

Pie Graphs

A "pie chart" is a circle graph from which one section has been partially removed to emphasize the importance of that particular event or cause. Figure 9–6 shows a pie graph or chart in which the defects caused by porosity (twenty-one of seventy-five, or 28 percent) have been accentuated.

Histograms

A histogram is used for two purposes. First, it shows the frequency (in number or as a percentage) with which an event occurs and helps to determine whether the problem that has been identified occurs more frequently during a specified interval (such as at a particular time, at a particular calibration). The second

FIGURE 9–2
Line Graph—Warehouse and Total Productivity Based on PPP Index Without Buybacks

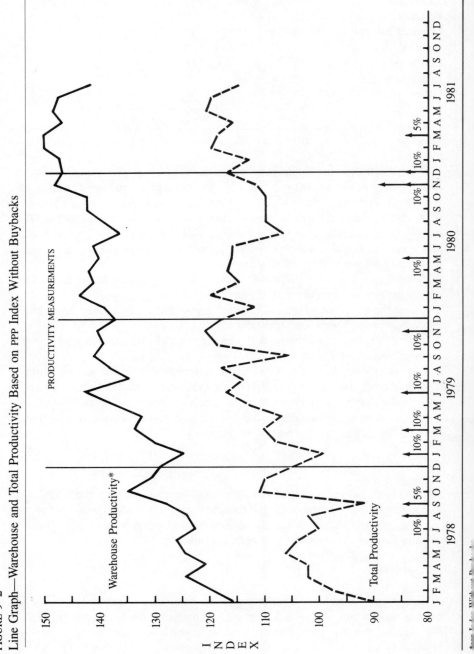

FIGURE 9–3
Vertical Bar Graph Showing Defects in Widget Department (L) by Sub-Cause During the Week of April 8, 198X to April 12, 198X

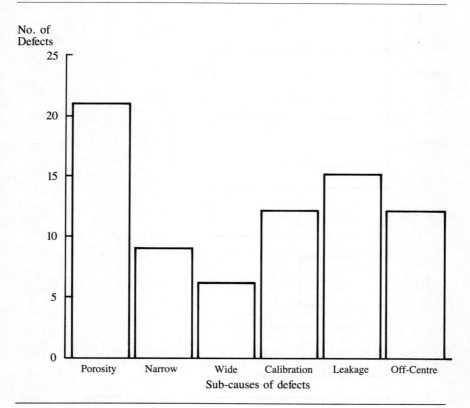

purpose of the histogram is to compare the shape of the distribution itself with some known distribution. For example, when a particular machine operates for more than eight hours without maintenance, defects increase by 10 percent every two hours. Quality circle members observe the machine and note the actual number of defects. This actual occurrence is compared with the expected distribution. To better illustrate this, the two distributions are plotted on the same graph paper using different colours or shading. In the same way, two or more machines, systems or operators can be compared.

A histogram is easy to construct. The following procedure can be used:

1. An observation is made, or available information is analyzed, to determine how frequently each sub-cause (defect, etc.) occurs at each point in time, at each calibration, and so on.

FIGURE 9–4

Horizontal Bar Graph Showing Defects in Widget Department (L) by Sub-Cause During the Week of April 8, 198X to April 12, 198X

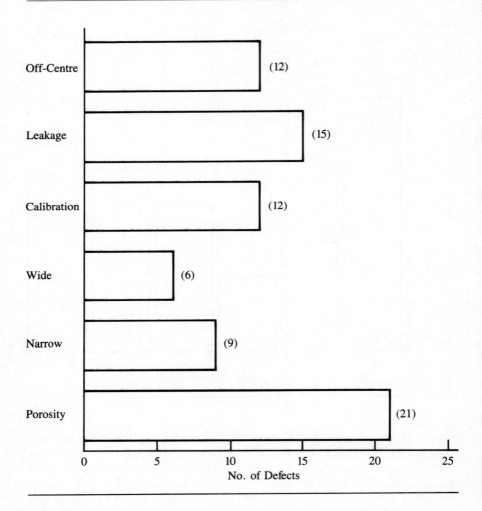

No. of Defects

2. A *continuous interval* of measurement (such as time or calibration) is decided on, and this is shown on the X-axis (horizontal axis) with equal distances between each number. For example, a quality circle on an automobile assembly line observed that the seventy-five defects mentioned previously occurred irregularly during the week as shown:

Day of week*	Time of day*	No. of defects
Monday	6:00 a.m. to 12:00 a.m.	10
Monday	12:00 a.m. to 6:00 p.m.	8
Monday	6:00 p.m. to 12:00 p.m.	4
Monday	12:00 p.m. to 6:00 a.m.	5
Tuesday	6:00 a.m. to 12:00 a.m.	3
Tuesday	12:00 a.m. to 6:00 p.m.	2
Tuesday	6:00 p.m. to 12:00 p.m.	2
Tuesday	12:00 p.m. to 6:00 a.m.	5
Wednesday	6:00 a.m. to 12:00 a.m.	1
Wednesday	12:00 a.m. to 6:00 p.m.	1
Wednesday	6:00 p.m. to 12:00 p.m.	1
Wednesday	12:00 p.m. to 6:00 a.m.	2
Thursday	6:00 a.m. to 12:00 a.m.	2
Thursday	12:00 p.m. to 6:00 a.m.	1
Thursday	6:00 a.m. to 12:00 a.m.	2
Thursday	12:00 p.m. to 6:00 p.m.	3
Friday	6:00 a.m. to 12:00 a.m.	5
Friday	12:00 a.m. to 6:00 p.m.	3
Friday	6:00 p.m. to 12:00 p.m.	7
Friday	12:00 p.m. to 6:00 a.m.	8

*In this instance, the X-axis is labelled with the days of the week and the time periods.

3. The number of occurrences (or percentages) is shown on the Y-axis (vertical axis) with an equal distance between each number. In this illustration, since defects range from 1 to 10, the numbers 0 to 10 are placed on the Y-axis (a graph begins at 0, if possible).

4. A vertical bar graph is drawn to show this. The bars are always adjacent to each other, that is, no space is left between them because time (or other variable chosen) is continuous. Generally the lines between the bars are not drawn but that is unimportant—it is convenient not to do so. Figure 9–7 shows a histogram of the number of defects which occurred during the week of April 8 to April 12 in the Widget Department at four different time periods of each day.

Pareto Diagrams

The Pareto diagram is based on the Pareto principle, which states that any effect is the result of a variety of causes which can be added together to produce the total effect and that, in many instances, only one or two causes, categories or

FIGURE 9-5
Steps in Drawing a Circle Graph

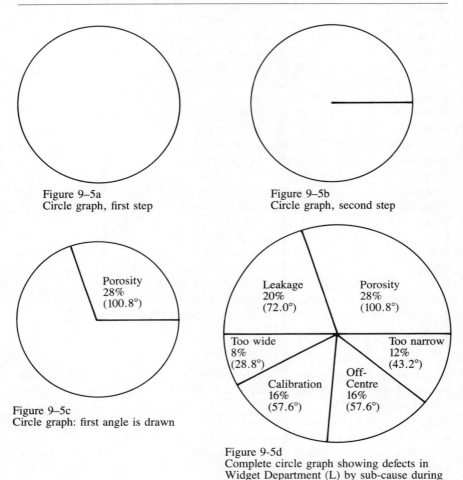

Figure 9–5a
Circle graph, first step

Figure 9–5b
Circle graph, second step

Figure 9–5c
Circle graph: first angle is drawn

Porosity
28%
(100.8°)

Leakage
20%
(72.0°)

Porosity
28%
(100.8°)

Too wide
8%
(28.8°)

Too narrow
12%
(43.2°)

Calibration
16%
(57.6°)

Off-
Centre
16%
(57.6°)

Figure 9-5d
Complete circle graph showing defects in
Widget Department (L) by sub-cause during
the week of April 8, 198X to April 12, 198X.

sub-processes are dominant, i.e., contribute more than one-half to the total effect
that occurs.

The diagram can indicate:
1. The degree to which one element or cause contributes to a problem.
2. Whether improvements have occurred.

A Pareto diagram is two graphs in one—a line graph and a bar graph. The

FIGURE 9–6
Pie Graph Showing Defects in Widget Department (L) by Sub-Cause and
Emphasizing Defects Because of Porosity During the Week of April 8, 198X
to April 12, 198X.

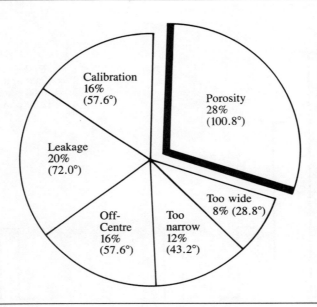

bar graph illustrates the variation, by frequency, percentage or cost, that occurs
in one variable in each of the different forms which that variable can take. The
line graph indicates the effect of all these variations, when cumulated one at a
time from largest to smallest.

An example will illustrate: The effect that is being examined is the number
of breakdowns caused by defects. These breakdowns occur seventy-five times
in total as shown:

	No. of defects	*Cumulative breakdowns*
Porosity	21	21
Leakage	15	36
Calibration	12	48
Off-centre	12	60
Opening too narrow	9	69
Opening too wide	6	75

FIGURE 9–7

Histogram Showing Number of Defects in Widget Department (L) During Four Time Periods Each Day for the Week of April 8, 198X to April 12, 198X

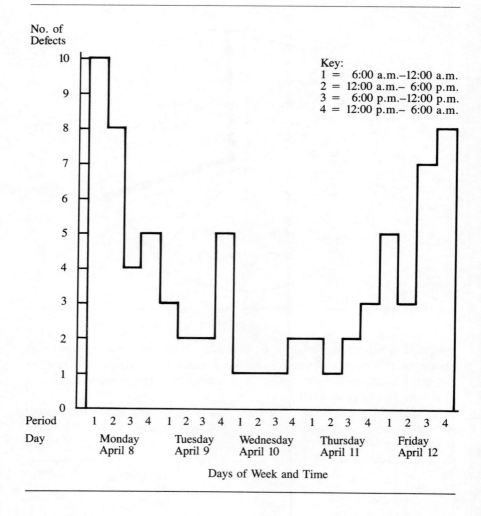

Days of Week and Time

Figure 9–8a illustrates the Pareto diagram (the line and bar graphs) that shows these relationships. The bar graph indicates the number of times each breakdown occurs and the types of defect which cause that breakdown. The line graph shows the cumulation of each of these breakdowns.

FIGURE 9–8a

Pareto Diagram Showing Contribution of Sub-Causes to Breakdown in Widget Department (L) for the Week of April 8, 198X to April 12, 198X

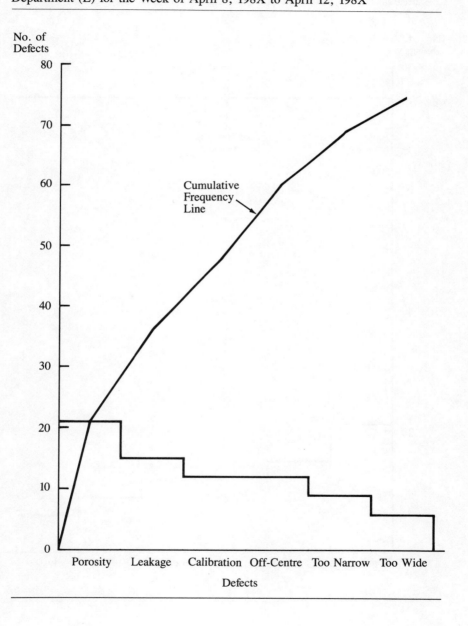

FIGURE 9–8b
Pareto Diagram Showing Contribution of Sub-Causes to Breakdown in Widget
Department (L) for the Week of April 8, 198X to April 12, 198X

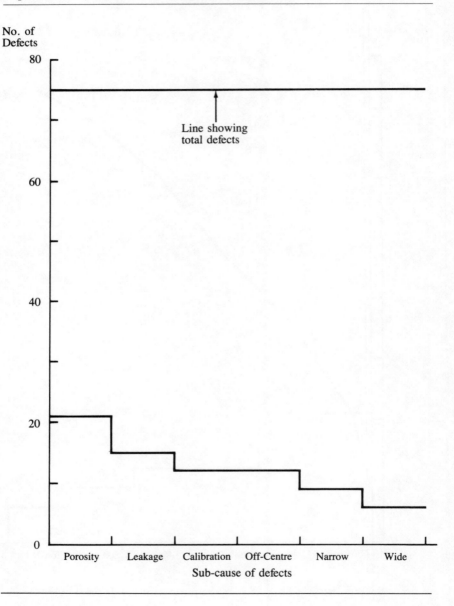

FIGURE 9–8c
Pareto Diagram Showing Contribution of Sub-Causes to Breakdown in Widget Department (L) for the Week of April 8, 198X to April 12, 198X

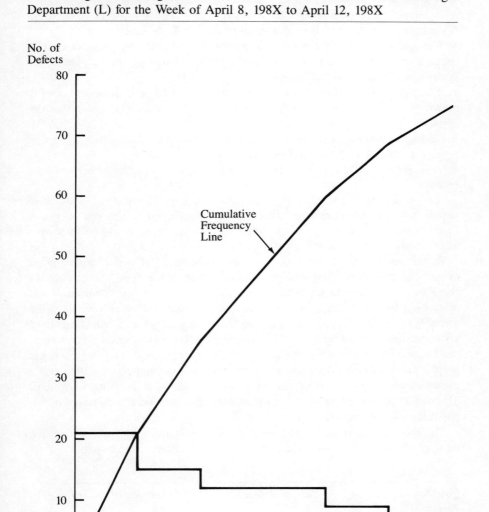

Pareto diagrams, which are easy to construct and interpret, are drawn as follows:

1. Possible sub-causes of an effect are identified using a fishbone diagram.

2. Information is gathered about a particular effect and its apparent sub-causes. A decision is made as to how this information should be categorized.

3. The X and Y axes are labelled. Generally the number, percentage or cost of occurrences is placed on the Y-axis; the categorization of the sub-causes or symptoms is placed on the X-axis.

4. The sub-cause or symptom which has the largest number of occurrences is drawn first. To do this, a bar graph is drawn at the origin (the far left of the graph).

5. Beside the first bar, a second bar is drawn to illustrate the sub-cause, symptom or defect which has the second greatest number of occurrences.

6. This process continues until all sub-causes, symptoms or defects are illustrated by bars.

7. The cumulative frequency is determined using sub-causes in the order in which they have been drawn on the graph, and the line indicating this is drawn. In this case, the line for porosity shows twenty-one defects; leakage is shown as thirty-six; calibration as forty-eight, and so on.

By convention, the cumulative line graph is generally drawn at the midpoint of each interval or bar graph (Figure 9–8a). When this is done, the cumulative frequency line is extended so that it begins at the origin (at 0 on both the X and Y axes). This, however, is not important, and Figures 9–8b and 9–8c show the same Pareto graph. In the first, the cumulative frequency line graph is drawn as a straight line, indicating the total number of defects; in the second illustration, the cumulative frequency corresponds to the extreme right edge of each bar graph. The technical details are not important; what is important is that circle members use one method or that each understands what is being illustrated. Through experience, study and training sessions, members become more sophisticated in the techniques that are used.

The three illustrations of the Pareto diagram (Figure 9–8) have utilized the number of defects. A Pareto diagram can use percentages, for example:

Cause of defect	No. of defects	Cumulative breakdowns
Porosity	28	28
Leakage	20	48
Calibration	16	64
Off-centre	16	80
Too-narrow opening	12	92
Too-wide opening	8	100

This illustration is shown in Figure 9–9.

Costs also could be used, for example:

Cause of defect	No. of defects	Unit cost of repair	Total repair cost	Cumula- tive costs
Porosity	21	$30	$630	$ 630
Calibration	12	20	240	870
Too-wide opening	6	30	180	1,050
Leakage	15	5	75	1,125
Off-centre	15	3	45	1,170
Too-narrow opening	9	3	27	1,197

This Pareto diagram is illustrated in Figure 9–10. It is a very different diagram from the other four. Defects attributable to some causes are very difficult to repair, and, while there may be few of them (too wide an opening, for example), the cost to the firm may be quite high. Quality circles should observe and illustrate the same problem from as many different perspectives as possible.

Although it is not noticeable in these examples because the same data is used to illustrate all cases, Pareto diagrams in the "real world" show that very few items contribute almost all of the value or variation. In fact, even in the above example of costs, three of the six items (porosity, calibration, too wide an opening) contribute about 88 percent of the value or variation. It is these "vital few" items that a quality circle analyzes and improves first.

Scattergrams

Scattergrams are utilized when it is believed that two occurrences are related to each other. If, for example, it is believed that raw material of a certain porosity causes the calibration of a particular part to vary excessively, a good way to examine this would be through the use of a scattergram. By examining the cluster of dots, it is possible to determine whether a relationship exists, whether this relationship differs as the variable changes, and whether certain conditions create or contribute to a deficiency. By examining the pattern of dots, as shown in Figure 9–11c, for example, it is not difficult to draw the conclusion that porous materials (porosity of 241, 242 and 243) tend to produce products that are calibrated improperly (at .0001, .0002, .0007, and .0008).

How is a scattergram constructed?

1. Observations are made over a period of time (hourly for a week, for example) of two or more variables or elements, one of which is suspected of causing the other, or both of which might be caused by a third as yet unidentified cause.

2. Figures, representing the respective number of occurrences of each element, are placed on the two axes of the graph and the axes are labelled. (Porosities of 236 to 243 have been placed on the Y-axis and calibrations of .0001 to .0008 have been placed on the X-axis).

FIGURE 9–9

Pareto Diagram Showing Contribution of Sub-Causes to Breakdown, by Percentage, in Widget Department (L) for the Week of April 8, 198X to April 12, 198X

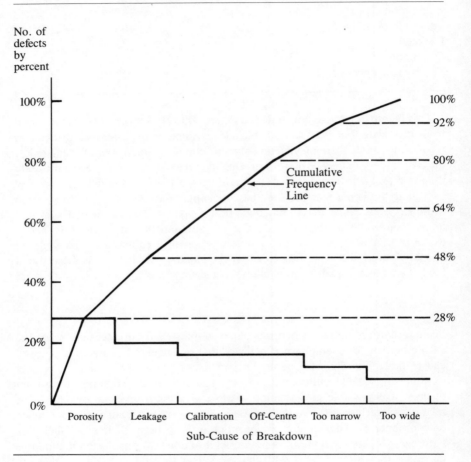

3. A dot is placed for each joint occurrence. Ten parts were produced on a particular day when the porosity of raw material is 237 and the ten parts cause calibrations of .0001, .0001, .0002, .0005, .0003, .0008, .0004, .0005, .0005 and .0004 (see Figure 9–11a). Porosity changed to 243 and three parts were produced with calibrations of .0008, .0007 and .0008 (see Figure 9–11b).

As pointed out earlier, Figure 9–11c shows that as the raw material becomes more porous, proper calibration becomes more difficult.

FIGURE 9–10

Pareto Diagram Showing Contribution of Sub-Causes to Breakdown, by Cost, in Widget Department (L) for the Week of April 8, 198X to April 12, 198X

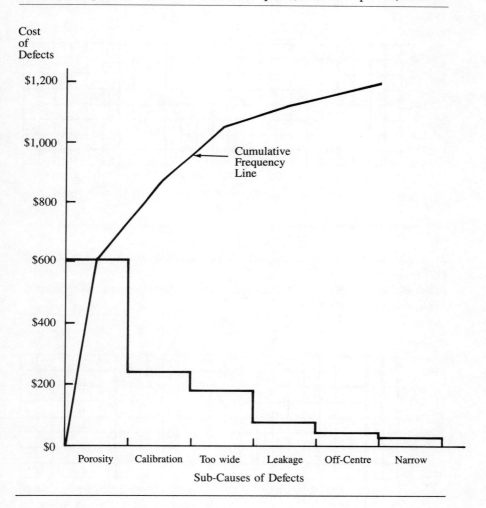

A Few Final Words

Graphs are easy to understand and easy to draw. Because the relationship can be visualized, circle members can more clearly understand the causes that produce a particular effect.

FIGURE 9–11a
Effect of Porosity of 237 on Calibration. Observations Taken April 8, 198X to April 12, 198X

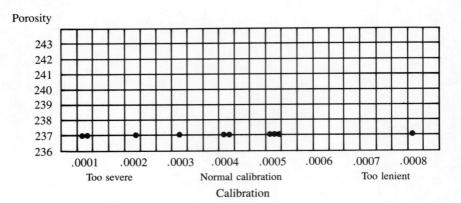

FIGURE 9–11b
Effect of Porosity of 237 and 243 on Calibration. Observations Taken April 8, 198X to April 12, 198X

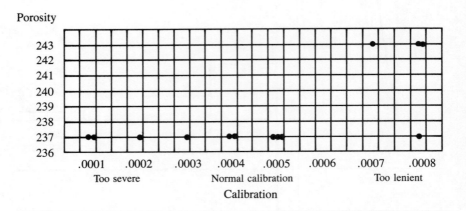

Some conventions exist that standardize what is done and help to better visualize the relationships that exist:

FIGURE 9–11c

Effects of Porosity on Calibration. Observations Taken April 8, 198X to April 12, 198X

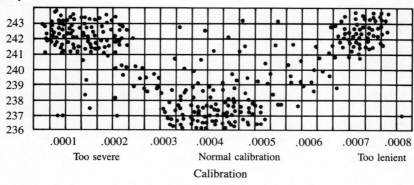

Porosity

Calibration

1. Generally graphs are placed on graph paper or grid paper.

2. The X and Y axes are always labelled. The X-axis is always horizontal; the Y-axis is always vertical.

3. A descriptive title is included with the graph. This title always includes a date and is so complete that the graph is immediately identifiable—even several years later.

4. Often graphs are initialled or signed by the person who researched the data and drew the graph. In that way, the individual assumes responsibility for the correctness of the information and illustration.

KNOW HOW TO CONSTRUCT:

Graphs
- line graph
- horizontal bar graphs
- vertical bar graphs

Circle graphs
- pie chart

Histogram

Pareto diagram can be drawn on basis of:
- number of defects
- percentages
- costs

Scattergram

10 *Sampling and Statistics*

Sampling is a process in which a small number of items are selected from an entire population for detailed examination and statistical analyses, because they are representative of that population. This is done so that decisions can be made about the characteristics of the whole population.

Before sampling or statistical procedures can be discussed in any detail, certain terms that are commonly used must be understood, such as: random sample, systematic sample, stratified sample, cluster sample, mean, mode, median, frequency distribution, cumulative frequency distribution, normal curve, kurtosis, skewness, area under the curve, dispersion, standard deviation and variance. It is also important to know how to sample and how many to sample, and to check whether the sample is representative of the population.

Sampling

Researchers may draw a random sample, a systematic random sample, a stratified sample, or a cluster sample. These terms simply refer to the method that has been chosen to select the units which will be examined in greater detail.

Random Sampling

When random sampling occurs, the units are selected without specifying any characteristics which the units must have or time intervals in which they must be selected (except that they are produced by the machine, operators or section of interest). If sampling is *systematic*, units are selected at regular intervals— for instance, every third, tenth or twentieth unit or one every fifteen minutes, half hour or hour. In other words, there is some system or pattern for selecting the units.

Stratified Sampling

A stratified sample is chosen when there is a desire to examine certain groups in detail and it is necessary to ensure that there are enough units in each of the groups. In the plant, stratified sampling is used when the quality circle decides that it will examine four units each day which are produced on each of four lathes by each of twelve operators for a one-week period. (The number of units selected during the week is 4 (units) × 4 (lathes) × 12 (operators) × 5 (days) = 960 units.) Under this selection process, it is relatively easy to give estimates of adequate or inadequate peformance for (1) each day of the week, (2) each of the four machines, and (3) each of the twelve operators. To do this, however, 960 units, assuming a five-day week, would have to be selected and examined.

This differs from random sampling because the machine and person have been specified. In random sampling, selection would be made at the end of the line without regard to operator or machine.

In using stratified sampling, it is necessary to decide on the number of groupings (strata) that are to be examined, whether the same proportion of units will be selected from each group or whether proportionately more units will be selected from some groupings than from others, and the total number of items or elements that is required.

Taking a larger sample from one group than from others may be justified because the group consists of a larger number (five units are made on Lathe 2 during the same time that one unit is made on Lathe 1 and on Lathe 3); because there is more variability (Lathe 2 appears to malfunction more frequently); or because it is cheaper to sample one group (for example: In order to sample and examine a unit, it must be destroyed. Lathe 3 and Lathe 1 produce parts which are made using an expensive alloy; Lathe 2 uses alloys that can be recycled). Under these circumstances, more Lathe 2 units are selected than Lathe 1 or Lathe 3 units.

Many formulas are given for selecting the number of units that will be examined and the total number of units. As circle members become more experienced, they will want to learn about these. At the beginning, some common-sense rules will suffice:

1. Enough units from one grouping must be examined so that circle members feel they have a reasonable knowledge of how a machine or operator is performing.

2. *As few units in each grouping as possible* should be selected. Sampling costs money because:

• Someone has to take time to examine each unit and do the analyses.
• It is often necessary to destroy the unit.
• Units which have been taken for the purpose of examination are not available for production purposes.

In short, because information costs money, it is never possible to be 100 percent certain about how an operation is proceeding. Because of this, small samples are taken and estimates about the characteristics of the entire population (such as quality) are made.

Cluster Sampling

In cluster sampling, the population is divided into sub-groups (for example, three lathes and twelve operators give thirty-six sub-groups or clusters). Not all thirty-six groups are examined if cluster sampling is used. Instead only specific subgroups which are perceived to be typical of the others are chosen (for example, Operators 3, 5 and 11 who work on Lathe 2; operator 1 on Lathe 1; Operator 7 on Lathe 3). A large number of units, however, are selected from each of these five sub-groups. On the basis of examination of the selected units, conclusions are made about the characteristics of the parts produced on all three lathes by all twelve operators.

Cluster sampling is especially useful if clusters are homogeneous (the work done on all lathes by all operators is of the same quality). Decisions that must be made concern the size of each cluster, whether an equal or unequal number of units should be selected from each of the sub-groups, and the total number of units that are to be selected.

Logical reasons must exist for selecting particular clusters. If there are none, clusters and units selected are chosen randomly.

The same common-sense rules of thumb can be used in cluster sampling—as few units as possible but a sufficient number so that some confidence can be placed in the estimates that are made.

Statistical Measures

Statistics can be extremely simple or extremely complex. Percentages, frequencies and cumulative frequencies are the simplest of statistical measures and describe the number of items that have been observed in a particular category. Other methods of describing a relationship, in statistical terms, are centrality measures and the normal curve.

Distributions

To describe a number or proportion of items which are in a specific category or grouping, the term "frequency distribution" is used. When the number of items in several categories are added together (summated or cumulated), the term "cumulative frequency distribution" is used.

For example:

	No. of Defects	Cumulative Frequency
Machine A	3	3
Machine B	6	9
Machine C	9	18

(cont'd)

	No. of Defects	Cumulative Frequency
Machine D	2	20
Machine E	5	25

The numbers 3, 6, 9, 2 and 5 represent the frequency or frequency distribution of defects by machine and the numbers 3, 9, 18, 20 and 25 represent the cumulative frequency distribution.

Centrality Measures

Centrality measures are those which indicate the centre, the middle or the average. Three measures are used most commonly—mean, mode and median.

Mean. The mean is the average of a group of numbers. If a worker wants to know his or her mean (average) monthly salary for the past year, he or she would add the value of all cheques received and divide by 12 (because there are 12 months).

Mode. Mode means fashionable, popular or chosen most frequently; it is the item, value, etc. that occurs the greatest number of times in a given series of observations. If the mode concerning defects produced on a particular machine is required and defects are examined on a daily basis for a month, the numbers from 0 to the largest number of defects which occur are written in a column. Each day a check mark is placed beside the number of defects that occur that day. The number with the most checks at the end of the month is the mode.

Median. A third measure of centrality is the median. If a worker wants to know the median salary which was received in the forty-nine weeks of the year in which he or she worked (three weeks were holidays), the salaries received in each of the weeks are arranged in order from smallest to largest or vice versa. The employee then counts to the halfway point (twenty-five in this case). The twenty-fifth number in the list is the median. If an even number of items appears in the list (say, the median salary for all fifty-two weeks), the employee again counts to the halfway point (in this case, between the twenty-sixth and the twenty-seventh items). The salaries which appear twenty-sixth and twenty-seventh are added together and are divided by two. The figure so obtained is the median.

The Normal Curve

Statisticians have determined, through experience, that any time thirty or more people or units are selected randomly and are examined on any one characteristic that can be measured on a continuous scale (height or weight, for instance) that there are some people who are very low on this characteristic and some that are very high. The majority are somewhere between very low and very high.

FIGURE 10–1a
Normal Curve

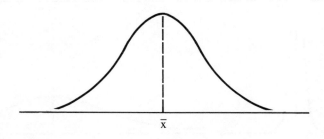

Through the examination of many such samples, statisticians have determined that the curve of the distribution of these characteristics is bell-shaped, as shown in Figure 10–1a. This distribution has become known as the normal curve.

The concept may be easier to understand by examining the manner in which a normal curve is constructed. The area under the curve represents very small bar graphs, each of which is drawn to represent the actual characteristics of the units under study. In other words, in drawing the normal curve of the heights of the entire population (or a large representative sample thereof) the frequency of all people from the shortest to the tallest, in one-quarter inch (or five-milli-meter) intervals, is calculated. These frequencies are each drawn as vertical bar graphs. The bar graphs, when squeezed together, assume the shape of the normal curve.

Mean, standard deviation, kurtosis and skewness are terms which describe the characteristics or properties of a distribution that can be shown by drawing a normal curve.

Kurtosis. What is kurtosis? Samples can be drawn from many types of groups. If a random sample of the general population is drawn and the heights of all the people are measured, the distribution appears like the one that is shown in Figure 10–1a. If, however, the sample is drawn only from professional basketball play-ers, there is relatively little difference between the heights, and the majority are grouped in a very small range. The normal curve of this group is shown at the left in Figure 10–1b. If almost an equal number of people are selected at each height, the normal curve is much flatter, similar to that shown at the right in Figure 10–1b. Kurtosis, then, is the relative degree of curvature near the mode of a normal curve.

Skewness. Normal curves can also be skewed, that is, have the largest portion to the right or left of centre, as shown in Figure 10–1c. In other words, using

FIGURE 10–1b
Kurtosis

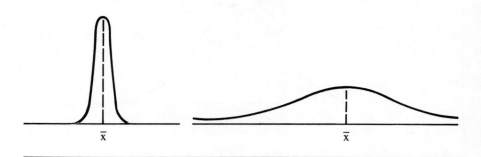

FIGURE 10–1c
Skewness

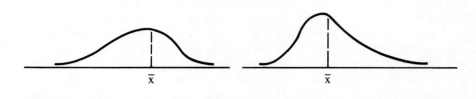

the example of height, although a random sample is drawn, the majority of the people that are selected in the sample are very tall or very short. Skewness is the state of being asymmetric or distorted.

Both kurtosis and skewness indicate that the sample which has been drawn varies from the usual or normal.

Mean. The mean (written as $\bar{x}$) can be calculated by adding together all the numbers which represent the characteristic in question (all the various heights, for example) and dividing by the number of units or people.

Standard Deviation. The mean is not the only measure that is needed to describe a normal distribution. As explained earlier, some normal curves are tall and some are very flat. For convenience, statisticians decided to draw a line under the curve and to divide this line into six approximately equal parts. They called the distance between each of these six parts a standard deviation. Three of the standard deviations are to the left of the mean (and hence represent people or units who have less of the characteristics than the mean person or unit has (for example, they are shorter than the average person). Three standard deviations are to the right of the mean. In Figure 10–1d, A and D are one standard deviation away from the mean; and B and E are two standard deviations away from the mean. Statistical textbooks give formulas for calculating standard deviation and variance. The variance formula appears like this: $\Sigma(x_i - \bar{x})^2/N$. Standard deviation is the square root of the variance.

To illustrate: A machine is observed for eight days. In those eight days, the following number of defects occur: 12, 10, 10, 9, 8, 7, 5 and 3. The mean number of defects for the eight days is $12 + 10 + 10 + 9 + 8 + 7 + 5 + 3$ divided by number of items (8) or 64 divided by 8 = 8 defects.

The variance is calculated as follows:

x_i	Mean ($\bar{x}$)	$x_i - \bar{x}$	$(x_i - \bar{x})^2$
12	8	4	16
10	8	2	4
10	8	2	4
9	8	1	1
8	8	0	0
7	8	−1	1
5	8	−3	9
3	8	−5	25
		$\Sigma(x_i - \bar{x})^2 =$	60

Variance = 60 divided by 8 or 7.5.
Standard deviation is the square root of 60/8 or 2.739.

What the formula is saying is that the mean is subtracted from each of the observations. This gives $(x_i - \bar{x})$. Each of these numbers is then squared $(x_i - \bar{x})^2$ and added together $\Sigma(x_i - \bar{x})^2$. (In statistics, the Greek letter sigma (Σ) indicates "to summate" or "to add together.") Finally, this value is divided by N (the number of observations). This is the value for variance. To obtain the standard deviation, it is necessary to take the square root of the variance.

Of course, it is not necessary to calculate the mean or the standard deviation manually; a computer can do it.

Interpreting Statistics

The area of any closed figure, such as a square, circle, triangle or octagon, can be calculated. A line under the curve makes the normal curve a "closed figure," and its area can be calculated. It may be redundant to say but important to do so: A triangle has 100 percent of its area within the triangle; the same is true for a square, a circle, and the area under the normal curve.

Statisticians have arbitrarily divided the line under the curve into six equal

FIGURE 10–1d
Relationship Between Normal Curve and Standard Deviation (SD)

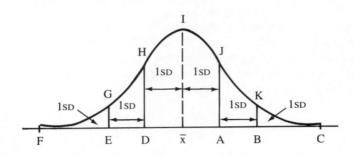

parts. They have called the distance between each of these one-sixth divisions a *standard deviation*. Because the area under the normal curve represents many bar graphs that are squeezed together, it is possible to select the specific bar graphs that fall at exactly the mean and at one and two standard deviations to the left or the right of the mean (or any other point). In Figure 10–1d, these are shown as x̄I, DH, AJ, EG and BK.

By examining many samples, statisticians have also determined that 2.3 percent of the area under the curve is to the left and to the right of the bar graphs which indicate the location of the second standard deviation from the mean, that is, the area circumscribed by FEG and by CBK.

Statisticians have also determined that the area under the curve which is bounded by the first and second standard deviations (EGHD and BKJA) is 13.6 percent of the whole of the area under the curve. Additionally, the area under the curve which is bounded by the mean and the first standard deviation to the left or to the right of the mean (x̄IHD and x̄IJA) is 34.1 percent of the whole of the area under the curve.

Why is this important?

If a unit (such as a machine or a person) in a particular sample has a certain amount of a characteristic and the amount of that characteristic is described as being one standard deviation to the left of the mean, that unit possesses more of the characteristic than 15.9 percent (2.3 percent plus 13.6 percent) of the other units in the sample. If a second unit has a certain amount of a characteristic and the amount of that characteristic is described as being one standard deviation to the right of the mean, the unit possesses more of that characteristic than 84.1 percent (2.3 + 13.6 + 34.1 + 34.1) of the other units in the sample.

An example may illustrate. A quality circle records the number of defects produced by one hundred machines at hourly intervals over a one-month period. A computer calculates the mean (x̄ is 10) and the standard deviation (SD is 2) for the entire sample. It also calculates the mean number of defects for each

FIGURE 10–1e
Relationship Between Standard Deviation and Area Under Curve

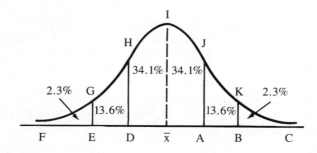

machine. For six machines the data given or calculated by members is as follows:

Average

Machine	Number of Defects	Standard Deviation
B1	6	2 (to the left)
L3	8	1 (to the left)
M6	10	0
P2	12	1 (to the right)
R9	14	2 (to the right)
W3	16	3 (to the right)

When the number of defects for all 100 machines are shown as bar graphs as a normal curve, Machine B1 can be described as being $(6-10)/2$ or 2 SD to the left of the mean. For Machine M6, this is $(10-10)/2$ or 0 deviations from the mean. For Machine W3, this is $(16-10)/2$ or 3 standard deviations to the right of the mean.

In other words, Machine B1 is a "good" machine; only 2.3 percent of the machines produced less defects than this machine did. Machine M6 is an average machine, but both R9 and W3 produced more than their share of defects. In the case of R9, it produced more defects than 84.1 percent of the machines in the sample. W3 is the worst machine; all 99 other machines produced less defects.

Within the work situation, it is necessary to correct a situation which produces or where there are too many deviants (for example, it is necessary to fix or replace a machine that produces too many defects). The mean and standard deviation also assist quality circle members in making decisions by allowing them to compare their findings with known or previously calculated standards through the use of statistical tests such as the t-test, analysis of variance or the chi-square (χ^2) goodness-of-fit test. Most companies have statistical packages for the computer which are used to compute these tests. All that is usually necessary is for quality circle members to list the results of their observations and the known or previously calculated mean and standard deviation.

The numbers chosen in this sample make the decision process very easy. Calculations are not required to reach the decision that Machine W3 is producing too many defects and should be replaced. If, however, a company can replace only one machine but must decide between three machines with means and standard deviations of:

Machine A ($\bar{x}$ = 10.369, SD = 2.613),

Machine B ($\bar{x}$ = 9.763, SD = 0.215), and

Machine C ($\bar{x}$ = 10.637, SD = 1.200), the decision is more difficult and the appropriate calculations and tests must be made.

Summary

In this chapter, three types of sampling and the concept of the normal curve and frequency distributions have been described. These statistics are sufficient to conduct the majority of analyses that will be required by circle members. The concepts are simple; the terminology that is used makes these appear more difficult than they really are. Circle members should be encouraged to learn and use statistical tools. As experience grows, more complex methods can be studied and the nuances can be appropriately interpreted.

STATISTICS

Sampling
- random
- systematic
- stratified
- cluster

Statistical measures
- percentages, frequencies, cumulative frequencies
- centrality measures: mean, mode, median
- normal curve
- standard deviation and variance

Normal curve
- kurtosis
- skewness
- area under the curve

11 *Evaluating the Circle*

After circles have been in operation for some time, even the most patient senior management will want assurances that money invested in this concept has been well spent. To show this, three types of measurements are necessary: objective productivity-type measures, subjective attitudinal measures regarding the impact that the circle has had on the organization, and an analysis of the internal processes of the circles.

Productivity Measures

The easiest way to measure success is through objective measures, that is, the concrete improvements which have occurred because of the work of quality circles. For this purpose, records are kept of improvements throughout the year. Additionally, one or two meetings are set aside at which past suggestions are examined and an action plan is set to investigate the long-range impact that the suggestions have had. Finally, a report is written by each quality circle outlining these benefits and improvements—placing, where possible, actual dollar figures on the savings that have accrued.

This objective productivity improvement analysis might address some of the following issues:

1. Better quality as measured by a reduction in rejects, fewer defective products, fewer recalls and fewer products which require rework.

2. Less scrap or waste.

3. Greater quantity of production.

4. Decrease in direct marginal cost (the cost of producing one unit).

5. Decrease in overhead or fixed costs.

6. Better equipment, machine and facility utilization.

7. Decrease in number and seriousness of accidents and more concern for safety and wearing of safety equipment.

8. Decrease in expenditures for maintenance of plant and equipment.

9. Less down time.

10. Increase in clients and customers, both in numbers and in value of purchases.

11. Greater customer satisfaction as shown by fewer customer complaints, less hostility and less office time allocated to problem solving.

12. For some or all employees, task procedures that have been simplified or improved.

No circle should feel, and no management should feel, that a circle has failed if there is little or no improvement in productivity—particularly in the first two or three years of circle operation. Even after the circle has become well established, improvement occurs in only one or two of the areas mentioned.

A more formal evaluation sheet used in Japan by Suzuki Motor Company is shown in Figure 11–1. Of interest are the eight criteria used and the weightings assigned to each:

• Number of suggestions made	2 points for each suggestion
• Length of time for which the circle meets	3 – 13 points times the number of meetings per month
• Attendance rate	2 – 5 points
• Money saved or the rank given the suggestion	10 points for suggestions up to 9,999 yen ($50); 170 points for suggestions of 200,000 yen ($2,000) or more
• Standards corrected	1 – 5 points for each correction
• Report presented at conference	40 points for each presentation
• Report published	40 points for each publication
• Standards violation	Deduction of 10 or 15 points for each violation

Each company and the circles in that company must decide whether such a formal evaluation serves a purpose. If the scheme is useful, the point system should be reached by a process of consensus decision making. Also, the system may have to change depending on the age of the circles and the unit or department in which they operate.

Relationship-Oriented Measures

Relationships, satisfaction, trust and cooperation are much more difficult to measure than productivity. Many problems exist in trying to quantify these aspects of organizational life and to prove, not only that there has been an improvement, but also that the improvement was attributable to circle operation. Relationships are long term in nature; U.S. and Canadian management, however, tends to be oriented to short-term results. Generally, no a priori measurements are made prior to circle introduction. External factors too affect internal processes. It is very difficult, for example, for trust to exist when the economy is in a severe downturn and massive layoffs are occurring or are imminent. Additionally, the validity of attitudinal surveys and organizational climate surveys has been questioned.

For those who may find it useful, a questionnaire developed to measure changes in attitudes which may result when quality circles are used is given at the end of this chapter. The questionnaire has five sections:

1. Questions about the circle and training.
2. Questions about circle processes.
3. Questions about the perceived effectiveness of the circle, namely which groups contribute to the success.
4. Questions concerning attitudes regarding the circle and the organization.
5. Questions about the respondent.

The questions about the circle processes centre on fifteen elements that play a part in circle success. These are examined to determine which are important. An additional nine statements attempt to determine the perceived purpose of the circle.

The attitudinal questions in Section 4 examine the feelings which members have about the circle, the work attitudes that exist, and whether members feel they are making a contribution. The last part of this section deals with commitment and loyalty to the organization, effort which the member would exert for the company, and the similarity in values which exists between company management and circle members.

The last section asks questions regarding age, gender, education, employment with the company and similar industries, position, department, union activities, participation as a member in and as a leader of a circle, and reasons for joining the circle.

Since the entire questionnaire is somewhat long, sections and questions should be selected carefully, depending on the desired purpose that a researcher has in mind. Several studies using this questionnaire are reported later in the book.

As relationships and trust improve, the amount of time that managers must spend resolving internal problems decreases. Interviews with managers in key positions therefore may also be useful in determining that attitudes have improved.

How can improvements be indicated to management? A section in the annual report of the circle always illustrates the manner in which at least some of the nine improvements listed below have occurred:

1. Greater trust and cooperation among employees, and particularly between management and rank-and-file employees, and between union executive members and company officials.
2. More open and meaningful communication, including better feedback and managerial responsiveness.
3. Better employee attitudes toward the company, toward management, and particularly toward the first-line supervisor.

FIGURE 11–1

Quality Circle Evaluation Sheet of Suzuki Motor Company

Month		Section Chief	
Section	Circle	Leader	

Item	Evaluation item	Weight	Points
Number of suggestions made	Number of improvements, ideas, opinions, and suggestions presented (Limited to Quality Circle suggestions)	2 ×	(cases)
Times circle met	15–29 minutes 30–59 minutes 60–89 minutes 90 + minutes	3 × 7 × 10 × 13 ×	(times) (times) (times) (times)
Attendance	–59 percent 60–79 percent 80 + percent	2 × 3 × 5 ×	(times) (times) (times)
Money saved	to 9,999 yen or 5th rank 10,000–49,999 yen or 4th rank 50,000–99,000 yen or 3rd rank 100,000–199,999 yen or 2nd rank 200,000 yen or 1st rank	10 × 30 × 70 × 100 × 170 ×	(cases) (cases) (cases) (cases) (cases)
SOS SIS	Correction of errors Formulation, revision	1 × 5 ×	(cases) (cases)
Report given at Quality Circle conference		40 ×	(cases)
Report published in		40 ×	(cases)
SOS SIS violation	Standard is correct but not conformed to	– 15 ×	(cases)
	Standard not correct and could not be conformed to	– 10 ×	(cases)
	TOTAL		
Details	SOS, SIS Division New No.	Entry error	

Note: 1. When the Quality Circle meets, this list must be submitted before the 10th of the following month. (If it is not submitted, the circle meeting will not be recognized as such.)

2. For the money saved in (4), supporting materials in written form must be submitted with this evaluation list

Registered members			
Remarks			
		File Number	
Type of suggestion			
(Data)	(Data)	(Data)	(Data)
(Data)	(Data)	(Data)	(Data)

Type of suggestion	File number	Money saved or suggestion for one case a month

Conference name
Name of magazine, issue
One check in three months

Revision	Enforcement

(except for suggestions).

Source: Tadao Koguri, "Providing Incentives to the QC Circle Through an Evaluation System," *Japan Quality Control Circles* (Tokyo: Asian Productivity Organization, 1982): 170.

FIGURE 11–2
Circle Meeting Assessment

	Never	Sometimes	Usually	Often	Always
Structure					
The group skips from subject to subject.					
Members of the group raise concerns and questions that are off the subject.					
Members know during the meeting where the meeting is on the agenda.					
So much information is discussed that group members become overwhelmed.					
Members come to the meeting knowing the purpose and/or agenda.					
Group members come and go at will during the meeting.					
The rules by which the meeting is conducted are clear.					
Discussions seem to go on endlessly.					
Influence					
Chosen solutions are what the leader wants rather than what the group wants.					
Participation by group members is encouraged.					
The leader power plays or rams decisions through.					
Most members of the group participate in discussions.					
Some members have concerns or ideas that never get on the agenda.					
All sides of an issue get aired.					
The same few members tend to monopolize discussion.					
Problem Solving					
The group divides or stalemates on issues.					
The group proposes solutions before thoroughly identifying causes.					
The same problems repeatedly emerge over the span of several meetings.					
Various alternatives are aired before a decision is reached.					
There is disagreement over the real issue or problem which is being considered.					
The problem under discussion is guise for another under-the-surface problem.					

Openness

Members tell the leader what he or she wants
to hear.

Members are willing to express their real
feelings about problems or issues.

Disagreement or discord is ignored or
avoided.

Members are subject to personal attack.

Members are open and willing to be critical.

Follow-Through

There is confusion about who is going to
make the decision or have the final say.

When a decision is reached, appropriate
action is taken.

The records of the meeting are available
before the next meeting.

There is confusion after the meeting over
who was to get things done and what was
to be done.

Adapted from: Steven Barney, *Quality Circles: Adapting Materials and Training to Organizational Needs* (unpublished paper prepared for Central Michigan University under the direction of Dr. Olga L. Crocker, December 1982).

4. Fewer short or suspect absences.

5. More interpersonal problems being worked out among employees so that there are fewer formal complaints and grievances.

6. More people being trained in company-needed skills on their own initiative and greater opportunities occurring for employees to use these skills.

7. Increase in number of employees who are interested in becoming members of quality circles.

8. Greater personal satisfaction regarding work, and feelings that the job offers opportunities to use abilities and skills and to perform work that is important, challenging and responsible.

9. Problems that quality circles are solving are increasing in number and in complexity.

Quality Circle Processes

Finally, some soul searching is in order. Members must analyze how effectively they have worked as a team. This analysis could include such things as the structure of the circle, the influence which the group and individual members have, their openness, follow-through, and problem-solving ability. Members may want to construct their own evaluation form; the thirty-item questionnaire developed by Barney (1982) may be helpful in this procedure (Figure 11–2).

After the questionnaires are completed, results must be analyzed. The circle must weigh the pros and cons of doing this internally or having the quality circle office do it for them. If the office does the analysis, members may be more honest in answering the questions because they are assured of the anonymity of their responses. On the other hand, circle members may learn more by bringing any differences of opinion into the open immediately. Some members could, however, feel intimidated and therefore not be willing to express their true opinions. Under either method, circle members must discuss problem areas and methods by which the internal processes can be improved.

Last but most important, after circle members have carried out objective, subjective, and process analyses, three things remain—self-congratulations, a pat on the back for fellow members, and a celebration for a job well done!

EVALUATION SHOULD INCLUDE IMPROVEMENTS IN:

Productivity
- quality
- scrap
- quantity
- marginal cost
- overhead
- equipment
- safety and accidents
- maintenance
- down-time
- sales
- customer satisfaction
- tasks

Attitude and relationships
- trust
- communication
- subordinate–supervisor relationships
- absenteeism
- complaints and grievances
- use of skills
- membership of circles
- personal satisfaction
- type and number of problems solved

Circle processes
- structure
- influence

- problem solving
- openness
- follow-through

A Questionnaire About Quality Circles

I. *Questions about the Technical Aspects of the Circle*

A. Check the correct answer.

1. To what type of circle or team do you presently belong?
___ shop-floor
___ clerical/office/white-collar
___ technical
___ professional
___ managerial
___ other (specify)

2. How often does the circle meet?
___ daily
___ more than once a week, but not daily
___ once a week
___ twice a month
___ once a month
___ less than once a month

3. How often would you like the circle to meet?
___ daily
___ more than once a week, but not daily
___ once a week
___ twice a month
___ once a month
___ less than once a month

4. Do you think the circle should meet:
___ on company time
___ after work but at time-and-a-half pay, double-time pay, etc.
___ after work at regular compensation
___ after work without compensation
___ a combination of without compensation and one of the others

5. For what length of time does the circle meet?
___ less than an hour
___ approximately one hour
___ between one and two hours
___ more than two hours
___ length of time varies

B. Prior to joining the circle, how adequately were you trained in each of the following skills? Please answer by selecting the correct option according to the following scale:

      1 not at all
      2 very little
      3 somewhat
      4 considerably
      5 more than adequately

____6 decision making
____7 fishbone analysis
____8 graphs
____9 statistics
____10 conducting a meeting
____11 team and interpersonal interaction
____12 managerial philosophy
____13 goal-setting processes
____14 On a scale of 1 (low) to 5 (high), overall how would you rate your training prior to joining the circle?

C. Since joining the circle, how adequately have you been trained in each of the following skills?
____15 decision making
____16 fishbone/process analysis
____17 graphs
____18 statistics
____19 conducting a meeting
____20 team and interpersonal interaction
____21 managerial philosophy
____22 goal-setting processes
____23 writing a report
____24 making an oral presentation
____25 On a scale of 1 (low) to 5 (high), overall how would you rate your training since joining the circle?

II. *Questions about Circle Processes*

D. Following are a number of factors which determine how successfully the circle is able to solve problems. Which of these have been important to your circle? Please answer by selecting the correct option according to the following scale:

      1 extremely unimportant
      2 somewhat unimportant
      3 neither unimportant nor important
      4 somewhat important
      5 extremely important

____26 Commitment to and participation in the circle by members

___27 Aggressiveness of the members

___28 Ability of the members

___29 Ability and commitment of the leader

___30 Ability and commitment of the facilitator

___31 Knowledge of the job by the members

___32 Effort of circle members and leader

___33 Cooperation among circle team

___34 Training received by members

___35 Technical assistance received

___36 Managerial attitude, support and responsiveness

___37 Managerial recognition of the circle

___38 Feedback provided

___39 Difficulty of the problem chosen

___40 Good luck

E. Rate each of the following statements according to how well the item describes the purpose of the circle of which you are a member:

       1 extremely unimportant

       2 somewhat unimportant

       3 neither unimportant nor important

       4 somewhat important

       5 extremely important

___41 to increase productivity

___42 to increase quality

___43 to decrease the number of defective parts

___44 to increase communication between workers and management

___45 to become competitive in national or world markets

___46 to improve the quality of work life for employees

___47 to increase employee participation

___48 to allow employees to use their intelligence, expertise and innovative ability

___49 to make employees think they are important

___50 to make management or the company look good.

III. *Questions about the Effectiveness of the Circle*

F. How effective the circle is depends upon many people. In your opinion, what is the contribution that each of the following make to the success of your circle? Rate each according to the following scale:

1 no contribution

2 very little contribution

3 moderate contribution

4 considerable contribution

5 a tremendous contribution

___51 You, yourself

___52 Other circle members

___53 Circle leader

___54 Facilitator

___55 Steering committee

___56 Unit supervisor

___57 Plant management

___58 Corporate management

___59 Union/union executive

___60 To what extent have improvements suggested by your quality circle been implemented? Choose the right answer from among the following:

        1 not at all

        2 a little

        3 moderately

        4 considerably

        5 to a great extent

        6 every suggestion has been implemented

IV. *Questions Concerning Feelings about the Circle and the Organization*

G. Following are statements which have been made about the operation of other circles. Based on your own experiences as a circle member, how strongly do you agree or disagree with each statement? Answer according to the following scale:

        1 strongly disagree

        2 somewhat disagree

        3 neither disagree or agree

        4 somewhat agree

        5 strongly agree

___61 I enjoy being a member of the circle.

___62 I would join another circle if I was moved to another unit or area of work responsibility.

___63 I would recommend to my friends that they join a circle.

___64 My experiences with the circle have been unpleasant and frustrating.

___65 I communicate with supervisors more easily than I did in the past.

___66 My relationship with my work group is better than it has been in the past.

___67 Our circle is doing important work.

___68 Our circle has made a worthwhile contribution to the organization.

___69 The company has profited financially from our circles' efforts.

___70 Our efforts are appreciated within this company.

H. Following are statements that have often been made by employees about the company for which they work. Based on your own experience with this company, how strongly do you agree or disagree with each statement? Use the 1 to 5 scale described above to give your answer.

___71 I am happy to put in extra effort for this company.

___72 I tell my neighbors and friends that this company is an excellent employer.

___73 This company is important to me.

___74 I would quit my job tomorrow if I could get an equal or better job.

___75 I do my best every day for the company.

___76 The goals and values that I have are similar to those of company management.

___77 I disagree with the company's policies and regulations.

___78 I am sorry that I went to work for this company.

___79 I would do any task or work which I was asked to do in order to remain with the company.

V. *Some Questions about You*

I. Please check the right answer.

1. Age

___ Less than 20 years of age

___ 20–25 years of age

___ 26–30 years of age

___ 31–35 years of age

___ 36–40 years of age

___ 41–45 years of age

___ 46–50 years of age

___ 51–55 years of age

___ 56–60 years of age

___ 61 + years of age

2. Gender ___Male ___Female

3. Education Level

___ Grade 8 or less

___ Grade 9 to 11

___ Completed high school (grade 12 or 13)

___ Some college training or education

___ Some university education

___ Received a diploma from a college

___ Awarded a degree

___ Awarded a master's degree

___ Awarded a doctoral degree

4. Length of employment with the company

___ Less than six months

___ 7 months to 12 months

___ 1 to 2 years

___ 3 to 5 years

___ 6 to 10 years

___ 11 to 20 years

___ more than 20 years

5. Length of employment in a similar industry (include employment for present company in the total)

___ Less than six months
___ 7 months to 12 months
___ 1 to 2 years
___ 3 to 5 years
___ 6 to 10 years
___ 11 to 20 years

6. Your position in this firm is:

___ Production worker (hourly pay)
___ Production worker (salaried)
___ Office worker (hourly pay)
___ Office worker (salaried)
___ Supervisory/first-line management
___ Middle management
___ Senior management
___ Technical
___ Professional
___ Other (specify) _____

7. The department in which you are employed is:

___ Production
___ Sales
___ Marketing
___ Finance
___ Accounting
___ Purchasing
___ Personnel/industrial relations
___ Design/research and/or development
___ Services to other employees (mailroom, cafeteria, etc.)
___ Other (specify) _____

8. How long have you participated in a circle or team?

___ Not at all
___ Less than 6 months
___ 7 to 12 months
___ 13 to 18 months
___ 19 to 24 months
___ 25 to 30 months
___ 30 to 60 months
___ More than 5 years

J. Why did you join the circle? Check all answers which apply:

___ 9. to get time off from work
___10. to meet or influence members of management
___11. because a friend, acquaintance or person with whom you share a ride did

___12. as a joke

___13. union asked/told me to do so

___14. management or supervisor asked/told me to do so

___15. for personal recognition

___16. because of peer pressure

___17. monetary reward

___18. to get some problems straightened out

___19. to help the company

___20. to keep my job (or jobs in general)

K. Select the three most important reasons. Place the number of the items (from 9 to 20) below.

21.___

22.___

23.___

L. Check the best answer

24. Do you enjoy being the team leader?

___ Yes

___ No

___ Not a team leader presently

25. If you are a leader or have been one in the past, what is the total period of time you have been/were a leader?

___ Not at all

___ Less than 6 months

___ 7 to 12 months

___ 13 to 18 months

___ 19 to 24 months

___ 25 to 30 months

___ 30 to 60 months

___ More than 5 years

26. If you are not presently a circle leader, would you like to be one?

___ Yes

___ No

___ Am presently a circle leader

27. The union that represents blue-collar workers in the firm can be described as being:

___ Extremely militant

___ Somewhat militant

___ In between militant and not militant

___ Somewhat non-militant

___ Extremely non-militant

___ Not applicable

28. The union that represents clerical workers in the firm can be described as being:
___ Extremely militant
___ Somewhat militant
___ In between militant and not militant
___ Somewhat non-militant
___ Extremely non-militant
___ Not applicable
(If this survey is being done in a variety of organizations):
29. The type of industry in which you are employed is:
___ Production/manufacturing
___ Professional (accounting, law, education, etc.)
___ Medical services
___ Civil service
___ Retail/wholesale sector
___ High technology
___ Service industry
___ Finance, insurance or real estate
___ Primary resource or basic industries (steel, coal, etc.)
___ Other (specify)_____
30. How many employees normally work in your company?
___ 20 or less
___ 21–100
___ 101–500
___ 501–1,000
___ 1,001–10,000
___ Over 10,000
___ Not applicable
___ Self-employed and only employee
___ Other

PART IV

CASE STUDIES AND CONCLUSION

12 Ford Motor Co. of Canada

The Ford Motor Co. of Canada, in Windsor, Ontario, is an excellent example of how a company can involve employees in the decision-making process in an effort to increase operating effectiveness and to improve employee working conditions.[1]

The Employee Involvement (EI) process originated in the United States during the 1979 national negotiations when Ford and the United Auto Workers (UAW) affirmed their intentions to jointly support an effort to increase employee participation on the shop floor. Operationalization of these intentions was initiated by establishment of the National Joint Committee on Employee Involvement (NJCEI).

Senior executives of both the company and the union have shown their commitment by being personally involved. The NJCEI, for example, was formerly chaired jointly by Donald F. Ephlin, UAW Vice-President and Director of the Ford Department (now Dennis Yokich), and by Peter J. Pestillo, Vice-President of Labor Relations, Ford Motor Company.

A quality circle structure has been suggested which management and union can establish at the local level (Figure 12–1). Reporting to the NJCEI (at least in the United States; a similar body does not exist in Canada) is the local plant steering committee. In Canada, EI coordinators assist problem-solving groups in shop-floor decision making.

The Employee Involvement concept has flourished. Presently, there are an estimated 10,000 employees who are participating actively in approximately eight hundred EI teams at sixty plants in Canada and the United States. Not only has operating performance risen, but employee attitudes and perceptions of the company have improved. Rank-and-file workers, for the most part, are positive and enthusiastic about the program.

This attitude is new. The climate at Ford Motor in the United States has been anything but conducive to cooperation. Historically the relationship between management and the union has been adversarial and hostile. Suspicion and distrust date back to the early and middle 1940s, when Henry Ford refused to recognize the UAW as the representative of the workers, and sit-down strikes were not only the rule but were characterized by bloodshed. The situation was

Photo by Ruth Kaplan

Hank Hunt headed the team that helped keep Ford's Engine Plant 2 open in Windsor, Ontario. With him are most of his former teammates. Front, from left: Charlie Warner, Hunt and Terry Souchuk. Middle: Corey Graham, Joe Clemente and Frank Ferrari. Back: Dave Macrow, Tim Hornsey, Ray Boulton, John Chick and Norm Zorzit.

no different in Canada. In fact, more recently, in 1979, labour–management relationships were strained because of revised practices that were implemented by management at the new Essex Engine Plant. As a consequence, at this plant, the union initially refused to support EI efforts because it felt that this was another method by which the company could take advantage of employees.

With the deepening recession, however, the situation changed. In order to stem the level of worker layoffs and the mounting threat of foreign competition, both sides, during the 1982 negotiations, agreed to cooperate. As Jerry Steele, Industrial Relations Manager for both the Windsor and Essex plants, points out: "We were not competitive from a cost, productivity, or quality standpoint; in

FIGURE 12–1
Ford's Quality Circle Organization

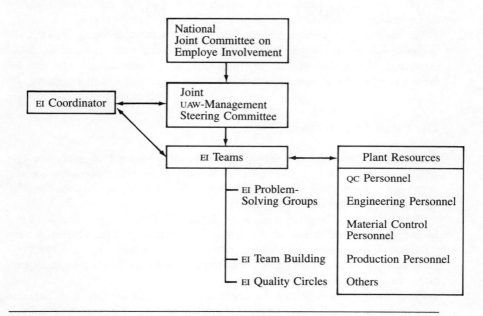

Source: Adapted from *A Handbook on the* UAW*-Ford Process for Local Unions and Management* (Dearborn, MI: UAW–Ford National Joint Committee on Employe Involvement, 1980): 26.

all the indicators or barometers of our industry, we were not competitive. We had to change.'' Ray Wakeman, President of UAW Local 200, which represents all Ford blue-collar employees in the city of Windsor, also admits that: ''we have to look at all the avenues because [the union's] primary function is to do things that would secure the workers a better place to work and not jeopardize their employment.''[2] Both union executive members and management agree, however, that EI is not a substitute for negotiations and that it does not infringe on issues that are negotiable.

As a result of these types of attitude changes, during the 1982 negotiations, Ford and the UAW agreed to establish a joint employee involvement program. As a consequence, a set of guidelines and structures were initiated. In the Windsor area there are six operations—Windsor Engine Plant #1 (WEP #1), Windsor Engine Plant #2 (WEP #2), Essex Engine Plant (EEP), Essex Aluminum Plant, Windsor Casting Plant (WCP), and Windsor Export Supply. Employee Involvement groups function in the first five operations. The WEP #1, WEP #2 and EEP have retained the name ''Employee Involvement''; the WCP has TOPP—

"Total Opportunity for People Participation." At the Aluminum Plant, four groups are tackling quality problems, and the groundwork is being laid to move to problem-solving teams. The last group—the all-salary employees at Export Supply—are being trained, and it is probable that in the near future a white-collar employee involvement team will begin to function.

The early negativism in the EEP makes it particularly interesting to examine. If quality circles (Employee Involvement) could make a difference in an organizational climate that was so far from ideal, it certainly has possibilities for firms where a more cooperative stance is taken by unions and management.

The Essex Engine Plant

The Essex Engine Plant is a capital-intensive and automated assembly line operation. Approximately 1,400 hourly-paid and 400 salaried employees are engaged in the production of standard V-6 engines which are used in the Cougar, the Thunderbird and other Ford models.

The plant did not begin operations until April 13, 1981. Later in that year, the EI concept was initiated—and discontinued. Unfortunately, the climate at that time was not conducive to cooperative ventures. Not until after the 1982 negotiations did EI teams officially begin to function again—with the blessing of both management and the plant union.

Plant management followed the example of Ford headquarters (U.S.) executives. Plant manager Leo Brown (and other plant officers), for example, endorsed the process from the outset and provided leadership and support in initiating the program. Today they continue to be actively involved.

Both the company and the union have chosen well-liked and respected people for the key positions. Company/Union appointees are: Gary Lesperance, EI coordinator for the Windsor operations (now Pat McKrow); Gene Gadzos, EI Facilitator for the salaried Windsor operations; Cleveland Magee, Hourly EI Facilitator for the EEP; John Rivard, Hourly Facilitator for the two WEPs; and Ken Gouin, TOPP Coordinator at the WCP. All have extensive labour relations backgrounds. More importantly, however, according to at least one blue-collar employee, they also "are great guys and are easy to work with."

EI teams at EEP are organized largely by work units on the basis of tasks which are performed. For example, each area has its problem-solving team which consists of eight to ten hourly-paid and salaried workers. The teams communicate with the Steering Committee and report their progress and problems on a regular basis. The Committee provides direction and assists teams on difficult projects. Most important of all, it publicizes the team's accomplishments (see Figure 12–1).

The Steering Committee is central to the organization and the implementation of EI. It consists of both company and union representatives. Curtis Davidson, Plant Union Chairperson, and Frank Morand, Bruce Magee and Sid Chase, UAW

FIGURE 12–2
Eight Basic Steps in Launching EI

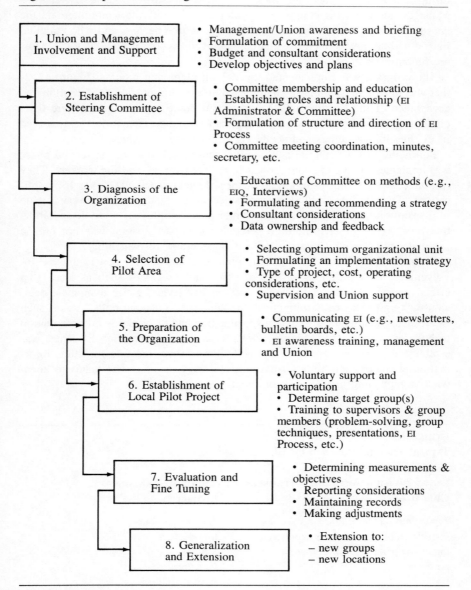

1. Union and Management Involvement and Support
- Management/Union awareness and briefing
- Formulation of commitment
- Budget and consultant considerations
- Develop objectives and plans

2. Establishment of Steering Committee
- Committee membership and education
- Establishing roles and relationship (EI Administrator & Committee)
- Formulation of structure and direction of EI Process
- Committee meeting coordination, minutes, secretary, etc.

3. Diagnosis of the Organization
- Education of Committee on methods (e.g., EIQ, Interviews)
- Formulating and recommending a strategy
- Consultant considerations
- Data ownership and feedback

4. Selection of Pilot Area
- Selecting optimum organizational unit
- Formulating an implementation strategy
- Type of project, cost, operating considerations, etc.
- Supervision and Union support

5. Preparation of the Organization
- Communicating EI (e.g., newsletters, bulletin boards, etc.)
- EI awareness training, management and Union

6. Establishment of Local Pilot Project
- Voluntary support and participation
- Determine target group(s)
- Training to supervisors & group members (problem-solving, group techniques, presentations, EI Process, etc.)

7. Evaluation and Fine Tuning
- Determining measurements & objectives
- Reporting considerations
- Maintaining records
- Making adjustments

8. Generalization and Extension
- Extension to:
  – new groups
  – new locations

Memo: It is important to note that this is a dynamic "non-linear" process, thus elements of any step will occur throughout the process.

Source: *A Handbook on the* UAW–*Ford Process for Local Unions and Management* (Dearborn, MI: UAW–Ford National Joint Committee on Employe Involvement, 1980): 18.

Committee, represent the union. Leo Brown, Plant Manager, Gifford Brown, Area Manager, Mel Rowe, Quality Control Manager, James Barry, Manufacturing and Plant Engineering Manager, and Jerry Steele, Industrial Relations Manager, represent the company. Working closely with the Committee are the coordinators and facilitators who act as the resource persons and who maintain liaison with all levels to ensure that communications are open and that the teams are functioning smoothly.

The program was implemented through an eight-step process (Figure 12–2) that was in two phases. Phase one focused on orientation and the promotion and acceptance of the EI concept. Managers and union representatives were thoroughly trained in the philosophy, the application, and the team processes involved in EI. Feasibility studies and needs assessments were conducted.

Following this managerial and union executive orientation, the second phase was implemented and the concept was introduced to rank-and-file workers. They responded with enthusiasm; a request for volunteers resulted in over 150 applications. Twenty-nine employees were selected, by random draw, to participate in a twenty-hour training program. While many employees were disappointed that they were not chosen, they perceived that participation was not only a privilege, but one which carried with it considerable responsibility.

Training consisted of units on the plant organization and on Employee Involvement. In addition, a variety of skills and processes such as leadership effectiveness, motivational theories, personality styles, group dynamics, decision-making processes, communication skills and "nuts and bolts" issues such as problem identification, problem specification and resolution, and presentation techniques were learned (Figure 12–3). To assist the teams, an EI centre was established. The centre houses the facilitator's office, meeting facilities, information about EI, and audio-visual aids. In short, anyone who wants to know what is happening in EI can learn about it at the centre.

FIGURE 12–3
Typical Training Program for EI Team Members

ENGINE DIVISION PARTICIPATIVE PROBLEM SOLVING GROUP TRAINING

Objective	**Content**
Topic: Introduction Plant Organization	*Time* = .5 hours
Provide employees with an understand-	Introduction
ing of the plant organization and its	Structure
products.	Functions
	Responsibilities
	Building an Engine

Topic: Communications
Emphasize the importance of listening and its impact on group participation.

Develop skills in active listening.

Increase the employees' awareness and skills for using two-way communication.

Time = 3.5 hours
Exercise "Group Listening"
Film "Power of Listening"
Discussion
Exercise "One-Way vs. Two-Way Communication"
Discussion/Critique

Topic: Motivation
Provide employees with an assessment of their own needs in the work environment.

Create an understanding of motivation and its impact on group participation.

Provide employees with an understanding of employee involvement and the conditions necessary for the successful implementation of problem-solving groups.

Time = 1.5 hours
Exercise "Motivation Feedback Opinionnaire." Discussion of Maslow, Herzberg

Topic: Leadership
Provide employees with group leadership concepts and techniques.

Develop an awareness of leadership styles and their impact on group participation.

Time = 2.5 hours
Discussion of McGregor
Discussion of Blake/Mouton
Case Study: "Mallard Airplane Company"
Discussion and summary of communications, motivation

Topic: Group Techniques
Develop an awareness of techniques that assist in the group decision-making process.

Develop skills for making more effective group decisions and recommendations.

Time = 3.0 hours
Handouts and discussion of group dynamics
Exercise "Subarctic Survival"
Discussion/Critique

Topic: Problem Identification
Identify Quality Control Measuring Techniques and Reports.

Time = 2.0 hours
QC Measuring Techniques
Discussion on QC Measuring Techniques

Develop the ability/skill to identify and separate problems in their work areas.	Stairstepping Techniques Practice Discussion
Topic: Problem Specification and Resolution Develop the ability and skills to more accurately define problems and identify their cause or causes.	*Time* = 5.0 hours Systematic Problem-Solving Techniques Practice Discussion Case Study Discussion Critique Brainstorming Techniques
Develop skills for making recommendations to management and/or Steering Committee for problem resolution.	Practice Discussion
Topic: Presentation Techniques Develop an awareness of the use of charts and graphics for effective presentations.	*Time* = 2.0 hours Use of Visuals Practice Discussion Platform Skills Practice Discussion
Develop effective presentation skills.	

Currently, the training program is being expanded. In addition to EI training, Ford in Windsor has instituted substance abuse awareness training, a twenty-hour upgrading (on company time) in statistical process control, safety, work practices, etc., and a five-evening pre-employment orientation program in which prospective employees (and other interested persons) are given the opportunity to hear about the company, safety and work practices, and where EI is thoroughly explained.

In addition, EI teams and middle management personnel have taken the initiative in sharing their expertise and knowledge not only with academics but with other firms in the Windsor community. As one union member stated, "This program makes us feel like people; we want to share that feeling with others."

The Process

To review, the complete eight-step process (shown in Figure 12–2) included:
1. The involvement of union and management personnel and their indication of support.
2. The establishment of the steering committee.
3. The diagnosis of the organization. This included establishing a committee on methods to be utilized, the formulation of a strategy, a discussion of the interrelationship between EI and Ford's existing suggestion system.
4. The selection of the pilot area. This involved an analysis of costs and benefits,

the extent of supervisory and union support and finally the formulation of an implementation strategy.
5. The preparation of the members of the organization for EI.
6. The establishment of the local pilot project.
7. The evaluation and fine tuning of the program.
8. Generalizing the program and extending it to other locations within the plant.

The Results

EI has been a success. Currently, the EEP has seven teams in which 55 employees participate. At the WEP and the EEP, sixteen teams are functioning and 160 employees are involved. Problems which have been resolved through EI include:
- reduction in kerosene usage in the Block Department at WEP #1
- quality and cost improvements in WEP #2
- energy savings at both WEPs
- reduction of rejects and improved efficiency in the testing areas at EEP

This last was an interesting problem. A stopper at the end of a vacuum tube sometimes became dislodged in testing. Since the tube then was drawing air, the part was rejected. This meant that it had to be sent to "repair," fitted with the plug and retested. Considerable tension between employees in repair and those who handled the part resulted because of the so-called "stupidity and carelessness" of that unit. The EI team determined that plugs, not employees, were at fault. A variety of solutions were tried: golf tees worked but had other drawbacks; taping was messy and time consuming. The solution: a longer plug. The result: a 17 percent increase in effectiveness of that unit.

Projects still in process include a number of improvements in materials, methods, quality and costs in all areas. Colour coding, instead of numbering, appears to be the solution to the matching problem that involves piston and bore size. Two hundred pairs of a new type of glove, which has a longer life and is cheaper and more flexible, have been ordered and will be examined during the next few weeks. Of great interest to team members is a van-pooling scheme. One team of employees is determined to resolve difficulties that have occurred in the past.

No company can long afford to sustain a loser. Employee Involvement is growing because it is not a cost burden; groups generate sufficient high-calibre ideas and suggestions to justify their existence. "They love solving problems," Gary Lesperance, EI coordinator, states. "Not the big ones—just the little ones; the kind that everybody used to walk by and say 'Somebody should do something about that.' " EI teams are doing that something. But more importantly, the barriers between plant employees and office employees are being broken down. The two groups are working together; engineers and managers are requesting assistance from shop-floor personnel to solve problems which they experience.

And from a labour relations point of view—Bill Johnston, Manager of Labour Relations and Hourly Personnel, Windsor Operations, has this to say: "EI is not a single program but a changing way to do business. It is one of a number of Ford programs aimed at communications, openness and an interest in our employees, not as a means to complete production schedules, but as people." When pressed, Johnston admits that grievances have dropped about 25 percent. This has resulted in considerable cost savings for the company and faster griev- ance resolution for the union in spite of the fact that 1,100 additional employees have been hired.

Unlike its U.S. Ford organization, the Essex Engine plant did not use outside consultants during the institutionalization of the change process. Instead, it mo- bilized only internal resources. Both union and company officials attribute much of the initial success to the need for cooperation between the two in resolving day-by-day EI problems.

An external study of the success of the EI program in this plant, conducted by the authors of this book, with the assistance of Local 200 of the UAW, is reported in the next chapter.

"SOS"

The 255 engine, which had been produced by Windsor Engine Plant #2, was being phased out in 1982, and the plant, which was down to eighty-three em- ployees and which the company said was unprofitable, was about to be closed. The employees, however, were determined to keep it open. To meet the challenge, a "Save Our Stampings" (SOS) team was established. Union and management working together

spearheaded improvements in productivity and quality control that turned the operation around. It is now efficient and profitable. The SOS team saved their own jobs, and created new jobs. (Editorial, *Windsor Star*, September 16, 1983)

Union and management are proud of the successes that have been accomplished. Some of these include: the plant is cleaner; lighting has been improved; a heated blow-off has been installed on the washer so that stamp parts dry and do not have to be derusted; there is improved cutting and stacking of oil pan blanks. Scrap has decreased from 18 percent to 2 percent; quality too has improved.

Plant Manager Leo Brown quickly agrees that employee team efforts have meant that the plant has continued to operate rather than being shut down. Furthermore, Brown says, "These efforts exemplify the kind of team action between employees, union and management which is necessary to keep our plants viable." The teams have been directly responsible for new business—the 3.8 litre rocker-arm cover press, assembly and paint operations. Recently pro- duction of the 3.02 five-litre engine was moved to this plant.

Employees and the union, too, are proud of their efforts. So enthusiastic is the SOS team that they have developed a presentation about their circle which they proudly deliver at other plants and organizations and to other groups that are interested. John Rivard, Hourly SOS Facilitator, proudly states that, "Our aim is no scrap and no rejects. We are determined to keep our plant open." Just recently, the team consisting of Henry (Hank) Hunt, Charlie Warner, Frank Ferrari, Charlie Cloutier, Joe Clemente, Ray Bolton and Bob Davis was one of five groups recognized for "outstanding business achievement" by the Ontario Chamber of Commerce.

The Future of EI

In spite of its success, both management and union continue to take a cautious approach to EI. It appears that senior management has not yet clarified the new role behaviours that they will be required to adopt—that of policy makers and not decision makers on day-to-day issues. This will be necessary if EI is to permeate the company.

There are reservations too. The economy and car sales have improved. The question which no one wants to voice is whether prosperity will work to the detriment of EI. Will the lessons of the past be forgotten by both management and the union? Both groups are quick to respond to this query, "EI is here to stay. The foundation has been carefully laid."

FORD MOTOR CO. OF CANADA

History
• relationships between union and management extremely poor
• 1979—National Joint Committee on Employee Involvement established
• 1982—Canadian EI established
Engine Plants
• steering committee of union and management members
• eight-step process of implementation
• twenty-hour training program
• additional twenty-hour training program in other facets for all employees
• sixteen teams and 160 employees participate at present
• many cost-saving improvements
• attitudes improved
SOS
• EI saved plant from being closed down

UAW–Ford Employee Involvement Survey

Generally, because of the underlying philosophy of quality circles, workers have a sense of participation at the shop-floor level. Through QCs, they can contribute their ingenuity, creativity, skills and talents to the attainment of organizational goals. In most cases, participants are intrinsically motivated because of the opportunities for self-development and accomplishment. It is not surprising, therefore, that most companies find a substantial improvement in worker attitudes and an increase in productivity after the introduction of quality circles.

Indeed, most of the literature has postulated that worker participation improves job satisfaction and productivity and that it stimulates psychological involvement. Blumberg (1968) reviewing the literature on this subject, stated:

There is hardly a study in the entire literature which fails to demonstrate that satisfaction in work is enhanced or that other generally acknowledged beneficial consequences accrue from a genuine increase in workers' decision-making power. Such consistency of findings . . . is rare in social research. (123)

Likewise, Locke and Schweiger (1979), following an examination of the subsequent literature, concluded that:

The benefits alleged to result from PDM (participation in decision making) by workers fall into two major categories. The first includes *increased morale and job satisfaction* and their frequent concomitants, reduced turnover, absenteeism, and conflict. The second category includes outcomes pertaining directly to *productive efficiency*, e.g. higher production, better decision quality, better production quality, and reduced conflict (again) and costs. (277)

Are the above comments true for the Windsor and Essex Engine Plants? A study conducted by Chiu and Crocker with the assistance of members of UAW Local 200 attempted to analyze the level of effectiveness of the UAW–Ford Employee Involvement Program.

Using an earlier version of the questionnaire shown in Chapter 11, data were obtained from two sources. First, thirty-six employees of the Windsor and Essex

Windsor Star Photo.

Members of the Ford SOS team receive Chamber of Commerce Award, September 1983.

Engine Plants responded. The second sample consisted of thirty-one employees from Canadian automotive and automotive parts manufacturing assembly line firms. All respondents in the second sample stated that they were not participating in an employee decision-making program.

Questionnaires for the Engine Plants were administered randomly by the union to EI members. The second set of questionnaires were administered to participants in a stress seminar and to students prior to night classes at a local college of applied arts and technology.

The demographic characteristics of the two samples do not differ significantly. All participants are male auto workers, predominantly in the thirty-one to fifty age group. Employees of both groups are, for the most part, shop floor workers. Both groups are also relatively well educated. Of the Engine Plant group, 63.9 percent reported that they had completed at least high school. Of the second group, 74.2 percent had completed at least high school. Almost all employees from both groups had more than ten years of seniority with their employers.

The study utilized a five-part questionnaire. One part requested personal and demographic information—age, sex, education level, length of employment with the company and degree of participation in shop-floor decision making or employee involvement. A second section, which was omitted by non–Engine plant employees, requested that participants give their opinions concerning the EI process by ranking twelve factors in order of their importance in assisting team members to solve problems. The twelve factors were: effort, training, ability of members, technical assistance from engineers, management responsiveness, co-operation among the circle members, active participation of members, recognition by the company, feedback, task difficulty, luck and use of job knowledge. In this section respondents also indicated, on a 5-point scale ranging from 1 (low) to 5 (high), their opinions with respect to those individuals who are responsible for the effectiveness of the circle or team.

In a third part of the questionnaire, the respondents were asked to indicate their experiences and perceptions with the circle or team. The items in a fourth section, which both sample groups answered, measured the degree to which respondents feel committed to the employing organization (Porter, 1974: 603–9). The nine items are divided into three categories: three items relate to the individual's involvement and satisfaction with the organization; three items relate to the individual's willingness to exert effort to achieve organizational goals, and the other three items relate to the individual's willingness to accept organizational values and policies.

The final section of the questionnaire provided respondents with the opportunity of making open-ended comments. These are given in Appendix 8.

The Findings

At the time of the study (April 1983), two-thirds of the Engine Plants' respondents had been participating in a circle or team for less than six months. A substantial group (ten of thirty-six, or 27.8 percent) had been involved for a period ranging from thirteen to twenty-four months. One person had participated for a period of seven to twelve months and one person was involved for more than twenty-four months.

Each circle or team member was involved in a shop-floor team which met weekly. Ten persons reported that they were currently leaders or had been leaders in the past. Of those who were not currently team leaders, eight of twenty-six (30.8 percent) stated that they did not wish to assume the leader's role. Each of the remaining eighteen (69.2 percent) would like to be a team leader.

All but one respondent felt that the circle or team should meet on company time. This other respondent indicated a desire to meet after work but with compensation. It must be pointed out, however, that EI teams do meet on company time; respondents may have been indicating that this arrangement was satisfactory.

Exactly one-half of the respondents felt that the purpose of EI was to improve quality. The next most popular response to the question regarding purpose was to improve communication (six replies or 16.67 percent). Five others (13.9 percent) responded that all seven items which were stated (to increase quality, productivity, quality of working life, communication and worker creativity, to decrease defects and to meet the Japanese challenge) were purposes of EI.

Why did participants join the teams? To what extent were the teams' suggestions implemented? To what extent did members feel that pre-training had been adequate? In answer to the first question—why the member had joined—fourteen (38.9 percent) did so for personal recognition. Another twenty-two reported other reasons for joining. Among the reasons given were being asked to do so, because buddies were joining, to improve the company, because of peer pressure, for monetary considerations and because it meant time off from work.

Interestingly, sixteen of the thirty-six respondents (44.4 percent) felt that the team's suggestions had been implemented to a great extent or to a very great extent. An additional thirteen of the thirty-six (36.1 percent) felt that suggestions had been implemented to some extent. Six respondents (16.7 percent) felt suggestions had been implemented to only a very slight extent.

Respondents split down the middle on the matter of training. Eighteen felt that pre-training was limited and eighteen felt that considerable pre-training had occurred. It was thought that perceptions of adequacy of pre-training would be a function of involvement time in a circle or team and whether the respondent was a leader or not. The results showed that time in the program did not significantly change perceptions of the adequacy of pre-training (chi-square = 1.33, degrees of freedom = 1, not significant). The data concerning leadership was more interesting. Of those respondents who were or had been leaders, eight of ten (80.0 percent) felt they had adequate pre-training; two of ten (20.0 percent) felt that they did not. Of the 18 who wanted to be future leaders, eleven (61.1 percent) did not feel that their training had been adequate. Seven of the eighteen thought pre-training had been adequate. The results are very similar for those eight respondents who did not wish to assume the leader's role. Five (62.5 percent) felt their pre-training had been inadequate; three (37.5 percent) felt it had been adequate. When the chi-square test of goodness was applied to these results, the differences were statistically significant; that is, results such as these could occur by chance once in each eleven times (chi-square = 5.00, degrees of freedom = 2, p = 0.09). This is sufficiently infrequent to conclude that the steering committee should carefully examine its pre-training programs, especially the training of rank-and-file workers. It appears that these employees perceive this aspect of the EI program as inadequate.

Who contributes to the greatest extent to the effectiveness of the circle or team? The results are summarized in Table 13–1. Not surprisingly, the majority of respondents felt that group members, the team leader, and they themselves contributed the greatest amount. The behind-the-scenes roles of both the steering committee and the union executive, generally speaking, were unrecognized. Only eleven of thirty-six persons (30.6 percent), in each case, felt that a substantial contribution was made by either of these two groups.

Twelve factors were named, and respondents were asked to rank each factor, in descending order of importance, regarding the circle's or team's ability to solve problems. Table 13–2 gives this summary in terms of number of responses together with the median.[1] The most important factors are job knowledge (median

208 CASE STUDIES AND CONCLUSION

TABLE 13–1
Extent to Which Members of the Organization are Responsible for Circle or
Team Success

Participant	Value Assigned*					Total
	1	2	3	4	5	
Yourself	0	1	16	11	8	134
Group Members	0	0	7	18	11	148
Team Leader	1	2	12	10	11	136
Facilitator	2	5	13	10	6	121
Steering Committee	7	9	9	7	4	100
Union Executive	7	7	11	10	1	99
Plant Management	5	2	8	14	7	124
Corporate Management	6	4	10	9	7	115

*According to contribution; 1 = little; 5 = great. Total possible score for any item is 180 (36 subjects times a high score of 5).

is 2.0), effort (median is 3.5), training (median is 4.0), ability of members (median is 4.5), cooperation (median is 5.0), and active participation (median is 5.0).

Two-thirds of respondents had extremely positive feelings regarding the teams or circles. Six persons (16.7 percent), however, had relatively negative or neutral feelings toward the teams. Did any similarities exist among the members of this group and did they differ from other members? The negative/neutral group was similar to the positive group in age, education, experience and length of partic-ipation in the EI program. The group included one leader, one individual who did not wish to assume a leader role and four persons who would accept this role if they were asked. These six people differed from the more positive group in their responses to the question on success of implementation of the team's suggestions (four of six felt that implementation was inadequate) and in their reasons for participating in the EI program. Four indicated that they had joined for "other" reasons but gave no clarification of that reason. One had joined to get two hours off from work; a second had joined to improve conditions at work. Again, if there is a message in these six responses, it may be that the steering committee or Engine Plants' management should be sensitive to the need for ensuring that implementation of teams' suggestions occurs, or, if it cannot, to better communicate the reasons for any delay or rejection.

The last objective section of the questionnaire was answered by Engine Plant and by non–Engine Plant employees. The nine items measure:
• involvement of the individual and satisfaction with the company (questions 72, 73, 74 of questionnaire given in Chapter 11)

TABLE 13–2

Factors Contributing to Teams' Abilities to Handle Problems, as Ranked by EI Participants (In descending order of importance)

| Factors | Ratings By Number of Respondents | | | | | Median Value* |
	1	2	3	4	5	
1. Use of job knowledge	11	8	3	2	2	2.0
2. Effort	3	5	10	5	2	3.5
3. Training	3	6	7	3	4	4.0
4. Ability of members	4	8	2	4	6	4.5
5. Cooperation	5	2	2	5	5	5.0
6. Active participation	4	2	5	5	5	5.0
7. Technical assistance	0	1	1	8	1	6.5
8. Management responsiveness	0	0	2	1	6	8.0
9. Recognition	1	0	1	1	3	9.0
10. Feedback	1	1	2	2	1	9.0
11. Task	1	1	1	0	1	10.0
12. Luck	2	0	0	0	0	12.0

*The median is the rating (ranking) on each item given by the "middle" person. In this case, it is the average of the ranking given by the eighteenth and nineteenth respondents.

- a willingness to exert effort to achieve company goals (questions 71, 75, 79)
- a willingness to accept organizational values and policies (questions 76, 77, and 78).

How do employees of the Engine Plants who are participating in EI feel about their organization as a place to work? How do their feelings compare to those of other employees who are not involved in a quality circle or similar program?

Responses to the items concerning the Windsor Essex Engine Plants as a place to work indicate that generally the plant is considered to be a good place to work (mean = 3.942, SD = 0.51). (The number "1" signifies strong disagreement with the positive statements and the number "5" indicates strong agreement with these same statements.) EI participants, however, are less willing to expend effort to achieve organizational goals (mean = 3.556, SD = 0.745) and are even less willing to adopt organizational values and policies (mean = 2.833, SD = 1.000).

Interestingly, however, the dispersion (standard deviation) is much greater for the items concerning effort and values. This indicates that much greater variability in responses exists, that is, that some members of the group agree very strongly with the positive statements while others disagree very strongly with the same statements. In other words, some members are extremely willing to expend effort

TABLE 13–3

Comparison of Responses—Ford Engine Plants (EI involvement) vs. Plants Not Involved in Quality Circles

	Engine Plant		Non–Engine Plant		t-test	Probability
	Mean	SD	Mean	SD		
Good place to work	3.942	0.515	3.624	0.479	2.602	0.008
Expend effort	3.556	0.745	3.779	0.572	1.357	NS
Accept values	2.833	1.000	2.349	0.776	2.177	0.020

*The mean is the average of all the scores; standard deviation (SD) has been explained in Chapter 9.

for the company; others are not. Also some members are extremely willing to adopt organizational values; others are strongly opposed to this.

Are these three averages significantly different from average responses given by the automotive and automotive parts respondents who are not involved in employee decision making? A summary table of the relevant information and the statistical tests is given in Table 13–3. The data indicate that the non–Engine Plants group had a mean = 3.624 (SD = 0.479) for satisfaction; a mean of 3.779 (SD = 0.572) for effort; and a mean of 2.349 (SD = 0.776) for acceptance of values and policies.

From this analysis it can be concluded that the two groups are significantly different in their perceptions of their company as a good place to work and in their willingness to accept the values of the organization. There is no statistically significant difference in their willingness to expend effort for their organization. In other words, the findings indicate that Ford employees who are participating in EI are significantly more satisfied with their organization and are significantly more willing to accept the values and policies of the company than are people who do not work for Ford and who are not involved in shop-floor problem solving (if our samples were representative of each group).

Previously, it was pointed out that six persons had negative or neutral feelings about circles or teams. Responses of these six employees were compared to the other thirty Ford employees. The results are given in Table 13–4. The data indicate that there is no difference between the two groups in their perception of Ford Motor Co. of Canada as a place to work. Both groups are relatively satisfied. The negative/neutral group, however, is significantly less willing to expend effort to achieve the goals of the organization or to accept the organizational values than is the group which perceives EI more favourably.

TABLE 13–4

Comparison of Responses Group which Perceives EI Positively vs. Group which Perceives EI Negatively

	Positive Group (N₁ = 30)		Negative Group (N₂ = 6)		t-test	Probability
	Mean	SD	Mean	SD		
Good place to work	3.980	0.496	3.750	0.610	1.000	NS
Expend effort	4.119	0.753	3.056	0.705	3.186	0.001
Accept values	2.983	1.043	2.084	0.783	1.995	0.020

Summary

In summary, the statistical analysis has indicated that:

1. The majority of respondents have been or are or would like to be a team leader.

2. Half of the respondents felt that the purpose of EI was to improve quality, suggesting that they are quality conscious. Others felt that EI was directed toward improving communication. Still others felt that the purpose could not be defined in one statement and chose instead all available categories.

3. Participants join the EI program for a variety of reasons. Most important is personal recognition.

4. Less than one-half of respondents felt that teams' suggestions are implemented reasonably frequently. One-sixth of the respondents felt implementation was "slight" or "very slight."

5. Leaders of teams perceive that they have been reasonably well trained prior to the introduction of EI. Rank-and-file employees, however, did not feel that they had been well trained.

6. Generally, EI participants felt that members, the leader and they themselves personally contribute most to the effectiveness of the team. The contributions of the union executive and the steering committee were less well recognized.

7. The ability to solve problems depends mainly on members' job knowledge, effort, training, ability and active participation, and on cooperation within the groups.

8. The majority of workers feel positive about EI.

9. Only six persons of the thirty-six sampled had negative or neutral feelings about EI. They also were less satisfied with the implementation process and most had joined the group for other, but unspecified, reasons. Furthermore, on the average, this group of six was less willing to expend effort to accomplish the

goals of the company and was less willing to accept organizational values and policies.

10. The EI implementation appears to be proceeding smoothly.

11. Participants in EI programs are more likely to perceive that their company is a good place to work than are non-participants. They are, on the average, also more willing to accept organizational values. The mean score for non-Ford workers on willingness to expend effort is somewhat higher than that of Ford employees; the difference is not significant.

Conclusions and Recommendations

Survey results suggest that EI has some impact on worker attitudes. EI participants are positive about the program and are willing to work with management to achieve corporate goals, that is, to improve the company's competitive position by increasing product quality and operating efficiency. It is important to remember that EI at the Essex Engine Plant has been in operation for less than a year and that generally even more positive results are experienced in the long run. Other Ford studies, namely the 1982 UAW–Ford Employee Involvement survey,[2] confirm that, since the introduction of EI, Ford employees have shown substantial improvement in attitudes concerning problem-solving, supervisory practices, job satisfaction, product quality and cost consciousness. This is in keeping with other research on quality circles. Northrup Corporation, Aircraft Division, for example, based on pre- and post-implementation data, also found that worker attitudes improved positively after QC participation.[3] Honeywell Corporation, in a 1982 survey, found that QC participants appeared psychologically committed to the company and that their perceptions and reactions were positive.[4] Quality circles do affect worker attitudes in a positive direction.

The findings of this study, however, point out two areas of weakness: the steering committee might do well to examine both the training program and the process and record of implementation of teams' suggestions.

One result in the findings was especially surprising. EI participants did not feel more willing to exert effort to achieve company goals than did employees from other auto-related firms that did not have a quality circle approach. A number of explanations come to mind. First, the EI program at the Essex Engine Plant is relatively new. Second, the previous few years have demanded substantial sacrifice from all employees in all automobile-related industries. Employees of other firms may not yet feel that their companies are economically secure. This could mean that greater effort continues to be required on their part to secure their own jobs. A third reason comes to mind. It is possible that employees feel that they had little or no part in determining the goals and values of the organization and that these do not represent them. If this is the case, as EI matures and the employees become more experienced at decision making, Ford management might wish to involve shop-floor people in strategic decision making—

the setting of organizational goals and values. Participation should increase commitment and the willingness to exert greater effort and to internalize the values of the company.

FINDINGS

Majority of members would like to be leaders.

Employees are quality conscious.

Many join EI teams for personal recognition.

Most feel suggestions are implemented reasonably frequently.

Leaders feel they are well trained.

Members feel they are not well trained.

Leaders, members, and individuals contribute most to EI success.

Union and steering committee perceived to contribute least to EI success.

Ability to solve problems depends on:
- job knowledge
- effort
- training
- ability
- active participation
- cooperation

Most members are positive about EI.

Only six respondents of the thirty-six sampled are not positive about EI.
- feel implementation process is unsatisfactory
- joined for other unspecified reasons
- feel training inadequate

EI participants feel:
- Ford of Canada is a good place to work
- less positive about willingness to expend effort
- even less positive about accepting organizational values
- significantly more positive regarding company and accepting organizational values than non-EI participants in other companies.

14 "PSI": Vickers Incorporated World Headquarters

With a core philosophy that emphasizes the dignity, self-worth, and contributions of employees, a company cannot help but succeed. Without such a philosophy, a company cannot hope to succeed.

These sentences, posted in the office of a member of the middle management team, express the philosophy and values of Vickers Incorporated World Headquarters management.

Vickers Incorporated operates in such diverse high technology growth industries as computer systems, farm equipment, aircraft and marine guidance and control, and fluid power. Vickers develops and manufactures hydraulic and pneumatic products and systems which provide power and control for industrial machinery, mobile vehicles, aircraft, ships, and land defence systems. Its products include hydraulic pumps, valves, motors, power units, transmissions, packaged systems, accessories, pneumatic products, solenoid valves, winches and planetary gear drives. The company employs 7,000 people and operates in forty-four countries, including Canada. World Headquarters (WHQ) is located in Troy, Michigan.

Vickers's quality circle teams are named PSI (an acronym for "pounds per square inch," adapted to stand for "People Seeking Improvement"). The PSI program began when the company was up for sale during a period of deepest decline. Personnel at the plants (and two at WHQ) were being put on indefinite layoff; others, and this included the headquarters staff, were being encouraged to take early retirement. Employees were impressed that a company at such a time would budget the funding necessary; this, to them, was proof of the commitment to PSI that exists.

Vickers's PSI groups are unique. While there are a few departmental teams, the majority of the fourteen circles, each with five to eight members (predominantly engineers), are cross-functional. No pilot project was established. Programs at various Vickers U.S. plants pioneered the way for quality circle implementation at WHQ. At these plants, teams have been in operation for over four years.

214

Courtesy Vickers, Inc.

A team captain presents ideas before the operating committee for approval. Presentations generally involve the entire team. Visual aids and presentation hand-outs accompany most ideas.

Vickers's management felt that productivity in the non-manufacturing sector had to be improved because:

1. A substantial portion of the cost of a product is attributable to overhead. It made little sense to streamline plant operations only to lose these gains in office areas—whether it was through the work of clerks or general managers.

2. In most industrial firms in North America, the number of people engaged in administrative duties is steadily increasing while the number of employees engaged in production is decreasing. Vickers is no exception. If this trend continues, the manufacturing labour segment could be too small to offset the administrative cost increases.

3. Office activity is labour-intensive. In addition, long-established, traditional methods exist for each function.

4. New types of machines in office operations are often inappropriate or are improperly used (e.g., computer output).

5. Savings attributable to improvements are difficult to quantify. If visible cost reductions are to be achieved, a continuous generation of ideas is required.

Management also recognized that, in addition to the usual resistance to change, other key problems had to be addressed:

1. If PSI groups were to quantify improvements, standards and output measure-

Courtesy Vickers, Inc.

A team holds an idea session. Groups are made up of persons from all disciplines. This heterogeneous make-up complicates the program, but permits better understanding of each function's problems.

Courtesy Vickers, Inc.

Question and answer sessions are an important part of a team presentation and help the operating committee make fast decisions.

ments would be required for office activities. Because these are more difficult to define than in manufacturing, few exist.

2. The setting of standards and of measurements would be perceived as regimentation or a taking away of individual freedom. Considerable resistance could be anticipated.

3. Certain aspects of administrative work depend upon "knowledge," and specially qualified people are hired for these jobs. A substantial portion of their

FIGURE 14–1
Plan for Implementing PSI at Vickers

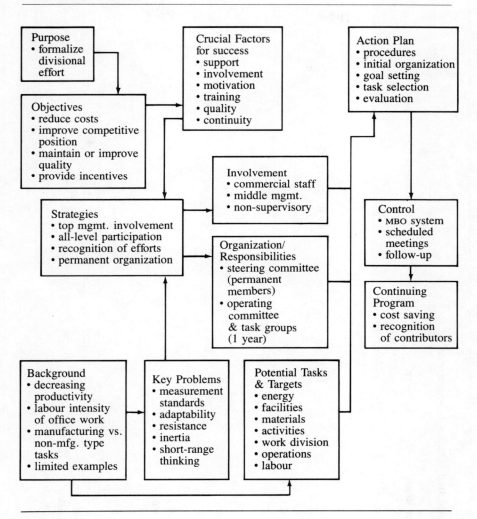

time, however, is spent on work activities that are clerical in nature and which could be done by lower-paid personnel. A resistance to a redistribution of these tasks could occur.

4. The PSI concept would be perceived as a threat by middle managers. This group undoubtedly would perceive that employees would be assuming their

FIGURE 14–2
Program Launch—Productivity/Quality Improvement

Business Plan Milestone Report　　　Business Plan _____

Symbols:
x —milestone target
□ —milestone complete
x -x revised target

Weeks —	1	2	3	4	5	6	7	8	9	10	11	12	13	14	15	16	17	18	19	20	21	22
Milestones																						
VP-General Manager																						
1. Approve implementation	x																					
2. Appoint program coordinator	x																					
Program Coordinator																						
1. Arrange for training program	x																					
2. Publish start of program			x																			
3. Attend meetings								(. . . . . all meetings . . . . .)														
Management Development																						
1. Prepare training program			x																			
2. Conduct sessions						x	x	x				x										
Steering Committee																						
1. First meeting	x																					
2. Appoint operating committee	x																					
3. Approve task group leaders			x																			
4. Approve task group organization				x																		
5. Approve group goals										x												
6. Approve group plans															x							

Milestones

Weeks	1	2	3	4	5	6	7	8	9	10	11	12	13	14	15	16	17	18	19	20	21	22
Operating Committee																						
1. First Meeting	x																					
2. Appoint group leaders	x																					
3. Training sessions			x	x																		
4. Appoint task group members				x																		
5. Assist in setting goals								x														
6. Approve task group goals									x													
7. Approve task group plans													x									
8. Write MBO's for goals															x							
9. Summary report to steering committee																	x					
Task Groups																						
1. Initial meeting					x																	
2. Training sessions						x	x															
3. Set goals									x													
4. Write plan												x										
5. Start investigation/research																						
6. Progress reports—monthly															x				x			

Comments:

decision-making role, usurping their position within the hierarchy, and that they (the managers) would be required to share their authority and power.

5. The heterogeneous, company-wide PSI teams would have a tendency, at least in the early experimental stages, to want to address problems in which their expertise and knowledge was limited and which other employees would have to implement (e.g., personnel policies).

These problems were discussed and plans and actions were taken to overcome their negative impact. Finally, an administrative plan for implementing the program was formulated (see Figures 14–1 and 14–2).[1]

Organization

The structure for PSI which was agreed upon was a three-tier type, that is, it had a steering committee, an operating committee, and task groups (circles).

Steering Committee

The general manager is chairperson of the steering committee which includes the department heads in charge of: manufacturing, marketing, engineering, finance, management and information systems, planning and product management, the corporate vice-president–personnel and the program facilitator. Figure 14–3 shows this structure in greater detail.

The steering committee appoints members to the operating committee, sets overall policy, assigns resources, arbitrates problems, provides backing and support to the program and the circles and, at times, establishes priorities.

Operating Committee

The operating committee has the key role in PSI success. It consists of nine employees, mostly middle managers, each representing a different department, and nine others, who are alternates. The program facilitator is chairperson. The term of office for this group has not yet been determined, and members are changed periodically but not more than once a year.

This committee establishes procedures; approves projects; reviews and approves the group's goals and procedures; provides guidance and direction for areas of cost reduction or productivity improvement to the task groups; monitors the progress of, and directs and controls, the activities of the task groups; reviews claimed successes and results; provides assistance as required to task groups; resolves cross-functional conflicts relating to credit for cost reduction improvements; contributes ideas for non-financial rewards for the task groups; and establishes annual goals for each department.

The operating committee, in general, is a communication vehicle. One member of this committee is the liaison to each of the teams. Most attend occasional meetings of their PSI circle(s), all are available as sounding boards and in an

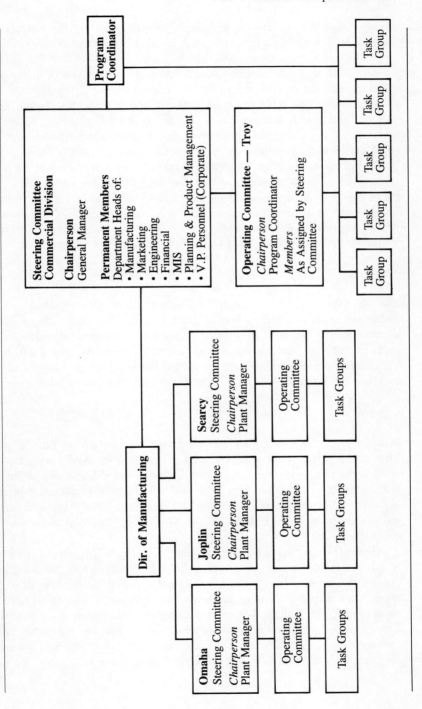

FIGURE 14-3
Vickers Productivity Quality Improvement Organization

advisory capacity. To ensure adequate communication up the hierarchy, one member is assigned as a liaison to each member of the steering committee.

Quality circle methods are new. There is little experience and few guidelines on which to draw. As a consequence, as in the majority of companies, top management was committed but not sufficiently prepared regarding the long-term nature of PSI. This has meant that the top management group, because they are pragmatic, has wanted results for expended monies. The operating committee must manage this impatience, must ensure that top management makes itself available for presentations, and that top executives really listen.

The operating committee must also ensure that circle members do not become discouraged. PSI circle members are impatient with the discussion, the research, the inability to structure solutions to (what appeared to be, at the beginning) very simple problems. "One of our [the operating committee's] more important tasks", says a committee member, "is to encourage circle members and to keep up their enthusiasm. Our job is to see that decisions get made quickly."

Facilitator

The job of the program facilitator, in addition to chairing the operating committee and acting as an ex-officio member of the steering committee, is to: coordinate communications between all committees and groups; ensure that training of circle captains and members occurs; act as liaison between PSI groups and the two committees; provide and monitor the record-keeping and reporting systems; and ascertain the progress (or lack of progress) which PSI groups are experiencing.

Captains

In some groups, captains (leaders) were appointed by the steering committee. The criteria which were used included personality, innovativeness, flexibility, willingness to take risks, aggressiveness, demonstrated leadership ability and a willingness to listen, to use peer participation and to allow freedom to members. In other circles, members elected their own captains. The majority of captains are those who have been subjected to considerable "baptism under fire"—the unit supervisors.

What role does the team captain have? According to the captain of PSI Team 8, this individual: organizes activities and logistics, monitors the meetings and ensures that all members of the team are participating, communicates with and assists team members between meetings, is careful not to impose his or her own ideas on the group and assists in monitoring implementation. Circles which are experiencing the greatest success are those which rotate secretarial and chairing responsibilities. In these circles, agendas are circulated in advance, and minutes are recorded and circulated. This is not true for all teams.

Operation

Each PSI circle meets for one hour each week on company time. (One circle holds meetings during the lunch hour.) Members are volunteers; each person who indicated a desire to participate was assigned by the steering committee to one of the heterogeneous PSI groups. New members also may join. Designated members may drop out if they wish; few have done so.

One of the first issues which each circle faced was how to select the problem that would be studied. The procedure varied among circles. Generally, following a brainstorming session in which many ideas were generated, each idea was discussed and evaluated. In some cases, a consensus approach was used to decide on the one problem. In other cases, a nucleus of problems was desired, so members were given the required number of votes, and democracy ruled. The most successful groups (about one-third, at this point) took on "bite-sized" problems.

Training

Leader training sessions include:
• an explanation of the program and its objectives and why it is necessary
• what teams are expected to do and how they are related to the steering committee and the operating committee
• logistics and procedures such as chairing meetings, agendas, minutes, types of reports and forms that can be developed and used
• how to establish goals
• value engineering concepts (cost benefit analysis) to help the groups identify areas where productivity improvement could occur
• calculation of and recognition of savings
• motivation of employees
• recognition

The training program was limited to these topics because the assumption was made that employees at WHQ, who are mostly professionals with degrees or post–high school training, had the necessary skills and knowledge that PSI required. Nothing could have been further from the truth, and the operating committee is currently attempting to develop more comprehensive training units.

Projects Undertaken and Implemented

Among the projects that have been undertaken and which presently are under study are:
• improving the quality and reliability of all products
• improving heat treating

- modifying performance and developing review forms
- reviewing of inter-office magazine circulation
- updating of job posting procedures
- examining mail and small packages transfer procedures, including mail to employees' homes and the usage of "confidential" envelopes
- reducing the number of in-house manuals
- providing a directory and information guide and refining the telephone directory
- providing recorded response to incoming calls during facility shutdown
- reducing proliferation of "unit model" releases
- reducing or eliminating rented cafeterias and their maintenance
- providing markers to assist in the relocation of removed microfilm records
- improving paper flow of shipper notifications
- assessing actions necessary to reduce tardiness and unauthorized early departures
- educating personnel to the features and benefits of the word processor
- improving computer terminal availability
- revising the processing and distribution of computer-produced invoices
- computerizing energy consumption and cost reports
- reducing the monthly phone expense, with a 5 percent reduction goal
- minimizing distractions within the workplace
- reducing employee time spent on scanning or reading bulletin boards
- improving copying services
- reviewing coffee-break procedures

About one-third of the circles, to date, have made suggestions which have been implemented. Completed projects include:

- modification of order procedures; savings of $600
- modification of "impending change" notices; savings of $24,000
- engineers trained in computer utilization; savings of $52,800 or 0.55 engineering person-years gained
- transfer of parts and service drawings; savings of $10,200 annually
- increased productivity of team members by holding team meetings on personal time rather than on company-paid time; potential savings are $4,050
- improved mailroom efficiency; three stages have been implemented to date with a resulting savings of $27,800
- reduction of electrical energy used by turning off one of two cooling system pumps; savings of $20,000 annually
- printing of graph paper in-house; savings of $553 annually
- review of engineering cost reporting system; projected minimum annual savings of $22,000
- expedition of "release pending" procedures; savings of $3,000 annually
- implementation of a standard engineering project filing system; potential cost savings of $50,000 to $70,000 annually

Figure 14 – 4 illustrates the cost savings report form that is currently being

FIGURE 14 – 4
Monthly Status Report

Monthly Status Report of Achievement

Team Identification _____   Steering Committee Approvals:
Team Leader _____   Project Nos. Approved _____
Month of _____   Project Nos. Rejected _____

Project Identification   Annual Goal   Achievements _____

1. Current Month $ _____
Year to Date $ _____
Percent of Project Goal:
Current Month   _____
Year to Date   _____
                                        0   25   50   75   100

2. Current Month $ _____
Year to Date $ _____
Percent of Project Goal:
Current Month   _____
Year to Date   _____
                                        0   25   50   75   100

Team Total Current Month $ _____
Year to Date $ _____
Percent of Project Goal:
Current Month   _____
Year to Date   _____
                                        0   25   50   75   100

used by quality circles within the manufacturing operations. Discussions at WHQ are continuing as to whether or not PSI teams want a similar format.

Recognition of Circles

Incentives for participation are necessary. These, however, do not have to be monetary in nature. In the manufacturing plants, monetary recognition includes

FIGURE 14–5
Letter Regarding an Accepted Proposal

Date: _____

To:
c/o Dept:
From:
Subject: *Quality & Cost Improvement Proposal—Accepted*
      Group # _____
      Team # _____
      Proposal # _____

Your proposal has been reviewed and approved by the Operating and Steering Committees.
A record of the annual savings amount of $ _____ will be placed in your personnel file.
The Steering Committee wishes to thank you for your participation and encourages you to submit additional cost improvement proposals in the future.
Attachment: Copy of Proposal

FIGURE 14–6
Letter Regarding an Unaccepted Proposal

Date: _____

To:
c/o Dept:
From:
Subject: *Quality & Cost Improvement Proposal—Not Accepted*
      Group # _____
      Team # _____
      Proposal # _____

Your proposal has been reviewed by the Operating and Steering Committees and was not accepted: [Reasons are given.]

The Steering Committee wishes to thank you for your participation and encourages you to continue to submit other ideas and suggestions to reduce our operating costs.
Attachment: Copy of Proposal

savings bonds, small prizes for the best team each month, trips for very significant achievements or ideas (or the best in a particular quarter). Non-monetary forms of recognition include dinners and baseball or football games for team employees and their spouses. A more "risky" activity includes a raffle for a number of prizes. A raffle ticket is given to the circle for each idea which is submitted during the month. The more tickets, of course, the better are the chances of winning.

These ideas have not been adopted at WHQ. Non-monetary recognition, however, is frequent and includes direct personal recognition by top departmental and divisional management and wall plaques for contributions made.

Additionally, achievement is noted in the employees' personnel records. Immediate feedback also is provided by acknowledging in writing the suggestion that has been made and the anticipated cost savings (See Figures 14–5 and 14–6).

In Retrospect

Progress to date has not been easy. With the PSI concept, WHQ management is in the early stages of a pioneering project; for them there are few guidelines and a continuous variety of different types of problems. Of course, everyone knew that the process would not fall into place immediately, and that there would be a very frustrating, painful growing period. "But," the facilitator reflects, "We underestimated how lengthy and frustrating that period would be. And we did make some mistakes." The mistakes were attributable to lack of knowledge and a desire to help teams accomplish early successes.

One of these mistakes was the setting of organizational goals for the groups. In an effort to help, management established goals, which, unfortunately, were perceived as being financial and qualitative in nature only, that is, they were cost-cutting targets. Resentment occurred. Again, in retrospect, a senior member of management muses, "If we had to do it all over again? First, we would avoid setting goals. You need to build harmony among the teams; they need a history of working together and of achieving success. Because there was no previous experience, our goals were set unrealistically high. Teams could not help but fall short. Management too had higher expectations. It was a no-win situation— a situation in which disappointment was programmed into the process."

Second, the training program for captains, which consisted of six sessions of one to one-and-a-half hours, and the indoctrination program for management were inadequate. The initial captain training program included familiarization with the PSI concept, the goals of the organization, the fundamentals of the change process, how to conduct a meeting, and techniques of problem solving. One middle manager, a member of the operating committee, states, "We were venturing into a new untried area. We had no history to fall back on and so were unable to anticipate all of the problems." Presently, Vickers is considering instituting periodic training sessions—on a continuing basis—mostly in additional techniques of group interaction and problem solving.

A third problem was experienced in the early stages. Circles were enthusiastic and felt that, at last, an opportunity was available which could help in eliminating the problems and bottlenecks. Projects selected, at times, tended to be difficult and far-reaching, and encompassed many departments of the organization. Circles generally underestimated the time that was required and the difficulty of conducting research and reaching consensus. In future, most of the circles will take on smaller, more manageable problems.

Lack of time to pursue circle activities has been a problem. Each circle is anxious to do an excellent job and to make the organization a better place to work and ensure that it remains competitive. This is not easy. Because of the adverse economic times, each person has had to assume additional functional duties and responsibilities. The lack of time to conduct required research is extremely frustrating.

A fourth problem concerns management style. Like that of other organizations that had their beginnings in the 1940s and 1950s, Vickers's management group is mature, and for the majority, the Theory-X style of management has worked well. The Theory-Z style requires considerable flexibility and adaptability. "No matter how hard a manager tries," states one member, "it is easy to slip back into the old ways."

In addition to problems, there have been many advantages. Among the most important is the tendency of circle members to believe that everything can be accomplished. They do not accept excuses and reasons; they just do it! To accomplish goals, protocol and organizational formality are ignored. The result has been a better communication system and a flattening of the hierarchy of the organization.

Management too has responded with enthusiasm. They are determined that this will be a grass-roots movement—loose, flexible and responsive. The direction and success will come from the members themselves. To this end, they are determined to avoid formalization and bureaucratic trappings. It is formalization and bureaucracy, says one senior management member, that "undermine incentive, thought and creativity. We have exceptional employees and are confident PSI teams will be successful."

PSI—PEOPLE SEEKING IMPROVEMENT

Why quality circles in an office situation?
- overhead contributes substantially to costs
- administrative staff increasing while production staff decreasing
- long-established practices exist

- machines used improperly
- savings for each suggestion difficult to quantify

Key problems:
- no standards or output measurements
- resistance to establishing these
- highly qualified people doing clerical work
- middle management apprehensive
- fear that teams would overextend their authority and expertise

PSI structure:
- steering committee
- operating committee—key to PSI group success
- facilitator
- fourteen PSI groups of five to eight members each
- cross-functional membership of groups

Annual cost savings of $250,000 currently achieved.
Incentives and recognition:
- acknowledgement letter
- notation in personnel file
- savings bonds
- trips for outstanding ideas
- wall plaques
- social events
- raffle

In retrospect:
- management set goals; this was a mistake
- training inadequate
- problems selected were too difficult
- lack of time
- management style

Circles believe they can make anything happen.

Management has been responsive.

15 In Conclusion: QCs—Success or Failure?

Are quality circles the answer to motivational and other problems which face the North American industrial world in the 1980s? The quality control circle and small group concept have assisted Japan in becoming the world trading nation that it is today. These activities, according to a survey done by the Kansai Productivity Centre, increase communication among members, make the workplace more humane and pleasant, provide workers with greater self-realization, decrease defects, increase efficiency and productivity, develop worker knowledge and skill; increase the number of group suggestions; decrease accidents, decrease production costs, increase product quality, and decrease absenteeism.[1]

Studies indicate that in North America, too, there have been benefits. For companies, QCs have resulted in: financial gain because of employees' concern for quality, their problem solving and their suggestions regarding the improvement of production processes and methods for decreasing costs; financial gain because of increased productivity; better union–management and employer–employee relationships; and fewer grievances and fewer conflicts. For employees, QCs have meant increased development of skills and abilities, greater challenges and learning opportunities and greater satisfaction.[2] Quality circles can assist both the organization and the employees. Why, then, are some applications of the method successful while others are not?

Japanese writers claim that the humanization of the workplace is the key to success:

Human beings . . . must become the central focus of the workplace. Despotic exercise of authority denies a worker an independent personality, turns him into a "cogwheel" or a "pebble." It inhibits productivity, results in the misuse of authority and naturally leads to the self-destruction of the company.[3]

But Japanese and American cultures and systems are very different, and the techniques that work in a company in Japan will not work—without adaptation—here. One vital idea, however, can be carried over: the way to humanize the workplace is to allow workers to participate in decision making in those areas which affect them and in which they have the expertise. "What the workers want most, as more than 100 studies in the last 20 years show, is to become masters of their immediate environments and to feel that their work and they themselves are important—the twin ingredients of self-esteem.''[4] A people-building process performs miracles.

Quality circles are people-builders. They allow employees to be human and not just robots or appendages of machines. Circles require workers to use their intelligence, creativity and ingenuity, not merely their physical efforts.

Second, quality circles present workers with challenge. This means that skills and abilities which they have learned are utilized. This, in turn, results in the need for new skills and knowledge and for additional training.

Third, quality circles increase communication between company employees. No longer does the company abdicate to the union the right to talk to its own workers. Management, engineers, and other white-collar employees solve problems with shop-floor workers. In doing so, they eliminate established stereotypes. Workers are no longer perceived as being illiterate, stupid people who are incapable of thinking and incapable of understanding instructions. Instead, they are individuals who love football, baseball and the latest hit tunes and movies, who live in the same environment and have the same problems, concerns and interests as managers have. The eye-opener works both ways—blue-collar workers discover that office personnel do not fritter away their time and that they do not intentionally try to make life miserable for those who "do the work." More importantly, blue-collar workers discover how inflexible the hierarchy is and how difficult it is to implement change. Circle members gain an understanding of the difficulties faced by supervisors and a new respect for this group. The communication process results in a better understanding of different groups within the organization, which in turn results in less conflict, higher self-esteem, better morale and a greater commitment to the organization.

Are QCs the key to all motivational problems? Although they have been used for these purposes, the degree of their influence on worker motivation cannot be determined. Motivation is an abstract construct; it is difficult to define and more difficult to measure. Eysenck explains it this way:

[N]o aspect of human behavior has proved more resistant to analysis and measurement. The effort of psychologists to grapple with drive and motivation has evoked a remarkable variety of unsatisfactory solutions, ranging from purely semantic exercises to pseudo-mathematical treatment of non-existent data. As a result there is still no generally accepted method of measuring the degree of motivation under which a person is working at any particular time.[5]

Only time will tell if quality circles are the missing link which, in the American environment, can inspire employees to put in a forty-hour week for forty hours of pay. The more important issue, however, is that it cannot hurt an organization to ensure that employees function in an environment that provides them with an opportunity to give their best efforts.

Steps to Ensure Failure

Will quality circles be a success or a failure? Only the personnel within an organization can determine this. Ten steps will help to ensure failure:

1. Management should have a hidden agenda in initiating circles. Failure will be ensured if management thinks of QCs as an easy way to make a buck without spending too much money, or as a union-busting technique. Another method that will assist failure is to make numerous promises to ensure that the union cooperates at the beginning, and then break the promises. Of course, there will be a special delight when the rug is pulled out and the union realizes that it has been tricked, that its members have been gullible, and that it was easy to "put one over on them." If there is no union, the hidden agenda can be that QCs are a good way to keep unions out.

One last method will guarantee that QCs fail. Management can use every opportunity to "screw" employees. Fishmarket haggling tactics are good for this purpose—even when the employee is right, has something coming and has been treated unjustly. This will show that management is really clever. Workers understand and respect that!

2. If failure is desired, management can rush into the program with a minimum of planning but insist that everyone, or only one pilot project, participate—at minimal cost, of course. In presenting the program, lots of flip charts and booklets should be used—in four colours. People, their problems, and listening to what they have to say are not important.

3. Very little time should be spent on training. After all, training takes money, and it means that people are away from their regular duties. All that talk about quality circles being successful because of training and the techniques used is just a lot of rubbish. Employees will catch on after a while—the important thing is that there is communication. Good old "rap sessions" are the key.

4. Management should also expect large dollar returns very quickly. After all, the name implies that there is going to be quality and, by implication, fast profits. If results are not coming quickly enough, pressure should be put on the circles. One good way to do this is to threaten to cancel the program. That will show everyone that the company means business.

5. Bureaucratization of the concept will help ensure failure. Lots and lots of paperwork is needed. If everything is written down, if paper flows up the organization, something is really happening. For failure, it is best to have a precise structure, to ensure that everyone understands this and does not deviate from it, and that there is an emphasis on bureaucracy and following the proper channels.

6. Management should permit circles to work only on problems which emphasize quality control and cost savings. After all, these are "quality" circles, and quality and cost are the only things that are important to the company.

7. The supervisor and other members of middle management are not important in the process—except that they should do a good job of quality circle manage-

ment with little or no time off from other duties. Besides, they are better educated; they already know these things and are paid to adjust quickly.

8. Non-responsiveness to circles helps to ensure failure. Circle suggestions that are costly or that management thinks are unnecessary should not be implemented. If circle suggestions are too good to turn down, slow response time will achieve the same purpose. Good day-to-day operating techniques include finding reasons for the circle to postpone its meetings or arranging work schedules in such a way that it will be difficult for all circle members to be present. Also, circles should not make presentations and send their reports to senior management; that violates the chain of command. If presentations are planned, members of management can make it a point to have something "come up" so that they do not attend the sessions.

9. When QC suggestions in a unit result in a need for fewer employee work-hours, people should be laid off.

10. The best way to ensure failure is to assume that quality circles will not work in North America. After all, this is a Japanese concept, and the Japanese are disciplined from childhood and will do everything that they are told.

Steps to Ensure Success

Just as the personnel within the organization can ensure that quality circles are a failure, they also have the power to ensure that they are a success. The steps are:

1. The quality circle concept is a people-building, not a people-using, philosophy. Open and trusting communication with employees and the union is required. If membership is voluntary, if the union is consulted, and if it shares the gains and the limelight, the union executive cannot object to quality circles.

2. Development should start slowly and the movement should be allowed to grow naturally. Extensive planning is needed before quality circles are launched. At first, it is very difficult for employees who in the past were expected only to "do" (as they were told) to begin thinking, talking, listening and caring as members of a circle. Also, care must be used in selecting steering committee members, the facilitator and circle leaders.

3. Training should be emphasized and re-emphasized. Communication and "rap sessions" are great, but a goal and a direction give purpose to the meetings. Success really does lie in the techniques—the ability of the group to organize a project, to gather and analyze data through brainstorming, cause-and-effect or process diagrams, statistical methods and the delphi technique. These give structure and direction to a circle's activities. They also remove the politicking.

4. Progress in the beginning stages is very slow. Circle members must learn the techniques and how to work with each other. When circle members are unable to meet established objectives, they become frustrated. Unrealistic expectations

also create a feeling among management members that circles have not been successful. Success, not failure, should be programmed into the process.

5. The emphasis should be on people solving problems and not on hierarchical pyramids or paperwork.

6. The other "quality"—quality of working life—is extremely important, and employees should be encouraged to solve problems that will mean added personal and group satisfaction.

7. The supervisor's role and that of other middle management members must change as the circle develops. Possible role expansion includes goal setting and policy making, training and mentoring, and being allowed to make those day-to-day decisions that affect their work area without consulting superiors. This means that these people's skills must be adequately developed, that a reward system which recognizes team and circle development must be in place, and that supervisory support systems must be built. Additionally, management must know how to positively reinforce participative behaviours. Time must be allocated into schedules to permit this group to perform activities that are expected of them. Quality circles work best if they are treated as a line, rather than a staff, responsibility.

In other words, circles must be part of a total organizational effort. Everyone, including senior management, middle management and supervisory staff, must be committed and involved. Crucial to success is the sharing of information that must occur among units and departments and hierarchical levels.

8. As many suggestions as possible should be implemented as quickly as possible. If this cannot be done, feedback should be provided to the circle regarding the reasons for the delay or the non-implementation. Also, senior management, as well as technical people, must be involved in presentations and must read and comment on the reports which are submitted.

9. Management should advertise its commitment that no employee will be laid off because of the implementation of quality circle suggestions. Instead, the organization should undertake to retrain employees and to reassign them to new jobs.

10. The idea that quality circles will not work in North America is nonsense. QCs will work in Canada and in the United States, and there are countless cases which show that they do (see lists in appendices). It is necessary, however, to adapt the concept to North American culture and to the specific organization.

There is nothing in the quality circle idea that is not applicable within the North American context. And there is much that is—the recognition of employees as people, the self-fulfilment, the knowledge that one is needed; these are the foundations of the Canadian and U.S. individualistic systems.

The quality control concept is not a Japanese idea. It is an American idea that was brought to Japan by Deming, Juran and others who followed. But even if it were a Japanese concept, multiculturalism has prepared people to learn from others, to take and adapt a wide variety of concepts and to build that new, better and bolder mousetrap or quality circle.

And so, in conclusion, if the proper people-developing philosophy exists, and if ideas to further it are followed thoughtfully and deliberately, managers may be surprised to discover in five, ten or fifteen years that success will come. That success involves all employees. Rank-and-file workers will be concerned about the well-being of the company and will solve problems and accomplish goals without management supervision and prodding. Management, on the other hand, will be willing and able to provide guidance, encouragement and support. Furthermore managers, engineers and white-collar and blue-collar employees, unionized and non-unionized, will cooperate to ensure that the company remains competitive, and that each employee has a rewarding and desirable job. On to the twenty-first century; quality circles are here!

Quality circles:
- Effect financial savings.
- Improve union–management relationships.
- Increase employee motivation and productivity.
- Increase individual development.
- Improve morale.

Because they:
- Are people builders.
- Present workers with challenge.
- Increase communication among employees.

Cure to motivational problems?
- Perhaps; but motivation is an abstract concept which is difficult to define and measure.

To ensure QCs are a failure:
- Use them as a union-busting technique.
- Do minimal pre-planning.
- Have minimal training.
- Expect large dollar returns quickly.
- Demand lots of paperwork.
- Allow circles to work only on quality and cost-savings problems.
- Ignore needs of supervisors and middle management personnel.
- Implement few suggestions, and those slowly.
- Lay off employees because of suggestion implementation.
- Believe that QCs won't work.

To ensure that QCs are a success:
- Use them to build people.
- Start slowly and let the movement grow naturally.
- Emphasize training.
- Be patient and expect little in the early stages.

- Emphasize people and people problems.
- Quality of working life is important and circles should address these types of problems.
- Plan new roles for supervisors and middle managers.
- Implement improvements quickly or provide feedback regarding the difficulties.
- Retrain and reassign employees who have become redundant because of circle idea implementation.
- Believe they do work and can work.

A P P E N D I C E S

APPENDIX 1
Training Programs

Length of Training Session

1. Top executives   2 days
2. Middle management   3 days
3. Union executive   3 days
4. Steering or advisory committee   4 days
5. Facilitators   10 days
6. Circle Leaders   8 days
7. Circle members   5 days

Length of Initial Training Session by Topic

	Time in Hours						
Group (as numbered above)	1	2	3	4	5	6	7
Introduction to Organization/Circles	1.0	1.0	1.0	1.0	1.0	1.0	1.0
a) Roles	.5	1.0	1.0	3.0	1.0	2.0	.5
b) Implementation process	.5	1.5	1.5	2.0	4.0	1.0	1.0
c) Cautions	.5	.5	.5	.5	.5	.5	.5
Human Resource Management							
a) Motivation	1.5	2.5	2.5	2.5	6.5	2.0	–
b) Leadership	1.5	2.5	2.5	2.5	6.5	3.0	–
c) Communication	1.5	3.5	3.5	4.0	6.5	3.5	3.5
d) Feedback	.5	1.0	1.0	1.5	1.5	1.0	1.0
Group Processes							
a) Group techniques	.5	1.5	1.5	2.5	6.5	3.0	3.0
b) Brainstorming	1.5	1.5	1.5	1.5	2.0	1.5	1.5
c) Decision Making	1.0	1.0	1.0	1.0	3.0	1.0	1.0

(cont'd)

(Appendix 1 cont'd)

Circle Skills (Appendix 1 cont'd)

a) Problem identification	1.0	1.0	1.0	1.0	6.5	6.5	6.5
b) Problem specification	1.0	.5	.5	.5	13.0	13.0	10.0
c) Presentation skills	.5	.5	.5	.5	4.5	6.5	1.5
d) Meeting logistics	–	–	–	–	2.0	6.5	1.5
TOTAL	13.0	19.5	19.5	24.0	65.0	52.0	32.5

Content of Initial Seminars and Emphasis on Topics

Orientation	1	2	3	4	5	6	7
What is a quality circle?	H	H	H	H	H	H	H
Costs and benefits	H	H	H	M	M	H	H
Philosophy of human resource management under QCs	H	H	H	H	H	H	L
Differences between Canada/U.S. and Japan	M	M	M	L	L	L	L
Union involvement	M	M	H	H	H	M	M
Threats posed to middle management and supervisors	H	H	–	H	H	H	–
Case studies of results achieved by QCs	M	M	M	M	M	M	M
Structure and responsibilities	H	H	M	H	H	–	–
Roles							
Executive	M	L	L	M	L	L	L
Middle management	H	H	L	H	M	L	–
Union executive	H	H	H	H	M	M	M
Steering (advisory) committee	H	H	M	H	H	H	H
Facilitators	H	H	M	H	H	H	H
Circle Leaders	L	M	M	H	H	H	H
Circle members	L	L	M	L	H	H	H
Implementing a Circle and Carrying out Recommendations							
Setting up objectives	L	L	L	M	H	H	H
Setting up a steering committee	M	M	M	–	–	–	–
Deciding on the number of quality circles	M	–	–	H	–	–	–
Choosing participants—steering committee	L	L	M	–	–	–	–
—facilitators	M	M	M	H	–	–	–
—leaders	L	M	M	H	H	–	–
—members	L	–	M	M	H	–	–
Getting involvement from the participants	M	M	M	M	H	H	–
Skills required	M	L	L	M	H	H	–
Selecting problems and issues	L	–	–	H	H	H	H
Analyzing costs/benefits of projects	H	–	–	H	H	H	H
Implementing recommendations	H	L	L	H	H	M	L

Some cautions

Steps to ensure that QCs are a success	H	M	M	M	M	M	–
Steps to ensure that QCs process functions well	–	–	–	M	H	H	H

Motivation

Theoretical background—hierarchical, two-factor, equity and expectancy	M	M	M	M	H	M	–
Reinforcement theory	M	M	M	M	H	M	–
Assessing personal needs and motives	M	M	M	M	H	M	–
Relationship of participation to motivation	H	H	H	L	H	H	–
Assessing environment	H	M	M	L	H	H	–

Leadership

Theoretical background—Theories X and Y; Theory Z	M	M	M	M	H	H	–
Theoretical—situational and contingency theory	M	M	M	M	H	M	–
Assessment of own leadership style	M	M	M	M	M	H	–
Awareness of leadership styles and their impact on group participation and performance	M	M	M	M	H	H	–
Group leadership concepts and techniques	M	M	M	M	H	H	–

Communication

Importance of listening and its impact on group participation	H	M	M	M	H	H	H
Development of active listening skills	H	M	M	M	H	H	H
Non-verbal communication	H	M	M	M	H	H	H
Skills required for meaningful two-way communication	H	M	M	M	H	H	H

Feedback, suggestions and criticism

Functional and dysfunctional types	H	M	M	M	H	H	H
Knowledge of results	H	M	M	M	H	H	–
Sources of performance feedback	H	L	L	L	H	H	H
Impact of goals and feedback on performance	H	M	M	M	M	H	H
Used as a managerial tool	H	M	–	M	H	H	–

Group dynamics and processes

Theory of group dynamics	H	H	H	H	H	H	H
Positive, neutral and negative modes of interaction	H	H	H	H	H	H	H
Negotiating skills	H	H	H	H	H	H	H
Arriving at consensus decision making	H	H	H	H	H	H	H
Brainstorming	H	H	H	H	H	H	H

Circle skills

Problem identification	L	L	L	M	H	H	H
Problem specification and resolution	L	L	L	M	H	H	H
Statistics: Techniques	L	L	L	M	H	H	H
Statistics: When to use	L	L	L	M	H	H	H
Statistics: How to construct and use	L	L	L	M	H	H	H

(cont'd)

(Appendix 1 cont'd)

Report preparation	L	L	L	H	H	H	L
Oral presentations	L	L	L	M	H	H	L
Meeting Logistics							
Chairing a meeting	–	–	–	–	H	H	L
Encouraging participation	–	–	–	H	H	H	M
Agendas	–	–	–	–	H	H	H
Keeping minutes of meetings	–	–	–	–	H	H	H
Other logistics	–	–	–	H	H	H	H

H means high content in this area.
M means moderate content in this area.
L means that, in the beginning stages, content in this area can be low.

APPENDIX 2

QC Education and Training Courses Promoted by Toyota Group

Courses	Frequency	Number of Participants
Middle Management		
Toyota QC Middle Management Course (51 hours)	once a year	198
Toyota Reliability Engineering Middle Management Course (30 hours)	once a year	176
QC Staff		
Toyota QC Basic Course (138 hours)	once a year	525
Toyota Reliability Engineering Basic Course (60 hours)	twice a year	657
Toyota Design of Experiments Course (78 hours)	twice a year	177
Superintendents		
Toyota QC Circle Promoter's Course (36 hours)	twice a year	276
Foremen and Group Leader		
Toyota QC Foremen's Problem-Solving Course (27 hours)	once a year	121

Source: *the wheel extended: A Toyota Quarterly Review* (Tokyo), Spring 1980, p. 26.

APPENDIX 3
U.S. Companies Using Quality Circles

The application of quality circles spans a wide variety of American industry. Among the organizations reportedly using circles are:

Abbott Labs (IL)
Advanced Micro Devices
Aerojet Ordnance
Alcan Aluminum Corporation
Allstate Insurance Company
American Airlines
American Biltrite, Inc.
American Can Co.
American Express
American Hoechst Corp.
AMF–Harley Davidson Corp.
AMP, Inc.
Anja Engineering Corp.
Applied Magnetics
Arco Sola, Inc. (CA)
Armco, Inc.
Automatic Electric Co.
Babcock & Wilcox Co.
Bank of America, San Francisco
Bank of California
Barber-Colman Co.
Bell Northern Research, Inc.
Bethlehem Steel
Blue Cross (WA, AK)
Wm. L. Bonnell Co.
Borg Warner—Spring Division
Braceland Bros. (PA)
Canadian Appliance Mfg. Co. Ltd.
C.B. Fleet Co. (VA)
Centerline Circuits (CO)
Central Pacific Bank (HI)
Champion Spark Plug Co.
Chase Manhattan Bank (NY)
Chemical Bank of New York
Chicago Title & Trust Co.
Citibank, N.A.
Continental Illinois National Bank

Copperweld Steel Co.
Cordis Dow Corp.
Corning Glass Works (PA)
Crocker Bank
Dana Corporation (IN)
Datapoint Corp.
Davidson Rubber Inc. (GA)
Dayton Tire & Rubber Co., Oklahoma City, OK
Dover Corporation
Duncan Industries
E.G. & G. Torque Systems
E.I. DuPont de Nemours Co.
Eaton Corporation
Estee Lauder Inc. (NY)
Eaton Engine Components Plant (MI)
Exxon Co.—Nuclear Division
Fairchild Bipolar LSI
Fairchild Digital Division
Fairchild Weston Controls
Federal Products Co.
Firemen's Fund Insurance Companies
First & Merchants National Bank
Fleetguard
Ford Motor Co.
Frolic Footwear Division, Wolverine
Galigher Company
Gates Learjet Corp. (KS)
G. E. Glass Plant (UT)
General Electric (RI)
General Motors Corporation
Gleason Works—Machine Div., Rochester, NY
Golden State Sanwa Bank
Goodrich Chemical Company
Graco, Inc.
Great Lakes Steel (MI)

Grove Valve, Oakland, CA
GTE Automatic Electric Company
Harper Wyman Co.
Hawaiian Dredging & Construction
Hazeltine Corporation
Hertz Corporation (CA)
Holiday Inn (FN)
Honeywell Inc.
Houston National Bank
Hughes Aircraft Co.
IBM (FL)
Ingersoll-Rand Research, Inc.
Intel Corporation
I.T.T. (MS, NJ, NY, TN)
I.T.T. Royal Electric Division (RI)
International Paper Co.
International Rectifier
Johnson & Johnson Products Inc.
Koppers World (MD)
The Kroger Co.
J. B. Lansing Sound Co.
Lincoln National Life Insurance Co.
Litton—Data Systems Division
Lockheed Missile & Space Corporation
Lumisistemas CM, S.A., Mexico
Marine Midland Bank
Marlin Rockwell—Division of TRW
Martin-Marietta Aerospace
Martin Marietta Chemicals Division
   (NC)
Massey Ferguson (MI)
McGraw-Edison (IL, NY)
Mellon Bank, N.A. (PA)
Memorex Corporation
Metropolitan Transit Authority (New
   York City)
Mid-Florida Technical Institute (FL)
Monsanto Chemical Co.
Morton Chemical Co.
Motorola
Mt. Sinai Medical Center of Greater
   Miami
Naval Air Rework Facility/No Island,
   San Diego, CA

New York Port Authority
C.A. Norgren Co.
Norris Industries—Vernon Division
Northern Telecom (NC)
Northrop Corporation
Oak Switch Systems, Inc. (IL)
Olin Brass Co.
Olin Paper & Film Group
Peabody Floway
Pentel of America
Pet Food Co.
Phelps Dodge Wire Magnet (IN, KY,
   OH)
Philips ECG (NY, OH)
Pittsburgh National Bank (PA)
Polaroid Corporation, Norwood, MA
Poly Chrome Corporation
Precision Shooting Equipment
Ralston Purina Co.
RCA—Distribution & Special Products
   Division
Robinson Brick & Tile
Rockford Products
Rockwell International Collins
   Communications Systems Division
Rockwell International Specifications
   Systems Group, Seal Beach, CA
Sacramento County, CA
Santa Clara Unified School District (CA)
Sargent and Lundy
Schering Plough, Kenilworth, NJ
Sealy Mattress Co. (MD, IL)
Security Pacific National Bank (CA)
Sennett Steel Corporation
Sherwin Williams Co. (CA)
Simplex Time Recorder
Smith Corona (NY)
Smith Kline Instruments, Inc.
Solar Turbines International
Spectrum Inc.
Sperry Gyroscope
Sperry Vickers
Standyne Distribution Center (IN)
Standyne Western (OH)

Sundstrand
Tektronix
Texize
Thor Electronics
3M Company, St. Paul, MN
Timex
Trane Air Conditioning—Lexington
  Manufacturing Division
The Trane Company, LaCrosse, WI
Tungsten Carbide Manufacturing
U.N.C.—National Automatic Tools
Unicore Federal Prison Industries, Inc.
  (NY)
Union Bank
Union Carbide, Greenville, SC
United California Bank
U.S. Department of the Army (CO)
U.S. Naval Aviation Logistics Center

U.S. Naval Ordnance Center,
  Louisville, KY
U.S. Naval Weapons Support Center
USA DARCOM Automated Logistics
The Upjohn Company—Varian Micro
  Tube Division
Verbatim
Vickers, Inc.
Voss Industries, Inc.
Warner-Lambert Co.—Consumer
  Products Group
Waters Associates
Waugh Controls Corporation
Western Wheel Corporation
Westinghouse Electric Corporation
Woodward-Governor Co.
Xerox Corporation
Yolo County, California

APPENDIX 4
Canadian Companies Using Quality Circles

Name and Address of Company	Date Initiated	No. of Circles	Contact Person
Aetna Canada Aetna Canada Centre 145 King Street West Toronto, Ontario M5H 3T7	June 1982	12	Brenda Butler Manager General Planning
Air BC 4680 Cowley Crescent Richmond, B.C. V7B 1C1	May 1983	8	Donna M. Hornsby Secretary
Allis Chambers 155 Dawson Road Guelph, Ontario N1H 1A4	July 1982	1	Peter Leslie Supervisor Employee Relations
Anca Inc. 111 Consumers Drive Whitby, Ontario	1982	2	Tessa Hogewaard
B.C. Tel 3777 Kingsway Vancouver, B.C. V5H 3Z7	1981	40	Sue Knot Personnel Manager Viki MacMillan QC Coordinator
Bell Canada 393 University Ave., 9th Floor Toronto, Ontario M5G 1W9	1982	30	Ron Deaken Section Manager Organization Development
Bonar Packaging Ltd. 2380 McDonnell Road Burlington, Ontario L7R 4A1	March 1983	14	Zenon Onufryk
Burroughs 51 Burmac Road Winnipeg, Manitoba R3C 2P7	1982	20	Carol Postineks Manager Training and Development
C.I.L. Box 10 Montreal, Quebec H3C 2R3			Michael Damphousse, H.R. Development Manager
CUNA of Ontario 895 Brand Street Burlington, Ontario		2	Ann Allan Facilitator

(cont'd)

(Appendix 4 cont'd)

Cardinal Meat Specialist Ltd. 2396 Stanfield Road Mississauga, Ontario L4Y 1S1	1983	4	Jack Boulet Controller
Champion Road Machinery P.O. Box 10 Goderich, Ontario N7A 3Y6	1981	16	Elgin Fisher Facilitator
City Bank Leasing P.O. Box 5060, South Service Road Burlington, Ontario			Richard P. Tailor
Claude Neon 1855 Hymus Dorval, Quebec H9P 1J8		7	Michel Bergeron Sales Supervisor
Claude Neon 555 Ellesmere Road Scarborough, Ontario M1R 4E8	1983	8	Tom Badani Facilitator
Constellation Assurance Company 26 Wellington Street East Toronto, Ontario M5E 1J6	December 1983	2	Jan Shuckard Asst. Vice-President Corporate Services
Control Data Canada 1855 Minnesota Court Mississauga, Ontario L5N 1K7	1982	22	William P. Murphy
Courtesy Chevrolet 3131 Main Street Vancouver, B.C. V5T 3G8	1982		Don Bannerman General Manager
Crush Canada, Inc. 1590 O'Connor Drive Toronto, Ontario M4B 2V4	March 1983	3	E. L. Marr QC Facilitator
Cumis Insurance P. O. Box 5065 Burlington, Ontario	March 1981	11	Anne Wright Training Specialist
Cyanamid Canada Inc. 2255 Sheppard Avenue East Willowdale, Ontario M2J 4Y5	1984		Jim Sands Director, H.R.

Dominion Directory 4400 Dominion Street Burnaby, B.C. V5G 4G4	1983	5	Doug Gavin
Dominion Life Assurance Co. Ltd. 111 Westmount Road South Waterloo, Ontario N2J 4C6	March 1983	33	Linda Lehtonew QC Coordinator
Dover Corp. (Canada) Ltd. Dover Elevator 126 John Street Toronto, Ontario M5V 2E3	1981	3	K. McCullough Manager of Engineering *or* D. Powers Supervisor of Quality Control
Duracel Inc. 2333 North Sheridan Way Mississauga, Ontario L5K 1A7	1981	4	Dwight S. Cameron QC Manager
EDP Industries 1313 Main Street Vancouver, B.C. V5T 3G8	1983	2	John Fysh
Equitable Insurance Company 200 Rue St-Jacques Montreal, Quebec H2Y 1M2	1983	3	Nicole Elbaz Supervisor
Esso Chemical Canada P. O. Box 3004 Sarnia, Ontario N7T 7M5	1980	1	R. W. Tully PVC Operations
Fisher Controls Co. of Canada 1039 Dundas Street Woodstock, Ontario N4S 7Z6	1981	7	Rick DeVleeschower
Foothills Hospital 1403 — 29 Street, N. W. Calgary, Alberta T2N 2T9	April 1983	5	Michael Oakes Staff Development Officer
Ford Motor Company of Canada No. 1 Quality Way Windsor, Ontario	Fall 1982	16	Pat McKrow QC Coordinator
General Foods 95 Moatfield Drive Don Mills, Ontario M3B 3L6	1983	2	Wendy Vinegar Supervisor H.R. Development and Recruitment

(cont'd)

(Appendix 4 cont'd)

Gould Outdoor Signs Brantford, Ontario		2	Paula McKay
Great West Life 60 Osborne Street North Winnipeg, Manitoba R3C 3A5	March 1982	30	Ed. J. Taylor Associate Manager Productivity Services
Hewlett Packard Canada Ltd. 6877 Goreway Drive Mississauga, Ontario L4V 1M8	June 1981	13	John T. Rooney Commercial Services Manager or Mark Borkowski Personnel Representative
Hiram Walker P. O. Box 250 Winfield, B.C. V0H 2C0	1982	3	Gene Levesque
Hook Signs 2335 — 30th Avenue N.E. Calgary, Alberta T2E 7C7	1983	6	Randy Otto
Hostess Chips P. O. Box 250 Kentville, N.S.	1983	8	Marlene McFarlane Personnel Manager
Hostess Food Products Ltd. 1001 Bishop Street North Cambridge, Ontario	March 1983	17	S. Cairns Vice President Operations
Hussman Store Equipment Limited P. O. Box 550 Brantford, Ontario N3T 5R2	February 1983	11	J. Al. Spence President
IBM Canada 3500 Steeles Avenue East Toronto, Ontario L3R 2Z1		700	Dennis Makepeace Program Manager Quality
Kaufman Footwear 410 King Street West Kitchener, Ontario N2G 4J8	1982	3	Phil Hendly Personnel Manager
Knape & Vogt Canada Inc. 340 Carlingview Drive Rexdale, Ontario M9W 5G5	1983	4	Joe Teixeira Distribution Manager

Lucerne Safeway 9256 - 198 Street Langley, B.C.	1982	2	Norm Reeve Director, Marketing
Mainland Magazine 9453 - 198th Street Langley, B.C. V3A 4P8	October 1982	4	Norm Reeve
McCain Foods P. O. Box 540 Hartland, N.B. E0J 1N0	1984	1	Ken Nichols V. P. Personnel and Training
Motorways P. O. Box 738 60 Eagle Drive Winnipeg, Manitoba R3C 2L8	December 1983		Don L. White Vice President Operations
Mountain City News P. O. Box 768 Hamilton, Ontario L8N 3N2	1983	2	Roli Pitalik
Nashua Canada Ltd. 550 Braidwood Avenue Peterborough, Ontario K9J 6X4	July 1979	10	J. J. Zeyen Vice President Manufacturing
Neon Products Box 2063 Vancouver, B.C. V6B 3F4	1982	8	Babs Babcock
New Balance 72 St. Leger Street Kitchener, Ontario N2H 6R7	1983	7	Margot Baird Facilitator
Northern Telecom Canada Ltd. (various locations)	1984	15	Sam Barnes Manager, Manufacturing and Training
Omark Canada Ltd. 505 Edinburgh Road North Guelph, Ontario N1H 6L4	February 1983	12	Al Rogers Training Manager
Otis Elevator McCaul Street Toronto, Ontario	1983		Dave Rhodes

(cont'd)

(Appendix 4 cont'd)

Overwaitea Foods P. O. Box 7200 Vancouver, B.C. V6B 4E4	October 1982	17	Art Van Pelt Employee Relations Manager
Jim Pattison Pontiac Buick 3434 Main Street, Vancouver, B.C. V5V 3N2	1983	3	Don Bannerman V. P.
Provincial News 14436 - 121A Avenue Edmonton, Alberta T5L 4L2	1983	2	Peter Kiernan Director, Marketing
Seaboard Advertising 1885 Clark Drive Vancouver, B.C. V6B 3S4	1982	8	Mike Jefferson
Toronto-Dominion Bank 55 King St. W. & Bay Street Toronto, Ontario M5K 1A2	Spring 1982	15	Ron Sinclair Coordinator Quality Program
Trans Ad 48 St. Clair Avenue West Toronto, Ontario M4V 2Z2			
Tridon Limited 2190 South Service Road, W. Oakville, Ontario L6L 5T8	October 1983	1	Ed Artuso QCC Facilitator
Vanguard P. O. Box 280 Winfield, B.C. V0H 2C0	1982	6	Jim Molyneaux
Venturetrans Manufacturing P. O. Box 100, Station A Kingston, Ontario	1983	3	Al Charlton
Weldwood of Canada Ltd. 1055 West Hastings Street Vancouver, B.C.	1984		Randy Schaeffer, Manager, Labour Relations
Westinghouse Canada Inc. P. O. Box 510 Hamilton, Ontario L8N 3K2	January 1980	57	R. McCormick Director Corporate Productivity Services

Wilfrid Laurier University	March 1983	4	Dr. J. Alex Murray
75 University Avenue, West			Dean
Waterloo, Ontario N2L 3C5			School of Business & Economics

Canadian Companies Which Have Reportedly Instituted Quality Circles

Alberta Children's Hospital   North American Life
Alcan Aluminum   Ontario Hydro
Excelsior Insurance   University of Calgary
McDonnell Douglas Corp.

APPENDIX 5
Selected List of Canadian Management Consultants in Quality Circles, and
Organizations Promoting QC/QWL in Canada

E & L Enterprises
(Ernie Long)
447 Patricia Drive
Burlington, Ontario L7T 1J9
Tel.: 1-416-525-2375

K. D. Frey & Associates
R. R. 2
Rockwood, Ontario N0B 2K0
Tel.: 1-519-856-9727

Institut National de Productivité
(Fernand Gauthier, Director-Général)
1 Complexe Desjardins, Tour Sud
C. P. 157, Suite 1509
Montréal, Québec, Canada H5B 1B5
Tel: 1-514-873-7601

Ontario Quality of Working Life Centre
(Hugh Auld)
400 University Avenue
Toronto, Ontario M7A 1T7
Tel.: 1-416-965-5958

Personnel and Productivity Management
(O. L. Crocker)
Faculty of Business Administration
University of Windsor
Windsor, Ontario N9B 3P4
Tel.: 1-519-253-4232; 1-519-734-7648

Qualitran Professional Services
(L. M. Galicinski)
Stroud, Ontario
Tel.: 1-705-722-8550

Thorne, Stevenson & Kellogg
(Cyril Charney)
2300 Yonge Street
Toronto, Ontario M4P 1G2
Tel.: 1-416-483-4313

Woods Gordon Management Consultants
(Dr. Pierre DuBois)
630, boul. Dorchester ouest
Montréal, Québec, Canada H3B 1T9
Tel.: 1-514-875-5835

Woods Gordon Management Consultants
(Colin Lockie)
Royal Trust Tower
Toronto, Ontario
Tel.: 1-416-864-1212

APPENDIX 6
Consultants in Quality Circles in the United States

There are several sources of information and/or consulting on the quality circle application in the U.S. They are:

Ann Arbor Consulting Assoc.
Philip Alexander
5204 Jackson Road
Ann Arbor, MI 48103
(313) 995-2404

American Quality Institute
4567 Gatetree Circle
Pleasanton, CA 94566
(415) 462-0493

Consulting Associates Inc.
Ron Kregoski & Ed Yaeger
21333 Haggerty Rd., Suite 311
Novi, MI 48050
(313) 348-0001

William Golombewski & Assoc.
593 Van Buren St.
Chicago, IL 60605
(312) 922-5985

Growing Organizations Unlimited
Carter Taylor
467 Tarrington Road
Rochester, NY 14609
(716) 482-1629

Juran Enterprises Inc.
Dr. Joseph Juran
866 United Nations Plaza
New York, NY 10017
(212) 832-3127

Organizational Dynamics
16 New England Exec. Park
Burlington, MA 01803
(617) 272-8040

Participative Systems, Inc.
Sidney Rubinstein
909 State Road, P.O. Box 18
Princeton, NJ 08540
(609) 452-1244

Productivity Quality Assoc.
Michael Clearey
7718 Normandy Lane
Dayton, OH 45459
(513) 274-7817

Quality Circle Institute
Donald Dewar
1425 Vista Way
Airport Industrial Park
P.O. Box Q
Red Bluff, CA 96080
(916) 527-6970

Quality Circle Systems
21 Tilton Lane
Andover, MA 01810
(617) 475-9563

Quest Associates Ltd.
P.O. Box 182
Park Forest, IL 60466
(312) 747-3663

Rath and Strong Inc.
Chuck Carter Jr.
P.O. Box 5001
Richardson, TX 75080
(214) 235-0210

(cont'd)

Reddy, Berger, Rosen and Woods, Inc.
Jack Reddy
2406 Massachusetts Ave.
Lexington, MA 02173
(617) 862-8888

Quality Control Circles Inc.
Wayne Rieker
Higgins and Root Bldg.
400 Blossom Hill Rd.
Los Gatos, CA 95030
(408) 358-2711

Stat-A-Matrix Inc.
Stanley Marash
P.O. Box 2152
Menlo Park Station
Edison, NJ 08817
(201) 548-0600

Robert Tate
1456 Tuscany Way
Germantown, TN 38138
(901) 754-6376

Training & Business Analysis
Gloria O'Meara
P.O. Box 24322, Edina Station
Minneapolis, MN 55424
(612) 478-6287

Visser Quality Assoc.
3 Mitchelle Ave.
New Brunswick, NJ 08816
(201) 828-2964

Wag and Assoc.
Eugene Lee
681 Market St., Ste. 1049
San Francisco, CA 94105
(415) 543-5262

APPENDIX 7
Organizations Promoting Quality Circles in the United States

American Management Association
Charles Ferris, Program Director
135 West 50th Street
New York NY 10020
Tel.: 1-212-586-8100

American Productivity Center
Jack Grayson, Chairman of the Board
123 North Post Oak Lane
Houston, TX 77024
Tel.: 1-713-681-4020

American Quality Institute
Paul Plum
4567 Gatetree Circle
Pleasanton, CA 94566
Tel.: 1-408-253-3038 or
        1-408-462-0493

American Society for Quality Control
Quality Circles Committee
Dr. Robert T. Amsden, Chairman
Suite 7000
2300 West Well Street
Milwaukee, WI 53203
Tel.: 1-414-272-8575

International Association of Quality
  Circles
801-B West Eighth Street, Ste. 301
Cincinnati, OH 45203
Tel.: 1-513-381-1959

International City Management
  Association
1120 G Street, N.W.
Washington, DC 20005
Tel.: 1-202-626-4600

Technological Transfer Institute
One Penn Plaza
Suite 1411
250 West 34th Street
New York, NY 10119
Tel.: 1-212-947-2648

APPENDIX 8

Open-Ended Comments of Ford EI Participants in Survey

"More effort in job. Management in quality before quantity. More feedback."

"Circle teams provide an outlet for creativity. It may be the only way to go in the future. It is an improvement from continual confrontation."

"I have seen results from stamping team, Plant 2, and block team, Plant 1. So I know they are doing a fine job. I believe the union should be more informed and involved in employee involvement as it will benefit us all."

"I believe that our team is really trying. But in my opinion we take leadership towards picking out a worthwhile task."

"I feel the concept is a good idea. I have found that in actual practice the management does not want to change the system, therefore, the employee involvement teams are doomed to fail."

"The team idea is a positive attitude in which the company gives its employees a chance to better the jobs and quality."

"Quality Circle Team Concept helps the company to solve some problems which it can't see or solve."

"The quality circle team (Ford's is Problem Solving Teams) is effective in improving quality, productivity and a better work environment because it utilizes the company's greatest asset — people. Every worker is given the opportunity to become involved in the general product. These are basic needs being answered, and job security is improved as a quality product improves sales, etc."

"Not enough important problems referred to our EI team from either management, our facilitator, union, or other. I don't think enough people on the floor are being trained in EI and therefore have negative reactions towards something they haven't experienced!"

"It works well."

"EI is an exceptional way of voicing your opinions as far workers' attitudes on job performance, boredom on line, changing management's opinion of quantity first instead of quality in most instances. If we are going to compete with the Japanese we must do something to keep our warranty down, e.g., changing machine drills in "x" amount of hours regardless of worn out or not, but not wait till tool's bit is worn or broken as most times happens now."

"If everyone pitches in and contributes, the EI concept can make our jobs easier as well as perpetuate them."

"I think it's a good idea and more people should be involved in it."

"We work as a team, to find out all kinds of quality problems on the engine line. We discuss and solve together, try to make more fun-loving, so people can come to work every day."

"The Circle Team Concept could be a vital tool if used properly. Only *bad* management can be the master link between success and failure."

"I agree wholeheartedly with the quality circle team concept. In practice something is obviously lacking. Certain areas feel the "Team's" efforts overlap their responsibility, thereby misinterpreting our intent, thus resulting initially in certain members losing interest and eventually resigning."

"I feel this type of team concept in the workplace is long overdue. To allow the workers to exchange information and ideas should benefit both workers and company. However, in a factory setting, the continuity of a group is a very hard thing to accomplish. As the group members move from job to job, plant to plant, area to area, maintaining the same members is quite impossible. The ability of these groups (with proper company support) to effect changes increasing both productivity and quality are limitless. While I feel all this is very positive, it should be carried further into the areas of re-educating the work force, i.e. instead of drawing skilled people out of school, draw a small percentage, say 5–10%, from existing workers through retraining."

APPENDIX 9
Quality Circle (Partners in Progress) Newsletter — American Motors
Corporation and United Auto Workers

Volume II, no. 1   January 10, 1983

Why P.I.P.

When we are in the plant on P.I.P. business, many employees stop us and ask how the P.I.P. process is developing and whether or not it is succeeding. During these conversations, we find that many employees do not understand the process and quite frankly are skeptical about its chances for success. In this regard, perhaps it would be appropriate to answer a few questions that hopefully will help you develop a better understanding of Partners in Progress.

Many changes have taken place within the society, the workforce and the industry over the last ten to twenty years. One only has to look at the automobile market to find the reasons for these changes.

The oil embargo probably had the greatest impact on the automobile market by causing consumers to search out and find a car that would give them greater gas mileage. This resulted in the great influx of foreign automobiles into our country. Additionally, the fluctuating economy caused people to become more quality conscious resulting in their search for greater utility for their dollar. In an effort to attain an even greater degree of product quality, Management began to put more emphasis on utilizing the expertise of their employees.

Thus, as a result of a sagging economy and a search by the consumer for increased quality and reliability, many companies and unions have re-evaluated their management philosophy and a new pattern of management within the United States is developing. The new patterns vary from company to company but basically they emphasize greater employee participation in dealing with the day-to-day problems and the decisions that are required to resolve them.

In order for American industries to remain competitive, changes in Management and Union philosophy should parallel changes in consumer attitudes. The Partners in Progress process is a step in the right direction because it gives employes the opportunity to voluntarily become involved in solving the problems that affect them and their work. This results in greater operational efficiency and improved product quality and reliability.

The primary key to a successful process, however, is communication and cooperation. We all recognize that when Management and the Union communicate and work together in a cooperative spirit, we begin to understand each other and through better understanding, we can build a more effective operation.

The Partners in Progress Coordinators and Editor of the Newsletter would like to help answer any questions you may have concerning the P.I.P. process. Therefore, please feel free to contact Gerry Wade, Bob Ludwig, Jerry Costello or Pat Mike at 7071, 7072 or 7073 and we will try to answer these questions by way of the P.I.P. Newsletter.

Dept. 808 — Press Room   1/5

Each member received a fact sheet containing PIP guidelines. The minutes from the last meeting were read and approved. The group then discussed who the next alternate admitted to the group would be. It was the consensus of the group that Jim Kane representing the die setters would be the next member admitted.

Reports

Sleeves

John Walauskis reported on difficulty in obtaining information. Coordinator Jerry Costello will find out who the purchasing agent is for the group. A sample of sleeves now being used in Milwaukee was inspected by the group. The group felt that the sleeves presently being used in the department are better than the sleeves being used in Milwaukee. The group will submit a sample of the most popular type of sleeves to the purchasing agent to aid in determining worker preference.

New Problems

Tony Perry will pursue the possibility of having in-plant television operating during the half hour breaks on weekends. There is special interest in sporting events.

Bad steel was then discussed. The group questioned why so much scrap is run before the load of steel is finally rejected. John Holland and Lenny Peden will investigate and report back at the next meeting. Tony Perry was welcomed as a new member of the group.

Dept. 1828 — Final Assembly   1/5

Coordinator Bob Ludwig reported that the communications from the group had been delivered to Mr. Austin and the Steering Committee. The next Steering Committee meeting will be on January 10, 1983. Action on the letters should be taken at that time.

Dan Vaccaro presented a new problem to the group. It is #56 — Fascia containers which do not stack properly. After discussing the rear suspension bolt problem, the group decided to keep it on hold for further monitoring. The group then discussed the condition of the restrooms within the department. Wes Schutz will contact Joe Zabrauskus about what can be done to clean them up. Problem #5 — Too many supervisors was considered solved as of 1/5/83.

The group then polled for a new problem. They decided that the only criteria to be applied to their decision was that the problem should concern product quality. It was decided to work on Problem #44 — Sealer–Brake Line Bracket, (Front Flex). The Coordinator was requested to find out which department and area is involved with this problem at Lakefront. They will make personal contact to investigate. It was felt that the group may go to Lakefront to try to find out what is causing the problem or send representatives to one of the Lakefront Group's meetings to discuss.

Dept. 2836 — Body Metal   1/6

Part of the group went to Dept. 808 to investigate the problem having to do with the dent in the rear quarter panel.

The group felt that perhaps it was originating in Dept. 808.

It was reported to the group that at this time there will be no alteration in the ventilation of Bldg. 101 2nd Floor. The group will monitor the problem and tests will be run to further investigate the situation.

The group also discussed the response they had received from Mr. Herrendeen concerning problems with the Gilman.

Dept. 2837 — Body Paint   12/14

Dave King, Fire Marshall was present to discuss the emergency aid system at AMC Lakefront plant. The group agreed that everything that can presently be done is being done. It was further decided that the group could not influence this situation so the problem was dropped for now.

The group brainstormed for new problems to handle. Problem #16 — Job Setups was added to the list.

12/21

The meeting began with a report by Mavis Wakefield from Dept. 2838. She stated that she had been shown several areas where they are having problems with excess sealer blocking holes. She gave the report to Jon Sebestyen. Improvements have been made but the group will continue to work on this.

Work was continued on new problem #12 — Eye wash in sealer area. It was decided to combine problems #11 and #12. Problem #11 concerns eye glass cleaning station. It was the consensus to have Jon contact the safety man on December 22 to see what can be done about these problems.

It was decided to work on Problem #10 No time bell. Bill Petit will contact Mr. Wheeler on this subject to see how long a bell has been on order.

The group also decided to work on Problem #15 — Gaps in seams. Jon will talk to Mr. Batassa to find out which is the worst and most recurring water leak.

1/4

There was a consensus to invite Mr. Visintainer to the next meeting to get a report on the door latch situation.

Dept. 2838 — Body Trim   1/5

Ken Hughes asked to be dropped from the Partners in Progress Program. Richard Foster will be the next person to enter the program. Carol Luciani was elected Recording Secretary for the group.

The group was notified that the women's washroom will be installed in Bldg. 190–1st floor in the near future.

Al Ellis reported on the sealer problems from the Paint Dept. The problem has improved very much but we will continue to monitor the problem from time to time.

Lorin Lichterman attended the meeting to observe the Partners in Progress Program in action.

12/22

Terry Keller has been installed as Facilitator with Elaine Janicek as Co-Facilitator.

The safety rail in the cushion room has not been completed as of this date. This will be followed up by the Committee.

It was decided that further investigation is needed to evaluate the need or desire for fixtures on scuff molding jobs. The committee will follow up and report back to the group.

Regarding water leaks in the trunk area, sealer problems still need monitoring and contact with 2836 and 2837. (Some improvements have been made but not on everything.)

Mavis Wakefield, Bill Petit and Dave Ruhl of 2837 P.I.P. group are helping solve some of the sealer problems.

NOTES

Chapter 1

1. This introduction is paraphrased from Eugene Guizzetti, *What Is Quality of Work Life?* (M.B.A. major paper prepared under the direction of Dr. Olga L. Crocker, Faculty of Business Administration, University of Windsor, Windsor, Ontario, 1983.

2. Masaaki Imai, "Quality Control and Small Group Activities: The Key to Improved Productivity," *When in Japan: An Introduction for Doing Business in and with Japan*, Vol. 3 (Tokyo: Planning and Promotion Division, Hotel Okura, April 20, 1982): 17.

3. Robert R. Rehder, "What American and Japanese Managers Are Learning from Each Other," *Business Horizons* 24 (March–April 1981): 68.

4. R. Lozano and Philip C. Thompson, "QC Implementation in the Space Shuttle External Tank Program at the Michoud Marietta Corporation," *ASQC 34th Annual Technical Conference Transactions*, 1980.

5. James Thompson, *Organizations in Action* (New York: McGraw-Hill, 1967): 151.

Chapter 2

1. Bando Satoshi, "Qualitative Change in the Labor Movement," *Japan Echo* 8 (1981): 30–37.

2. Hitoshi Kume, "Quality Control in Japan's Industries," *the wheel extended*: A Toyota Quarterly Review (Tokyo), Spring 1980, p. 21.

3. Upon the recommendation of JUSE Managing Director Dr. K. Koyanagi, who had received a donation from Dr. Deming of the royalties from the published transcripts of his lectures, the Board of Directors of JUSE approved setting up a fund for the Deming Prize. Subsequently, Dr. Deming again donated a portion of the royalties from the Japanese edition of his work *Some Theories of Sampling* to this fund.

4. *JSA Technical Reports*, nos. 1–4 (Japanese Standards Association, 1963–1969).

5. JUSE did not define the term "pan-industrial," but seems to have used it to mean "including all industries."

6. "QC Circle Activities and the Suggestion System," *Japan Labor Bulletin*, January 1982, p. 5.

7. J. M. Juran, "International Significance of the QC Circle Movement," *Quality Progress*, November 1980, pp. 18–19.

8. Patricia Fisher Foley and Thomas J. McGuire, eds., *World Almanac and Book of Facts* (New York: Newspaper Enterprise Association, 1983), p. 151.

9. Kaoru Ishikawa, "QC Circle Activities," *QC in Japan Series No. 1* (Tokyo: Union of Japanese Scientists and Engineers, April 1968).

10. Itajime Karatsu, *Quality Control to Extend a Company: From Top Management to the Factory Floor* (Tokyo, 1966), p. 132.

11. Masaaki Imai, "Policy Development: Japanese Management's New Strategic Tool." *The Japan Economic Journal*, February 22, 1983, p. 12.

12. Robert E. Cole, *Work, Mobility and Participation* (Berkeley, CA: University of California Press, 1979), p. 138.

13. J. M. Juran, "Product Quality: A Prescription for the West. Part II: Upper Management Leadership and Employee Relations," *Management Review* 70 (June 1981): 58.

14. "U. S. Executives Look at Japanese QC," *Quality Progress* 13 (February 1980): 8.

15. Susumu Takamiya, "The Characteristics of Japanese Management," *Management Japan* 14 (Summer 1981): 8.

16. George A. De Vos, "Apprenticeship and Paternalism." In *Modern Japanese Organization and Decision-Making*, edited by Ezra F. Vogel (Berkeley, CA: University of California Press, 1975), p. 217.

17. Edwin D. Reischauer, *The Japanese* (Cambridge, MA: Harvard University Press, 1977), pp. 131–32.

18. Chie Nakane, *Japanese Society* (Berkeley, CA: University of California Press, 1970), p. 19.

19. "QC Circle Activities and the Suggestion System," *Japan Labor Bulletin*, January 1982. p. 5.

20. Peter F. Drucker, "Behind Japan's Success," *Harvard Business Review* 59 (January–February 1981): 83–90.

21. Tadashi Hanami, *Labour Relations in Japan Today* (Tokyo: Kodansha, 1981), p. 92.

22. Except for the fact that women are generally temporary rather than permanent employees, little mention is made in the literature regarding their role in industry. It is therefore not clear whether women have supervisory positions.

23. William Bowen, "Japanese Managers Tell How Their System Works," *Fortune*, November 1977, p. 128.

24. Yoshi Tsurumi and Rebecca Tsurumi, "A Closer Look at Japan's 'Lifetime' Employment System," *Pacific Basin Quarterly* 8 (Fall 1982): 5.

25. Ibid.

26. Conversation with Japanese trade consulate officials.

27. Christopher Byron, "How Japan Does It," *Time*, March 30, 1981, pp. 44–50.

28. Bando Satoshi, "Qualitative Change in the Labor Movement," *Japan Echo* 8 (1981): 30–37.

29. Kiyoaki Murata, "What Makes Japan Tick," *The Japan Times Weekly*, February 27, 1982, p. 3.

30. Yoshitaka Fujita, "The Workers' Autonomous Small Group Activities and Productivity in Japan," *Management Japan* 14 (Summer 1981): 18.

31. Masaaki Imai, "Small Group Activities: The Key to Improved Productivity," *The Japan Economic Journal*, February 23, 1982, p. 12.

32. Charles J. McMillan, "Production Planning and Organization Design at Toyota," *Business Quarterly*, Winter 1981, pp. 22–30.

33. The word *kanban* means "signboard" or "label." In production processes, such as Toyota's engine plant, a *kanban* is attached to each unit. When the unit has been processed at a particular stage in the production process, the *kanban* is returned and serves as a reorder instruction. There is no warehouse of supplies and raw materials in large Japanese production companies. Instead suppliers deliver goods on demand, that is, just in time to be used in production. The *kanban* indicates that another unit (or units) is needed.

34. Masaaki Imai, "Quality Control and Small Group Activities: The Key to Improved Productivity," *When in Japan: An Introduction for Doing Business in and with Japan*, Vol. 3 (Tokyo: Planning and Promotion Division, Hotel Okura, April 20, 1982), p. 17.

35. Yoshinobu Nayatani as quoted by Masaaki Imai, "Policy Deployment: Japanese Management's New Strategic Tool," *When in Japan: An Introduction for Doing Business in and with Japan*, Vol. 4 (Tokyo: Planning and Promotion Division, Hotel Okura, February 14, 1983), p. 26.

36. Robert E. Cole, *Industry at the Crossroads, Michigan Papers in Japanese Studies*, no. 7 (Center for Japanese Studies, University of Michigan, 1982), pp. 100–101.

37. Yoshitaka Fujita, "Participative Work Practices in the Japanese Auto Industry: Some Neglected Considerations," in *Industry at the Crossroads, Michigan Papers in Japanese Studies*, No. 7, edited by Robert E. Cole (Ann Arbor, MI: University of Michigan, Center for Japanese Studies, 1982), p. 84.

38. Tadao Koguri, "Providing Incentives to the QC Circle Through an Evaluation System." *Japan Quality Control Circles* (Tokyo: Asian Productivity Organization, 1982), p. 170.

Chapter 3

1. Edgar H. Schein, "SMR Forum: Does Japanese Management Style Have a Message for American Managers?" *Sloan Management Review* 23 (Fall 1981): 55.

2. "Talking in Circles Improves Quality," *Industry Week*, February 14, 1977, p. 62.

3. Ibid. and *Quality Circles at Honeywell: A Study of Participant Perceptions* (Minnetonka, MN: Corporate Human Resources Development Department, Corporate Conference Center), unpaginated.

4. *Quality Circles at Honeywell*.

5. Barry A. Stein and Rosabeth M. Kanter, "Building the Parallel Organization: Creating Mechanisms for Permanent Quality of Work Life," *The Journal of Applied Behavioral Science* 16 (1980): 371–86.

6. Frank M. Gryna, Jr., *Quality Circles: A Team Approach to Problem Solving* (New York: AMACOM, a division of American Management Association, 1981), p. 45.

7. *Toronto-Dominion Quality Programme Introductory Kit* (Toronto: Toronto-Dominion Bank of Canada, 1982), p. 10.

8. Mignon Mazique, "The Quality Circle Transplant," *Issues & Observation*, May 1981, p. 2.

9. David Soyka, "Honeywell Pioneers in Quality Circle Movement," *World of Work Report*, September 1981, p. 66.

10. A recent survey by the American Management Association indicated that 65 percent of companies had employed consultants to help on a portion or on all of the circle activity. Morris (1981) also reports that 70 percent of the thirty-three organizations surveyed had received assistance from consultants and that half of them had contracted for total implementation packages.

11. Joyce MacDonald and Carol Robinson, "Concept for Management," *The Quality Circles Journal* 4 (November 1981): 13–15.

12. Douglas McGregor, *The Human Side of Enterprise* (New York: McGraw-Hill, 1960); idem, *The Professional Manager* (New York: McGraw-Hill, 1967). For completeness, it should be pointed out that two additional views exist: the "blank state" theory and the view that "there is no such thing as human nature." The first dimisses any inherent characteristics as myths. Those who subscribe to this theory maintain that characteristics which exist are a product of environment and circumstance. The second view is that of behaviourists (a philosophy originated by B.F. Skinner). Basically, behaviourists repudiate the concept of human nature, attitudes, needs, and other internal aspects of human nature with the assumption that "If you can't see it, it isn't there."

13. William Ouchi, *Theory Z: How American Business Can Meet the Japanese Challenge* (Reading, MA: Addison-Wesley, 1981).

14. See for example: R. R. Blake and Jane S. Mouton, "The Dynamics of Influence and Concern," *International Journal of Social Psychiatry* 2 (1957): 263–65; A. C. Filley and A. J. Grimes, "The Bases of Power in Decision Processes," in *Academy of Management Proceedings: 27th Annual Meeting*, edited by R. W. Millman and M. P. Hottenstein (1967): 133–60; and C. J. Lammers, "Power and Participation in Decision Making in Formal Organizations," *American Journal of Sociology* 73 (1967): 201–16.

15. See for example: H. C. Kelman, "Compliance, Identification and Internalization: Three Processes of Attitude Change," *Journal of Conflict Resolution* 2 (1958): 51–60; Ronald J. Ebert and Terence R. Mitchell, *Organizational Decision Processes: Concepts and Analysis* (New York: Crane, Russak & Company, 1975), pp. 239–40; and A. Zander and T. Curtis, "Effects of Social Power on Aspiration Setting and Striving," *Journal of Abnormal and Social Psychology* 64 (1962): 63–74.

16. See any organizational behaviour textbook. Two examples are: R. Dennis Middlemist and Michael A. Hitt, *Organizational Behavior: Applied Concepts* (Palo Alto, CA: Science Research Associates, 1981); and Terence R. Mitchell, *People in Organizations: Understanding Their Behavior* (New York: McGraw-Hill, 1978).

17. Conversation with Ernie Long, formerly with Cumis Insurance Co., Burlington Ontario.

18. The United Auto Workers, which represents employees at Ford of Canada, has in the past taken a stand against quality circle implementation. At this point, the union has

left the decision to the union local which represents employees of each plant. Also, in the days of Henry Ford, the relationship between the union and management was not always pleasant. Today, the aftermath of this relationship exists.

19. Paper prepared for Central Michigan University by Michael Nastanski under the direction of Dr. Olga L. Crocker, October 1983.

Chapter 4

1. Solomon B. Levine, *Industrial Relations in Postwar Japan* (Urbana, IL: University of Illinois Press, 1958), p. 36.

2. Kubota, Akira, "Japan: Social Structure and Work Ethic," *Asia Pacific Community* 20 (Spring 1983): 8.

3. Ibid., p. 7.

4. Charles J. McMillan, "Production Planning and Organization Design at Toyota," *Business Quarterly*, Winter 1981, p. 24.

5. Charles J. McMillan, "From Quality Control to Quality Management: Lessons from Japan," *Business Quarterly*, Spring 1982, pp. 37, 38.

6. Masaaki Imai, "Small Group Activities—Five Times ROI? The Case of Nissan Chemical Industries," *When in Japan: An Introduction for Doing Business in and with Japan*, Vol. 4 (Tokyo, Japan: Planning and Promotion Division, Hotel Okura, June 14, 1982), p. 17.

7. Charles J. McMillan, "Is Japanese Management Really So Different?" *Business Quarterly*, Autumn 1980, pp. 27–28.

8. In addition to references previously cited, comparative Japanese information which is given here is based on: "The New Economy," *Time*, May 30, 1983; Tadashi Hanami, *Labor Relations in Japan Today* (Tokyo: Kodansha International Ltd., 1981); M. Sumiya, "The Emergence of Modern Japan," in *Workers and Employers in Japan: The Japanese Employment Relations System*, edited by K. O. Kochi, B. Karsh, and S. B. Levine (Princeton, NJ: Princeton University Press, 1974); Clark Kerr, John T. Dunlop, Frederick Harbison, and Charles A. Myers, *Industrialism and Industrial Man* (New York: Oxford University Press, 1964); and John W. Bennett and Iwao Ishino, "Paternalistic Economic Organizations and Japanese Society," in *Paternalism in the Japanese Economy: Anthropological Studies of Oyabun–Kabun Patterns*, edited by Bennett and Ishino (Minneapolis: University of Minnesota Press, 1963), p. 243.

Chapter 6

1. William J. Gordon, "An Operational Approach to Creativity," *Harvard Business Review* 34, (November–December 1956): 41–51.

2. Sydney Dauer and Alice Dauer, "A New Approach to Creative Thinking and Idea Development," *IBM Engineering Seminar*, 1956.

3. Tom Alexander, "Synetics: Inventing by the Madness Method," *Fortune*, August 1965.

4. John W. Haefele, *Creativity and Innovation* (New York: Van Nostrand Reinhold, 1962), p. 151.

5. Carl E. Gregory, *Management of Intelligence* (New York: McGraw-Hill, 1967), p. 200.

Chapter 8

1. Some good books for those who wish to know more about reports and oral presentations are: Ronald Adler, *Communicating at Work: Principles and Practices for Business and the Professions* (Mississauga, Ont.: Random House, 1983); Abne M. Eisenberg, *Understanding Communication in Business and the Professions* (New York: Macmillan, 1978); Jerry W. Koehler, Karl W. E. Anatol, and Ronald L. Applbaum, *Public Communication: Behavioral Perspectives* (New York: Macmillan, 1978); Raymond V. Lesikar, *Basic Business Communication* (Georgetown, Ont.: Richard D. Irwin, Inc., 1979); John J. Makay, *Speaking with an Audience: Communicating Ideas and Attitudes* (New York: Crowell, 1977); J. H. Menning, C. W. Wilkinson, and Peter B. Clarke, *Communicating Through Letters and Reports* (Georgetown, Ont.: Richard D. Irwin, Inc., 1979); Robert L. Montgomery, *A Master Guide to Public Speaking* (New York: Harper & Row, 1979); and Don B. Morlan and George E. Tuttle, Jr., *An Introduction to Effective Oral Communication* (Indianapolis, IN: Bobbs-Merrill, 1976).

Chapter 9

1. A book which is very practical and which explains graphs succinctly is Vernon Clover and Howard Balsley, *Business Research Methods* (Columbus, OH: Grid, Inc., 1974).

Chapter 12

1. The content material given in this chapter is based on interviews conducted by Dr. Olga Crocker or Johnny Sik Leung Chiu with: Mr. Curtis Davidson, UAW Plant Chairperson of Essex Engine Plant and other union members; Mr. Gary Lesperance, former Coordinator of EI Programs, Windsor Operations; and Mr. Bill Johnston, former Manager of Labor Relations and Hourly Personnel, Windsor Operations; and on information provided in "Guidelines for Implementing UAW–Ford Employe Involvement Programs" (Dearborn, MI: UAW–Ford National Joint Committee on Employe Involvement, September 1980); and *A Handbook on the UAW–Ford Process for Local Unions and Management* (Dearborn, MI: UAW–Ford National Joint Committee on Employe Involvement, 1980).

2. *The Windsor Star*, March 3, 1983.

Chapter 13

1. The median is obtained by placing all responses for each factor in order from 1 to 12, and counting to the mid-point and looking at the response which this individual has given. For example, for the second item in the table, effort, all responses were ranked (placed in a column in order) from 1 to 12. Halfway down our column was between the eighteenth and nineteenth responses (there are thirty-six in total). The eighteenth respondent had answered 3; the nineteenth respondent had answered 4. The median therefore is 3.5.
2. *UAW–Ford Employe Involvement: A Special Survey Report* (Dearborn, MI: UAW–Ford National Development and Training Center, March 1983).
3. Robert I. Patchin, *Quality Control Circles in an Office Environment* (Northrup Corporation, Aircraft Division, April 1981), p. 5.
4. *Quality Circles at Honeywell: A Study of Participant Perceptions* (Minnetonka, MN: Corporate Human Resource Development Department, Honeywell, Inc., July 1982).

Chapter 14

1. The information for this chapter is based on interviews by Dr. Olga L. Crocker with: Mr. Donald Young, Coordinator of the PSI Program; Mr. John Olaja, Director of Advertising; Mr. Derek Millet, engineer; Mr. Bob Brown; Mr. Bob Immel; and other individuals within the company who asked that they not be identified. Two Vickers publications also were utilized: *Plan for Productivity/Quality Improvement, Commercial Division* (Troy, MI: July 1980) and *Quality Fluid Power Components and Systems to Meet Industry's Needs, the World Over* (Troy, MI: n.d.).

Chapter 15

1. Yoshitaka Fujita, "The Workers' Autonomous Small Group Activities and Productivity in Japan,"*Management Japan* 14 (Summer 1981): 17.
2. Zane K. Quible, "Quality Circles: A Well Rounded Approach to Employee Involvement," *Management World*, September 1981, p. 10.
3. J. E. Struthers, *Canada–Japan Essay: Long Road Back* (Canada–Japan Council, Summer 1981), p. 6.
4. *Work in America*, Report of a Special Task Force to the Secretary of Health, Education and Welfare (Cambridge, MA: The MIT Press, 1973).
4. H. J. Eysenck, "The Measurement of Motivation," *Scientific American* 208 (May 1963): 130.

BIBLIOGRAPHY

ABEGGLEN, JAMES C. *Management and Worker: The Japanese Solution.* Tokyo: Kodansha International, 1973.

ABERNATHY, WILLIAM J., and KIM B. CLARK. "Notes on a Trip to Japan: Concepts and Interpretations." In *Industry at the Crossroads,* Michigan Papers in Japanese Studies No. 7, edited by Robert E. Cole. Ann Arbor: University of Michigan, Center for Japanese Studies, 1982.

ABRAMS, JIM. "What You Train Is What You Get." *The Japan Times Weekly,* March 5, 1983: 3.

"Action Exchange." *American Libraries* (December 1982): 714.

ALEXANDER, C. PHILIP. "Learning from the Japanese." *Personnel Journal* 60 (August 1981): 616–19.

ALEXANDER, TOM. "Synetics: Inventing by the Madness Method." *Fortune,* August 1965.

AMSDEN, DAVIDA M., and ROBERT T. AMSDEN. "Problem-Solving Comparisons: QC Circles, KT, ZD, and Others." *ASQC 32nd Annual Technical Conference Transactions.* Milwaukee: American Society for Quality Control, 1978.

AMSDEN, DAVIDA M., and ROBERT T. AMSDEN, eds. *QC Circles: Applications, Tools, and Theory.* Milwaukee: American Society for Quality Control, 1976.

AMSDEN, DAVIDA M., and ROBERT T. AMSDEN. "The Research Aspects of QC Circles." *IAQC 1st Annual Conference Transactions.* Cincinnati: International Association of Quality Circles, 1979.

AMSDEN, DAVIDA M., and ROBERT T. AMSDEN. "Results of Research on QC Circles." *ASQC 34th Annual Technical Conference Transactions.* Milwaukee: American Society for Quality Control, 1980.

AMSDEN, DAVIDA M., and ROBERT T. AMSDEN. "Statistics Applied to and by QC Circles." *ASQC 32nd Annual Technical Conference Transactions.* Milwaukee: American Society for Quality Control, 1978.

AMSDEN, ROBERT T., and DAVIDA M. AMSDEN. "A Look at QC Circles." *Tooling & Production,* June 1980.

"An Aging Work Force Strains Japan's Traditions." *Business Week,* April 20, 1981: 72–85.

ANTILLA, SUSAN. "East Meets West: The Quality Circle." *Working Woman,* October 1981: 88–91.

AONUMA, YOSHIMATSU. "The Japanese and the Organization." *the wheel extended: A Toyota Quarterly Review* 9 (Tokyo), Spring 1980, pp. 9–19.

AUBREY, CHARLES A. II, and LAWRENCE A. ELDRIDGE. "Banking on High Quality." *Quality Progress* 14 (December 1981): 14–19.

AUBREY, CHARLES A. II, and WENDY CAROL FENCL. "Management, Professional and Clerical Quality Circles." *ASQC 36th Annual Technical Conference and Exposition Transactions*. Milwaukee: American Society for Quality Control, 1982: 54–61.

AZUMI, KOYA, and CHARLES MCMILLAN. "Worker Sentiment in the Japanese Factory: Its Organizational Determinants." In *Japan: The Paradox of Progress*, edited by Lewis Austin. New Haven: Yale University Press, 1976.

BABBIT, ROBERT C. "One Company's Approach to Quality Circles." *Quality Progress* 14 (October 1981): 28–29.

BALDWIN, DAVID, and DAVID GROMES. "EI at Canton Forge." *Work Life Review* 2 (March 1983): 17–21.

BALL, R. A., and S.P. BARNEY. *Quality Circle Project Manual*. Rawsonville, MI: UAW–Ford Employe Involvement, 1982.

BANDO, SATOSHI. "Qualitative Change in the Labor Movement." *Japan Echo* 8 (Spring 1981): 30–37.

BARNEY, STEPHEN. *Quality Circles: Adapting Materials and Training to Organizational Needs*. Unpublished paper, Central Michigan University, December 1982.

BARRA, RALPH J. *Putting Quality Circles to Work: A Practical Strategy for Boosting Productivity and Profits.*. New York: McGraw-Hill, 1983.

BEARDSLEY, JEFFERSON F. "Ingredients of Successful Quality Circles." *IAQC 2nd Annual Conference Transactions*. Cincinnati: International Association of Quality Circles, 1980.

BEARDSLEY, J. F. "The Quality Circle Steering Committee." *The Quality Circles Quarterly* 1 (Fourth Quarter 1978): 26–30.

BEARDSLEY, J. F. "Training is the Heart of the Lockheed QC Circle Program." In *ASQC 30th Annual Technical Conference Transactions*. Milwaukee: American Society for Quality Control, 1976.

BENEDICT, RUTH. *The Chrysanthemum and the Sword: Patterns of Japanese Culture*. New York: New American Library, 1967.

BENNETT, J. W., and IWAO ISHINO. "Paternalistic Economic Organizations and Japanese Society." In *Paternalism in the Japanese Economy*. Minneapolis: University of Minnesota Press, 1963.

BIEBER, OWEN. "UAW Views Circles: Not Bad at All." *The Quality Circles Journal* 5 (August 1982): 6.

BINSTOCK, S. L. "Americans Express Dissatisfaction with Quality of U.S. Goods." *Quality Progress* 14 (January 1981): 12–14.

BIRD, ALLAN. "A Comparison of Japanese and Western Management." *Management Japan* 15 (Autumn 1982): 21–24.

BLAKE, R. R., and JANE S. MOUTON. "The Dynamics of Influence and Concern." *International Journal of Social Psychiatry* 2 (1957): 263–65.

BLUESTONE, IRVING. "Labor's Stake in Improving the Quality of Work Life." *Interna-

tional Conference on the Quality of Working Life, Toronto, 1981. Available from Work in America Institute, Scarsdale, NY.

BLUMBERG, PAUL. *Industrial Democracy: The Sociology of Participation*. New York: Schocken Books, 1969.

BOCKER, HANS J., and HERMAN O. OVERGAARD. *Quality Circles: An Answer to the Productivity Challenge*. Research Paper Series No. 3281. Waterloo, Ontario: Wilfrid Laurier University, 1982.

BOCKER, HANS J., and HERMAN O. OVERGAARD. *Quality Circles: A Managerial Response to the Productivity Problem*. Research Paper Series No. 3381. Waterloo, Ontario: Wilfrid Laurier University, 1982.

BROOKE, KEITH A. "QC Circles' Success Depends on Management Readiness to Support Workers' Involvement." *Industrial Engineering* 14 (January 1982): 76–79.

BRUCE-BRIGGS, B. "The Dangerous Folly Called Theory Z." *Fortune*, May 17, 1982.

BRUNET, LUCIE. "Quality Circles: Can They Improve QWL?" *The Canadian Scene* 4 (1981): 1–2.

BRYANT, STEPHEN, and JOSEPH KEARNS. " 'Workers' Brains as Well as Their Bodies': Quality Circles in a Federal Facility." *Public Administration Review* 42 (March–April 1982): 144–50.

BUBACK, KENNETH, and JAROSLAV I. DUTKEWYCH. "Quality Circles in Health Care: The Henry Ford Hospital Experience." *IAQC 4th Annual Conference Transactions*. Cincinnati: International Association of Quality Circles, 1982.

BYRON, CHRISTOPHER. "How Japan Does It." *Time*, March 30, 1981.

CANDY, WARREN L. "Maintenance Groups Make and Implement Own Suggestions for Improving Productivity." *Industrial Engineering* 14 (February 1982): 44–48.

CLARK, GREGORY. "Western Reindustrialization and Japan: Why Japan Works (1)." *The Japan Economic Journal*, March 9, 1982: 24.

CLARK, RODNEY. *The Japanese Company*. New Haven: Yale University Press, 1979.

CLELAND, D.I. "Matrix Management (Part II): A Kaleidoscope of Organizational Systems." *Management Review* 70 (December 1981): 48–56.

CLINE, NANCY, and DALIA PALAU. "Quality Circles in the Recovery Room." *Nursing and Health Care* 3 (November 1982): 494–96.

CLOVER, VERNON, and HOWARD BALSLEY. *Business Research Methods*. Columbus, OH: Grid, Inc., 1974.

COLE, ROBERT E. "Common Misconceptions of Japanese QC Circles." *ASQC 35th Annual Technical Conference and Exposition Transactions*. Milwaukee: American Society for Quality Control, 1981.

COLE, ROBERT E. "Diffusion of New Work Structures in Japan." *IAQC 1st Annual Conference Transactions*. Cincinnati: International Association of Quality Circles, 1979.

COLE, ROBERT E. *Japanese Blue Collar: The Changing Tradition*. Los Angeles: University of California Press, 1971.

COLE, ROBERT E. "Japanese Quality Control Circles: Are They Exportable to U.S. Firms?" *World of Work Report* 4 (June 1979): 42, 46.

COLE, ROBERT E. "Learning from the Japanese: Prospects and Pitfalls." *Management*

Review 69 (September 1980) 22–28.

COLE, ROBERT E. "Made in Japan—Quality Control Circles." *Across the Board* 16 (November 1979): 72–78.

COLE, ROBERT E. "Made in Japan: A Spur to U.S. Productivity." *ASIA Magazine*, May–June 1979, pp. 18–24.

COLE, ROBERT E. "QC Warning Voiced by U.S. Expert on Japanese Circles." *World of Work Report* 6 (July 1981): 49–51.

COLE, ROBERT E. "Quality Control Practices in the Auto Industry: United States and Japan Compared." *Ann Arbor Observer*, February 1982: 27–28.

COLE, ROBERT E. *Industry at the Crossroads. Michigan Papers in Japanese Studies, No. 7.* Ann Arbor: University of Michigan, Center for Japanese Studies, 1982.

COLE, ROBERT E. "Rationale for Financial Incentives for Quality Circle Members." *The Quality Circles Journal* 4 (February 1981): 8.

COLE, ROBERT E. "Will QC Circles Work in the U.S.?" *Quality Progress* 13 (July 1980): 30–33.

COLE, ROBERT E. *Work, Mobility, and Participation: A Comparative Study of American and Japanese Industry.* Los Angeles: University of California Press, 1979.

COLE, ROBERT E., and ANDREW G. WALDER. *Structural Diffusion: The Politics of Participative Work Structures in China, Japan, Sweden, and the United States.* Ann Arbor: University of Michigan, Center for Research on Social Organizations, 1981.

COLLARD, R. "The Quality Circle in Context." *Personnel Management* (U.K.) 13 (September 1981): 26–30, 51.

COMSTOCK, VIVIAN C., and GERALD E. SWARTZ. "Predictable Developmental States in the Evolution of a Quality Circle." *IAQC 2nd Annual Conference Transactions.* Cincinnati: International Association of Quality Circles, 1980.

COURTRIGHT, WILLIAM. "Hughes Circles: An Update." *The Quality Circles Journal* 4 (August 1981): 30–34.

CUTTS, ROBERT E. "The Productivity Proposition: Notes on the Japanese Approach." *Japan Airlines Travel Magazine*, October 1980: 4.

DAILEY, JOHN J. JR., and RUDOLPH L. KAGERER. "A Primer on Quality Circles." *Supervisory Management* 27 (June 1982): 40–43.

DAVIDSON, WILLIAM H. "Small Group Activity at Musashi Semiconductor Works." *Sloan Management Review* 23 (Spring 1982): 3–14.

DAUER, SYDNEY, and ALICE DAUER. *A New Approach to Creative Thinking and Idea Development.* Syracuse: IBM Engineering Seminar, 1956.

DEMING, W. EDWARDS. "Improvement of Quality and Productivity Through Action by Management." *National Productivity Review* 1 (Winter 1981–82): 12–22.

DEMING, W. EDWARDS. "On Some Statistical Aids Towards Economic Production." *Interfaces* 5 (August 1975): 1–15.

"Dr. W. Edwards Deming—The Statistical Control of Quality, Part I." *Quality*, February 1980: 38–41.

"Dr. W. Edwards Deming—The Statistical Control of Quality, Part II." *Quality*, March 1980: 34–36.

DE VOS, GEORGE, A. "Apprenticeship and Paternalism." In *Modern Japanese Organi-*

zation and Decision-Making, edited by Ezra F. Vogel. Berkeley: University of California Press, 1975.

DEWAR, D. *The Quality Circle Handbook*. Red Bluff, CA: Quality Circle Institute, 1982.

DEWAR, DONALD L. "If Japan Can—We Can Too." *IAQC 3rd Annual Conference Transactions*. Cincinnati: International Association of Quality Circles, 1981.

DEWAR, DONALD L. "Implementing Quality Circles in Your Organization." *IAQC 2nd Annual Conference Transactions*. Cincinnati: International Association of Quality Circles, 1980.

DEWAR, DONALD L. "Measurement of Results—Lockheed QC Circles." *ASQC 30th Annual Technical Conference Transactions*. Milwaukee: American Society for Quality Control, 1976.

DEWAR, DONALD L. *The Quality Circle Guide to Participation Management*. Englewood Cliffs, NJ: Prentice-Hall, 1982.

DI GEORGIO, BRENT S. "Management and Labor Cooperate to Increase Productivity." *Supervision* 43 (January 1981): 5–7.

DOI, TAKEO. *The Anatomy of Dependence*. Translated from the Japanese by John Bester. Tokyo: Kodansha International, 1973.

DONOVAN, J. MICHAEL. "Building Management Support for Quality Circle Programs." In *IAQC 3rd Annual Conference Transactions*. Cincinnati: International Association of Quality Circles, 1981.

DONOVAN, J. MICHAEL. "New Tools For Problem Solving in Quality Circles." *IAQC 3rd Annual Conference Transactions*. Cincinnati: International Association of Quality Circles, 1981.

DONOVAN, J. MICHAEL. "Quality Circles—Goldmine or Fad? Skillful Management of the Program Can Make the Difference." *IAQC 1st Annual Conference Transactions*. Cincinnati: International Association of Quality Circles, 1979.

DONOVAN, J. MICHAEL. "Quality Circles Help School Through Financial Crises." *The Quality Circles Journal* 2 (Third Quarter 1979): 14–17.

DONOVAN, J. MICHAEL. "A Roadmap for Solving Problems in Quality Circles." *The Quality Circles Journal* 2 (Fourth Quarter 1979): 16–22.

DONOVAN, J. MICHAEL. "Skillful Management of the Program Can Make the Difference." *IAQC 2nd Annual International Conference Transactions*. Cincinnati: International Association of Quality Circles, 1980.

DONOVAN, J. M., and WINGATE SIKES. "QC Circles: An Explosive Formula for Cutting Costs." *The Quality Circles Journal* 1 (Fourth Quarter 1978): 19–22.

DORE, RONALD. *British Factory—Japanese Factory: The Origins of National Diversity in Industrial Relations*. London: Alden & Mowbray, 1973.

DRUCKER, PETER F. "Behind Japan's Success." *Harvard Business Review* 59 (January–February 1981): 83–90.

DUBOIS, PIERRE. "Quality Circles: A Valuable Tool for Effective Management." *Canadian Banker and ICB Review* 90 (April 1983): 38–43.

East Asian Studies Program, Ohio State University. *Business and Society in Japan: Fundamentals for the Businessman*. Bradley M. Richardson, ed. New York: Praeger, 1981.

EBERT, RONALD J., and TERENCE R. MITCHELL. *Organizational Decision Processes: Concepts and Analysis*. New York: Crane, Russak & Company, 1975.

EI UAW-Ford Employe Involvement. *A Handbook On the UAW-Ford Process for Local Unions and Management*. Dearborn, MI: UAW–Ford National Joint Committee on Employe Involvement, 1980.

EISENBERG, ABNÉ. *Understanding Communication in Business and the Professions*. New York: Macmillan, 1978.

EMORY, C. WILLIAM. *Business Research Methods*. Homewood, IL: Richard D. Irwin, Inc., 1980.

Employe Involvement Process Workshop. Dearborn, MI: UAW–Ford National Development and Training Center, March 1983.

EPSTEIN, EUGENE. *People and Productivity: A Challenge to Corporate America. A Study from the New York Stock Exchange, Office of Economic Research*. New York: New York Stock Exchange, 1982.

ERICKSON, TOM, and JANICE G. SPROUL. "How Do You Know You Have Arrived at Where You Thought You Were Going?" *IAQC 1st Annual Conference Transactions*. Cincinnati: International Association of Quality Circles, 1979.

EYSENCK, H. J. "The Measurement of Motivation." *Scientific American* 208 (May 1963): 130–40.

"Father of Quality Control Circles Doubts Their Long-Term Viability in the West." *International Management*, August 1982: 23–25.

FENNEY, E. "Quality Circles: Using Pooled Effort to Promote Excellence." *Training and Human Resource Development*, January 1980.

FILLEY, A. C., and A. J. GRIMES. "The Bases of Power in Decision Processes." In *Academy of Management Proceedings: 27th Annual Meeting*, 1967, edited by R.W. Millman and M.P. Hottenstein: 133–60.

FITZGERALD, LAURIE, and JOSEPH MURPHY. *Installing Quality Circles: A Strategic Approach*. San Diego, California: University Associates, 1982.

FOLEY, PATRICIA FISHER, and THOMAS J. MCGUIRE, eds. *The World Almanac and Book of Facts*. New York: Newspaper Enterprise Association, 1983.

Ford Casting Division Japanese Productivity Study Group. *A Report on the Japanese Automotive Foundry Industry*. Windsor, Ont.: December 1980.

FUJITA, YOSHITAKA. "Participative Work Practices in the Japanese Auto Industry: Some Neglected Considerations." In *Industry at the Crossroads*, edited by Robert E. Cole. Michigan Papers in Japanese Studies No. 7. Ann Arbor: University of Michigan, Center for Japanese Studies, 1982: 75–86.

FUJITA, YOSHITAKA. "The Workers' Autonomous Small Group Activities and Productivity in Japan." *Management Japan* 14 (Summer 1981): 16–18.

FUKADA, RYUJI. "Japanese Management Not Magic, But Science." *The Japan Times Weekly*, March 13, 1982: 5.

GELINAS, MARY V. "A Systems Approach to Quality Circles." *IAQC 4th Annual Conference Transactions*. Cincinnati: International Association of Quality Circles, 1982.

General Electric Company. *Quality Circles Leading and Facilitating Manual*. Bridgeport,

CT: General Electric Company Quality Projects, 1981.

GIBSON, PRICE. "Assess Readiness, Measure Change and Survive." *The Quality Circles Journal* 5 (May 1982): 19–31.

GIBSON, PRICE. "Challenges for Quality Circles and Quality of Work Life." *IAQC 4th Annual Conference Transactions*. Cincinnati: International Association of Quality Circles, 1982.

GIBSON, PRICE. "Full-Time Facilitation." *The Quality Circles Journal* 4 (August 1981): 9.

GIBSON, PRICE. *Quality Circles: One Approach to Productivity Improvement*. Work in America Institute Studies in Productivity. New York: Pergamon, 1982.

GIBSON, PRICE. *Quality Circles Facilitator Education and Development Needs. A Report on Research Conducted in Northeastern Ohio Organizations*. Kent, OH: Kent State University, College of Special Programs, March 1981.

GIBSON, PRICE. "Questions and Challenges for Quality Circles Implementors." *Creativity Week V Proceedings*. Greensboro, NC: Center for Creative Leadership, 1982: 60–77.

GIBSON, PRICE. "Short-Term Fad or Long-Term Fundamental? The Need for Research into the Quality Circle Process." *The Quality Circles Journal* 4 (May 1981): 25–26.

GOODFELLOW, MATTHEW. "Quality Control Circle Programs—What Works and What Doesn't." *Quality Progress* 14 (August 1981): 32–33.

GORDON, WILLIAM J. "Operational Approach to Creativity." *Harvard Business Review* 34 (November–December 1956): 41–51.

GOW, ERNEST. "Would Our Use of the Japanese 'Quality Circle' Bring Cost Savings?" *Management Accounting* 58 (February 1980): 18.

GREEN, R.R. "Productivity Improvements for J. C. Penney Catalog." *AIIE Proceedings*, Spring 1981: 489–93.

GREGORY, CARL E. *Management of Intelligence: Scientific Problem Solving and Creativity*. New York: McGraw-Hill, 1967.

GRYNA, FRANK M., JR. *Quality Circles: A Team Approach to Problem Solving*. New York: AMACOM, A Division of the American Management Association, 1981.

GUEST, ROBERT H. "Quality of Work Life: Learning from Tarrytown." *Harvard Business Review* 57 (July–August 1979): 76–87.

Guidelines for Implementing UAW–Ford Employe Involvement Programs. UAW–Ford National Joint Committee on Employe Involvement, September 1980.

GUIZZETTI, EUGENE. "What is Quality of Work Life?" M.B.A. major paper, University of Windsor, 1983.

HAEFELE, JOHN W. *Creativity and Innovation*. New York: Van Nostrand Reinhold, 1962.

HALL, FRANK. "Made in Japan." *Plastics Engineering*, November 1980: 38–48.

HALL, FRANK. "Participation Improves Quality . . . Because it Changes Attitudes." *Machinery*, July 1971: 46–50.

HALL, JAMES L., and JOE K. LEIDECKER. "Is Japanese-Style Management Anything New? A Comparison of Japanese-Style Management with U.S. Participative Models." *Human Resource Management* 20 (Winter 1981): 14–21.

HANAMI, TADASHI. *Labor Relations in Japan Today*. Tokyo: Kodansha International, 1982.

Handbook on the UAW–Ford Process for Local Unions and Management. UAW Ford National Joint Committee on Employe Involvement, 1980.

HANLEY, JOSEPH. "Our Experience with Quality Circles." *Quality Progress* 13 (February 1980): 22–24.

HATTRUP, COLLEEN. "The Changing Roles of Participants in a Self-Facilitation Mode." *IAQC 4th Annual Conference Transactions. Cincinnati: International Association of Quality Circles, 1982.*

HATVANY, NINA, and VLADIMIR PUCIK. "Japanese Management Practices and Productivity." *Organization Dynamics* 9 (Spring 1981): 4–21.

HAZAMA, HIROSHI. "Characteristics of Japanese Corporate Management." *the wheel extended: A Toyota Quarterly Review* (Tokyo), Special Supplement, Winter 1979, pp. 1–8.

HAYES, ROBERT H. "Reflections on Japanese Factory Management." *Harvard Business School Working Paper*, January 1981.

HAYES, ROBERT H. "Why Japanese Factories Work." *Harvard Business Review* 59 (July–August 1981): 56–66.

HEGLAND, RONALD E. "Quality Circles: Key to Productivity with Quality." *Production Engineering*, June 1981: 26–31.

HERIP, WALTER M. "Forging Ahead." *The Quality Circles Journal* 5 (November 1982).

HERZENBERG, STEPHAN A., and WILLIAM A. SCHWARTZ. "UAW: Loosening the Chains." *The Harvard Crimson* 21 (February 21, 1979): 3.

HILL, C., and W. CARTWRIGHT. "Quality Circles Work." *The Quality Circles Journal* 1 (Third Quarter 1978): 27–36.

HOFFMAN, FRANK O. "A Quality Atmosphere: Quality Circles Demand a Supportive Business Philosophy." *Management World* 12 (January 1983) 44.

"Honeywell Quality Circles: Part of a Growing American Trend." *Journal of Organizational and Behavior Management* 3 (1981–82): 97–101.

HOWARD, NIGEL, and YOSHIYA TERAMOTO. "The Really Important Difference Between Japanese and Western Management." *Management International Review* 21 (February 1981): 19–30.

HUNT, BONNIE. "Measuring Results in a Quality Circle Pilot Test." *Quality Circles Journal* 4 (August 1981): 26–29.

HUTCHINS, DAVID. "How Quality Goes Round in Circles." *Management Today*, January 1981: 27–28.

IMAI, MASAAKI. "Plant-Wide Campaigns: Voluntary Activities Extended Beyond Small Group." *The Japan Economic Journal*, July 27, 1982: 12.

IMAI, MASAAKI. "Policy Development: Japanese Management's New Strategic Tool." *The Japan Economic Journal*, February 22, 1983: 12.

IMAI, MASAAKI. "Productivity in Disarray: Its 'Hard' and 'Soft' Aspects." *The Japan Economic Journal*, January 26, 1982: 12.

IMAI, MASAAKI. "Quality Control and Small Group Activities: The Key to Improved Productivity." *The Japan Economic Journal*, April 27, 1982: 12.

IMAI, MASAAKI. "Small Group Activities—Five Times ROI? The Case of Nissan Chemical

Industries." *The Japan Economic Journal*, June 14, 1982: 12.

IMAI, MASAAKI. "Small Group Activities: The Key to Improved Productivity." *The Japan Economic Journal*, February 23, 1982: 12–13.

IMAI, MASAAKI. "From Taylor to Ford to Toyota: 'Kanban' System—Another Challenge from Japan." *The Japan Economic Journal*, March 30, 1982: 12.

IMAI, MASAAKI. "Total Quality Control as Corporate Strategy." *The Japan Economic Journal*, December 28, 1982: 12.

IMBERMAN, WOODRUFF. "Why Quality Control Circles Don't Work." *Canadian Business*, May 1982: 103–6.

INGLE, SUD. *Quality Circles Master Guide: Increasing Productivity with People Power.* New York: Prentice-Hall, 1982.

INGLE, SUD. "How to Avoid Quality Circle Failure in Your Company." *Training and Development Journal* 36 (June 1982): 54–59.

IRVING, ROBERT R. "QC Circles Spur Productivity, Improve Product Quality." *Iron Age* 221 (June 5, 1978): 61–63.

IRVING, ROBERT R. "QC Payoff Attracts Top Management." *Iron Age* 222 (August 20, 1979): 64–65.

ISHIKAWA, KAORU. "Cause and Effect Diagram—CE Diagram—Tokusei Yo-In Zu-Ishikawa Diagram." In *QC Circles: Applications, Tools, and Theory*, edited by Davida M. Amsden and Robert T. Amsden. Milwaukee: American Society for Quality Control, 1976: 91–94.

ISHIKAWA, KAORU. *Guide to Quality Control.* Tokyo: Asian Productivity Organization, 1976.

ISHIKAWA, KAORU. *QC Circle Activities: QC in Japan.* Series No. 1, Tokyo: Japanese Union of Scientists and Engineers, April 1968.

ISHIKAWA, KAORU. "Quality in Japan: QC Circle Activities." *Quality*, May 1980: 97.

JACKSON, MICHAEL. *Productivity Improvement*: A Study of Selected Approaches. M.B.A. major paper, University of Windsor, May 1982.

Japan Quality Control Circles. Tokyo: Asian Productivity Organization, 1982.

"Japanese Managers Tell How Their System Works." *Fortune*, November 1977: 126–38.

Japanese Standards Association. *JSA Technical Reports*, No. 104, 1963–1969.

"Japan's High-Tech Challenge." *Newsweek*, August 9, 1982: 48–54.

"Japan's Industrial Competitiveness: The Human Factor." *Japan Labor Bulletin*, May 1982: 5–8.

JENKINS, K. M., and J. SHIMADA. "Quality Circles in the Service Sector." *Supervisory Management* 26 (August 1981): 2–7.

JOCH, ALAN. "Quality Circles: The Key to Better Management?" *Metal Center News*, June 1982: 64–69.

JOHNSON, BRYAN. "Brave New World of Nissan—U.S.A." *The Globe and Mail*, June 18, 1983.

JOHNSON, RICHARD TANNER, and WILLIAM G. OUCHI. "Made in America (Under Japanese Management)." *Harvard Business Review* 52 (September–October 1974): 61–69.

JUECHTER, W. MATTHEW, and TOM UTNE. "Wellness: Addressing the 'Whole' Person." *Training and Development Journal* 36 (May 1982): 112–16.

JURAN, JOSEPH M. "International Significance of the QC Circle Movement." *Quality Progress* 13 (November 1980): 18–22.

JURAN, JOSEPH M. "Japanese and Western Quality: A Contrast." *Quality Progress* 11 (December 1978): 10–18.

JURAN, JOSEPH M. "Product Quality—A Prescription for the West. Part I: Training and Improvement Programs." *Management Review* 6 (June 1981): 9–14.

JURAN, JOSEPH M. "Product Quality—A Prescription for the West. Part II: Upper-Management Leadership and Employee Relations." *Management Review* 7 (July 1981): 57–61.

JURAN, JOSEPH M. "Quality Control of Service—the 1974 Japanese Symposium." *Quality Progress* 8 (April 1975): 10–13.

KARATSU, HAJIME. *Quality Control to Extend a Company: From Top Management to the Factory Floor*. Tokyo: Japan, 1966.

KARATSU, HAJIME. "What Makes Japanese Products Better?" *SAM Advanced Management Journal* 47 (Spring 1982): 4–7.

KEEFE, JOHN P. "Part-Time Facilitation." *The Quality Circles Journal* 4 (August 1981): 8.

KEEFE, JOHN, and WILLIAM A. KRAUS. *Building Effective Quality Circles: A Research Report*. Hendersonville, NC: General Electric Company Quality Projects, 1982.

KELMAN, H. C. "Compliance, Identification and Internalization: Three Processes of Attitude Change." *Journal of Conflict Resolution* 2 (March 1958): 51–60.

KERR, CLARK, JOHN T. DUNLOP, FREDERICK HARBISON, and CHARLES A. MYERS. *Industrialism and Industrial Man*. New York: Oxford University Press, 1964.

KIDA, HIROSHI. "Life-Long Learning: Education for All People at All Ages." *Look Japan*, December 10, 1981: 1–3.

KIKUCHI, SEIICHI. "Japanese Quality Control Method Increasingly Finds Its Way Abroad." *The Japan Economic Journal*, June 1, 1982: 11

KLEIN, GERALD D. "Implementing Quality Circles: A Hard Look at Some of the Realities." *Personnel* 58 (November–December 1981): 11–21.

KLEIN, WALTER F., and THOM SCHAMBERGER. "Part-Time Facilitators and Quality Control Circles in the Hospital Environment." In *IAQC 4th Annual Conference Transactions*. International Association of Quality Circles, 1982: 528–40.

KNIGHT, L. J. "Quality Circles in Action: A Canadian Experience." *CTM: The Human Element*, February 1983, 20–21.

KOEHLER, JERRY W., KARL W. E. ANATOL, and RONALD L. APPLBAUM. *Public Communication: Behavioral Perspectives*. New York: Macmillan, 1978.

KOGURI, TADAO. "Providing Incentives to the QC Circle Through an Evaluation System." *Japan Quality Control Circles*. Tokyo: Asian Productivity Organization, 1982.

KONARICK, RONALD B., and WAYNE REED. "A Military Approach: Work Environment Improvement Teams." *The Quality Circles Journal* 4 (August 1981): 35–40.

KONDO, YOSHIO. "Company-Wide Quality Control in Japanese Industries and its Impact on Quality of Work Life." *International Conference on the Quality of Working Life.* Scarsdale, NY: Work in America Institute, 1981.

KONDO, YOSHIO. "The Role of Managers in QC Circle Movement." In *QC Circles: Applications, Tools, and Theory*, edited by Davida M. Amsden and Robert T. Amsden. Milwaukee: American Society for Quality Control, 1976: 41–54.

KONZ, STEPHAN. "Quality Circles: Japanese Success Story." *Industrial Engineering* 11 (October 1979): 24–26.

KONZ, STEPHAN. "Quality Circles: An Annotated Bibliography." *Quality Progress* 14, (April 1981): 30–35.

KOSHIRO, KAZUYOSHI. "The Quality of Working Life." *the wheel extended: A Toyota Quarterly Review* (Tokyo), Special Supplement, June 1981, pp. 1–8.

KRAAR, LOUIS. "The Japanese Are Coming—With Their Own Style of Management." *Fortune*, March 1975: 116–21, 160–64.

KUBOTA, AKIRA. "Japan: Social Structure and Work Ethic." *Asia Pacific Community* 20 (Spring 1983).

KUME, HITOSHI. "Quality Control in Japan's Industries." *the wheel extended: A Toyota Quarterly Review* 9 (Tokyo), Spring 1980.

LAMMERS, C. J. "Power and Participation in Decision Making in Formal Organizations." *American Journal of Sociology* 73 (1967): 201–16.

LANCIANESE, F. W. "Small Plant's Safety Success Formula." *Occupational Hazards* 43 (July 1981): 45–48.

LAW, JOE M. "Quality Circles at a Naval Shipyard: Employee Involvement Ups Productivity." *World of Work Report* 6 (January 1981): 3–4.

LEE, YONG Y., and LARRY W. FEGLEY. "How QC Circles Were Started in AMP, Inc." In *IAQC 1st Annual Conference Transactions*. Cincinnati: International Association of Quality Circles, 1979.

LESIKAR, RAYMOND V. *Basic Business Communication*. Homewood, IL: Richard D. Irwin, Inc., 1979.

"Lessons from Japan, Inc." *Newsweek*, September 8, 1980: 61–62.

LEVINE, SOLOMON B. *Industrial Relations in Postwar Japan*. Urbana, IL: University of Illinois Press, 1958.

LINDSAY, WILLIAM M. "Can Quality Circles Bridge the Japanese/American Culture Gap?" In *IAQC 4th Annual Conference Transactions*. Cincinnati: International Association of Quality Circles, 1982.

LOCKE, E. A., and D. M. SCHWEIGER. "Participation in Decision Making: One More Look." In *Research in Organizational Behavior*, edited by B. M. Staw. Greenwich, CT: JAI Press, Inc., 1979.

LOHR, STEVE. "Overhauling America's Business Management." *The New York Times*, January 4, 1981: VI, 15. For letters about this article, see February 15, 1981: VI, 102.

LOZANO, ROBERT. "Quality Circles—Blue-Collar, White-Collar and Other Hues." In *ASQC 36th Annual Technical Conference Transactions*. Milwaukee: American Society for Quality Control, 1982.

LOZANO, ROBERT, and PHILIP C. THOMPSON. "QC Circle Implementation in the Space

Shuttle External Tank Program at the Michoud Marietta Corp." In *ASQC 34th Annual Technical Conference Transactions*. Milwaukee: American Society for Quality Control, 1980.

MACDONALD, JOYCE, and CAROL ROBINSON. "Concept for Management." *The Quality Circles Journal* 4 (November 1981): 13–15.

MAGUIRE, MARY A., and RICHARD T. PASCALE. "Communication, Decision Making and Implementation Among Managers in Japanese and American Managed Companies in the United States." *Sociology and Social Research* 63 (1978): 1–23.

MAIN, JEREMY. "The Battle for Quality Begins." *Fortune*. December 29, 1980, 28–33.

MARKS, MITCHELL LEE. "Conducting an Employee Attitude Survey." *Personnel Journal* 61 (September 1982): 684–91.

MARSH, ROBERT M., and HIROSHI MANNARI. *Modernization and the Japanese Factory*. Princeton, NJ: Princeton University Press, 1976.

MARTIN, WALLACE. "What Management Can *Expect* From an Employee Attitude Survey." *Personnel Administrator*, July 1981: 75–79.

MASER, MARJORIE. "Mount Sinai Invests in Quality Circles." *Health Services Manager* 14 (February 1982): 44–48.

MAZIQUE, MIGNON. "The Quality Circle Transplant." *Issues and Observation* 1 (May 1981): 1–3.

MCCLENAHAN, J. S. "Bringing Home Japan's Lessons." *Industry Week* 208 (February 23, 1981): 69–73.

MCGREGOR, DOUGLAS. *The Human Side of Enterprise*. New York: McGraw-Hill, 1960.

MCGREGOR, DOUGLAS. *The Professional Manager*. New York: McGraw-Hill, 1967.

MCMILLAN, CHARLES J. "From Quality Control to Quality Management: Lessons from Japan." *Business Quarterly* 47 (Spring 1982): 31–40.

MCMILLAN, CHARLES. "Is Japanese Management Really So Different?" *Business Quarterly* 45 (Autumn 1980): 26–31.

MCMILLAN, CHARLES J. "Production Planning and Organization Design at Toyota." *Business Quarterly* 46 (Winter 1981): 22–30.

MENNING, J. H., C. W. WILKINSON, and PETER B. CLARKE. *Communicating Through Letters and Reports*. Homewood, IL: Richard D. Irwin, Inc., 1976.

METZ, EDMUND J. "Diagnosing Readiness." *The Quality Circles Journal* 4 (November 1981): 16–20.

METZ, EDMUND J. "The Verteam Circle." *Training and Development Journal* 35 (December 1981): 78–85.

MEYER, ROBERT P. "Marriage of Your P's and Q's Through Quality Circles." In *ASQC 36th Annual Technical Conference Transactions*. Milwaukee: American Society for Quality Control, 1982.

MIDDLEMIST, R. DENNIS, and MICHAEL A. HITT. *Organizational Behavior: Applied Concepts*. Palo Alto, CA: Science Research Associates, 1981.

MILLS, TED. "Human Resources: Why the New Concern?" *Harvard Business Review* 53 (March–April 1975): 120–34.

MITCHELL, TERENCE R. *People in Organizations: Understanding Their Behavior*. New

York: McGraw-Hill, 1978.

MITO, TADASHI. "The Internationalization of Japanese Management." *the wheel extended: A Toyota Quarterly Review* 9 (Tokyo), Summer 1981, pp. 2–9.

MONTGOMERY, ROBERT L. *A Master Guide to Public Speaking.* New York: Harper & Row, 1979.

MORLAND, JULIA. *Quality Circles.* London: Industrial Society, 1981.

MORRIS, ROSEMARY. *Quality Circles Consulting: Marketing Survey and Industrial Analysis.* San Jose, CA: FMC Corporation, Ordnance Division Engineering, 1981.

MURATA, KIYOAKI. "What Makes Japan Tick?" *The Japan Times Weekly*, February 27, 1982: 3.

The Motorola Participative Management Program. Corporate Offices, Motorola Inc., 1983.

NAKANE, CHIE. *Japanese Society.* Berkeley: University of California Press, 1970.

NAKAYAMA, ICHIRO. *Industrialization and Labor–Management Relations in Japan.* Translated by Ross E. Mouer. Tokyo: The Japan Institute of Labor, 1975.

NAYATANI, YOSHINOBU. As quoted by Masaaki Imai. "Policy Deployment: Japanese Management's New Strategic Tool." *When in Japan: An Introduction for Doing Business in and with Japan.* Vol. 4. Tokyo, Japan: Planning and Promotion Division, Hotel Okura, February 14, 1983: 24–26.

National League for Nursing. "The Quality Circle Process." *Nursing and Health Care* 3 (November 1982): 492–93.

"The New Economy." *Time*, May 30, 1983.

"The New Industrial Relations." *Business Week*, May 11, 1981: 85–87, 89–90, 92–93, 96, 98.

ODAKA, KUNIO. *Toward Industrial Democracy: Management and Workers in Modern Japan.* Cambridge, MA: Harvard University Press, 1975.

OISHI, O. "The Concept of Perfect Production." *CTM: The Human Element*, February 1981: 14–16.

ORBAUGH, PAMELA K., and TIM ORBAUGH. "Is Your Lab Ready for Quality Circles?" *Medical Laboratory Observer*, February 1983: 41–45.

ORFAN, CONSTANTINE. "In-Process and End-Product Goals of Quality Circles." *The Quality Circles Journal* 4 (February 1981): 26–27.

OUCHI, WILLIAM. *Theory Z: How American Business Can Meet the Japanese Challenge.* Reading, MA: Addison-Wesley, 1981.

OZAWA, TERUTOMO. *People and Productivity in Japan.* Work in America Institute Studies in Productivity. New York: Pergamon Press, 1982.

PABST, WILLIAM R. JR. "Motivating People in Japan." *Quality Progress* 5 (October 1972): 14–18.

PASCALE, RICHARD T., and ANTHONY G. ATHOS. *The Art of Japanese Management: Applications for American Executives.* New York: Simon & Schuster, 1981.

PASCARELLA, PERRY. "Fad or Philosophy? QCs May Have Become Too Popular." *Industry Week*, March 22, 1981: 23–24.

PASCARELLA, PERRY, *Industry Week's Guide to Tomorrow's Executive: Human Man-*

agement in the Future Corporation. New York: Van Nostrand Reinhold, 1981.

PASCARELLA, PERRY. "Quality Circles: Just Another Management Headache?" *Industry Week*, June 26, 1982: 50–55.

PATCHIN, ROBERT I. "Consultants: Good and Bad." *The Quality Circles Journal* 4 (May 1981): 11–12.

PATCHIN, ROBERT I. "Facilitators, Facilitation and Ownership." *The Quality Circles Journal* 4 (February 1981): 13–14.

PATCHIN, ROBERT I. "Stairway to the Stars." *The Quality Circles Journal* 5 (February 1981): 10–15.

PATCHIN, ROBERT I., and ROBERT CUNNINGHAM. *The Management and Maintenance of Quality Circles.* Homewood, IL: Dow Jones–Irwin, 1983.

PERRY, BERNARD J. "Problem Identification: What's the Best Way." *IAQC 2nd Annual Conference Transactions.* Cincinnati: International Association of Quality Circles, February 1980.

PETERS, THOMAS J. "Putting Excellence Into Management." *Business Week*, July 21, 1980: 196–205.

Plan for Productivity/Quality Improvement, Commercial Division. Sperry-Vickers Corp., July 1980.

PORTER, L. W., R. M. STEERS, R. T. MOWDAY and P. V. BOULIAN. "Organizational Commitment, Job Satisfaction, and Turnover Among Psychiatric Technicians." *Journal of Applied Psychology* 59 (1974): 603–9.

Productivity and Quality Control: The Japanese Experience. Tokyo: Japan External Trade Organization, 1980.

"QC Circle Activities and the Suggestion System." *Japan Labor Bulletin*, January 1982: 5–8.

"Quality Circle Boom Part of Growing American Trend." *Supervision* 43 (September 1981): 8–11.

Quality Circles at Honeywell: A Study of Participant Perceptions. Minnetonka, MN: Corporate Human Resource Development Department, Honeywell Inc., July 1982.

Quality Fluid Power Components and Systems to Meet Industry's Needs, the World Over. Troy, MI: Sperry Vickers Corp., n.d.

"Quality and Productivity: America's Revitalization." *Business Week*, November 8, 1982: 19–20, 25–26, 30.

"Quality: The U.S. Drives to Catch Up." *Business Week*, November 1, 1982: 66–69, 70, 77, 80.

QUIBLE, ZANE K. "Quality Circles: A Well-Rounded Approach to Employee Involvement." *Management World* 10 (September 1981): 10–11, 38.

REED, THOMAS W., and MARK R. OLSON. "Circle Quality—Members Remembered." In *IAQC 4th Annual Conference Transactions.* Cincinnati: International Association of Quality Circles, 1982.

REHDER, ROBERT R. "What American and Japanese Managers Are Learning From Each Other." *Business Horizons* 24 (March–April 1981): 63–70.

REHDER, ROBERT R. "Japan's Synergistic Society: How It Works and Its Implications for the United States." *Management Review* 70 (October 1981): 64–66.

REID, LAURA. "Nashua: Using Statistics to Solve Hidden Problems." *The Financial Times of Canada*, November 22, 1982: 11–13.

REISCHAUER, EDWIN O. *The Japanese*. Cambridge, MA: Harvard University Press, 1977.

RENDALL, ELAINE. "Quality Circles: A 'Third Wave' Intervention." *Training and Development Journal* 35 (March 1981): 28–31.

RENDALL, ELAINE , and MARJORIE MASER. "Using Quality Circles in the Health Service." *Human Resource Development* 4 (June 1980): 12–14.

Report on the Survey of Labor-Management Consultation Systems at Work as of 1980. Tokyo: Japan Productivity Center, April 1981.

RIEKER, WAYNE S. "Management's Role in QC Circles." In *IAQC 2nd Annual Conference Transactions*. Cincinnati: International Association of Quality Circles, February 1980.

RIEKER, WAYNE S. "The QC Circle Phenomenon: An Update." In *ASQC 33rd Annual Technical Conference Transactions*. Milwaukee: American Society for Quality Control, 1979.

RIEKER, WAYNE S. "What Is the Lockheed Quality Control Circle Program?" In *ASQC 30th Annual Technical Conference Transactions*. Milwaukee: American Society for Quality Control, 1976.

RIEKER, WAYNE S., and SHAUN J. SULLIVAN. "Can the Effectiveness of *QC* Circles Be Measured?" *The Quality Circles Journal* 4 (May 1981): 29–31.

RINGLE, WILLIAM M. "The American Who Remade Made in Japan." *Nation's Business* 69 (February 1981): 67–70.

ROHLEN, THOMAS P. "The Company Work Group." In *Modern Japanese Organization and Decision-Making*, edited by Ezra F. Vogel. Berkeley: University of California Press, 1975: 185–209.

ROLLAND, I., and R. JANSON. "Total Involvement as a Productivity Strategy." *California Management Review* 24 (Winter 1981): 40–48.

ROSOW, JEROME M. "Productivity and the Blue-Collar Blues." *American Management Associations Annual Conference Transactions*. New York: American Management Association, February 1971.

ROSS, JOEL E., and WILLIAM C. ROSS. *Japanese Quality Circles & Productivity*. Reston, VA: Reston Publishing Company, 1982.

Royal Bank of Canada. *The Communication of Ideas. A Collection of Monthly Letters.* Montreal, 1972.

RUBENSTEIN, SIDNEY P. "New Management Concepts From Japan: A Tale of Two Conferences." *Paperboard Packaging*, January 1970: 44–45.

RUBINSTEIN, SIDNEY P. "Participative Quality Control." *Quality Progress* 4 (January 1971): 24–27.

RUBINSTEIN, SIDNEY P. "QC Circles and U.S. Participative Movements." In *QC Circles: Applications, Tools, and Theory*, edited by Davida M. Amsden and Robert T. Amsden. Milwaukee: American Society for Quality Control, 1976: 157–62.

RUBINSTEIN, SIDNEY P. "QWL and the Technical Societies." *Training and Development Journal* 34 (August 1980): 76–81.

SANDHOLM, LENNART. "Japanese Quality Circles—A Remedy for the West's Quality Problems?" *Quality Progress* 16 (February 1983): 20–23.

SATO, KINKO. "More & More Japanese Women are Hoping to Get Lifetime Jobs." *The Japan Economic Journal*, March 30, 1982: 11.

SCHEIN, EDGAR H. "SMR Forum: Does Japanese Management Style Have a Message for American Managers?" *Sloan Management Review* 23 (Fall 1981): 55–68.

SCHMIDT, JERRY L. "Participative Management—Challenge to Competition." *ASQC 34th Annual Technical Conference Transactions*. Milwaukee: American Society for Quality Control, 1980.

SCHMITT, G. A., N. P. PRESTON, and B. S. MITCHELL. "Successful Application of a Quality Circle Program in a Utility Environment." *AIIE Proceedings, Fall Annual Conference*, Fall 1980: 365–71.

SEDAM, SCOTT M. "QC Circle Training Process Should Cover Relating, Supporting, Problem Solving Skills." *Industrial Engineering* 14 (January 1982): 70–74.

SEDERBERG, GEORGE W. "The Role of the Steering Committee." In *IAQC 4th Annual Conference Transactions*. Cincinnati: International Association of Quality Circles, 1982.

SEELYE, H. NED, EDWARD C. P. STEWART, and JOYCE A. SWEEN. *Evaluating Quality Circles in U.S. Industry: A Feasibility Study*. Arlington, VA: U.S. Department of Defense, Office of Naval Research, 1982.

SHAW, ROBERT J. "Middle Management's Role in Quality Circles." *Management Focus* 29 (May–June 1982): 34–36.

SHEARMAN, ROBERT W. "How Can America Increase Productivity in the Next Decade?" *Quality Progress* 12 (January 1979): 22–26.

SIEGEL, IRVING H. *Productivity Measurement: An Evolving Art*. New York: Pergamon, 1982.

SINGLETON, JACK. "Quality Circles in a State Psychiatric Hospital." In *IAQC 4th Annual Conference Transactions*. Cincinnati: International Association of Quality Circles, 1982.

SOKOL, MARC, and V. HURWITZ. "Evaluation Equals Growth and Survival." *The Quality Circles Journal* 5 (August 1982): 15–20.

SORGE, MARJORIE. "Work Smarter, Not Harder, Advises Quality Consultant." *Automotive News*, July 27, 1981: 6.

SOYKA, DAVID. "Honeywell Pioneers in Quality Circle Movement." *World of Work Report* 6 (September 1981): 65–67.

SPROW, EUGENE E. "Made in USA." *Tooling and Production*, February 1982: 73–80.

SPROW, EUGENE E. "The Quality Commitment." *Tooling and Production*, March 1982: 73–80.

STANSBURY, JAMES F. "Financial Incentives For Circles?" *The Quality Circles Journal* 4 (February 1981): 7.

STEIN, BARRY A., and ROSABETH MOSS KANTER. "Building the Parallel Organization: Creating Mechanisms for Permanent Quality of Work Life." *The Journal of Applied Behavioral Science* 16 (1980): 371–86.

STRUTHERS, J. E. *Canada–Japan Essay: Long Road Back*. Canada–Japan Council, February 1981: 6–10.

SUGIMOTO, YASUO. "The Advancing QC Circle Movement." *Japan Quality Control Circles*. Tokyo: Asian Productivity Organization, 1972.

SUMIYA, M. "The Emergence of Modern Japan." In *Workers and Employers in Japan: The Japanese Employment Relations System*, edited by K. Ōkochi, B. Karsh, and S.B. Levine. Princeton, NJ: Princeton University Press, 1974.

SWARTZ, GERALD E., and VIVIAN C. COMSTOCK. "One Firm's Experience with Quality Circles." *Quality Progress* 12 (September 1979): 14–16.

TAGLIAFERRI, L. E. "As Quality Circles Fade, a Bank Tries Top Down Teamwork." *ABA Banking Journal* 74 (July 1982): 98–100.

TAKAMIYA, SUSUMU. "The Characteristics of Japanese Management," *Management Japan* 14 (Summer 1981): 6–9.

TAKEDA, YUTAKA. *Autonomous Self-Management Activity: A Key to High Productivity at Nippon Steel Corporation*. A paper presented at the Japan Society, May 9, 1980.

TAKEUCHI, H. "Productivity: Learning from the Japanese." *California Management Review* 23 (Summer 1981): 5–19.

"Talking in Circles Improves Quality." *Industry Week* 192 (February 14, 1977): 62–64.

TAVERNIER, GERARD. "Awakening a Sleeping Giant: Ford's Employee Involvement Program." *Management Review* 70 (June 1981): 15–20.

TAYLOR, FREDERICK W. *Scientific Management*. New York: Harper & Row, 1911, 1947.

TAYLOR, MARK. "BankCal Quality Circles." In *IAQC 4th Annual Conference Transactions*. Cincinnati: International Association of Quality Circles, March 1982.

THOMPSON, JAMES. *Organizations in Action*. New York: McGraw-Hill, 1967.

THOMPSON, PHILIP C. "Management Circles—No!" *The Quality Circles Journal* 4 (November 1981): 7.

THOMPSON, PHILIP C. *Quality Circles: How To Make Them Work in America*. New York: AMACOM, a Division of American Management Association, 1982.

THOMPSON, PHILIP C. "Voluntary Circles." *The Quality Circles Journal* 4 (May 1981): 9.

Toronto-Dominion Quality Programme Introductory Kit. Toronto: Toronto Dominion Bank of Canada, 1982.

TORTORICH, R., R. THOMPSON, C. ORFAN, D. LAYFIELD, C. DREYFUS, and M. KELLY. "Measuring Organizational Impact of Quality Circles." *The Quality Circles Journal* 4 (November 1981): 26–33.

TOWNSHEND, ROLPH. "Why the Japanese Are So Successful." *Management Review* 69 (October 1980): 29–47.

TSURUMI, YOSHI, and REBECCA TSURUMI. "A Closer Look at Japan's Lifetime Employment System." *Pacific Basin Quarterly* 8 (Fall 1982): 5–6.

TUTTLE, HOWARD C. "The Shortest Distance to Employee Ideas is a Circle." *Production*, June 1971, pp. 73–75.

UAW–Ford Employe Involvement: A Special Survey Report. Dearborn, MI: UAW–Ford National Development and Training Center, March 1983.

"U.S. Executives Look at Japanese QC." *Quality Progress* 13 (February 1980): 8.

VARLEY, PAUL H. "An Inquiry Into the Chrysanthemum and the Sword of Japanese Civilization." *Look Japan*, March 10, 1982, pp. 10–11.

VOGEL, EZRA. *Japan as Number One: Lessons for America*. Cambridge, MA: Harvard

University Press, 1979.

VOGEL, EZRA, ed. *Modern Japanese Organization and Decision-Making*. Berkeley and Los Angeles: University of California Press, 1975.

WELLSTOOD, SYBIL A., and LINDA WRIGHT. "Using Quality Circles to Spot and Solve Lab Problems." *Medical Laboratory Observer*, February 1983: 32–37.

WERTNER, WILLIAM B., JR. "Quality Circles: Key Executive Issues." *Journal of Contemporary Business* 11 (Second Quarter 1982): 17–26.

"Why Industrial Productivity Is as Important as Military Arms." *Government Executive* 13 (October 1981): 38–40.

WIDTFELDT, JAMES R. "How IES Can Contribute to, Gain from a Quality Circle." *Industrial Engineering* 14 (January 1982): 64–68.

"Will the Slide Kill Quality Circles?" *Business Week*, January 11, 1982: 108–9.

Windsor Star, March 3, 1983.

Work in America. Report of a Special Task Force to the Secretary of Health, Education and Welfare. Cambridge, MA: MIT Press, 1973.

"Worker Motivation in Japan (II)." *Japan Labor Bulletin*, March 1982: 5–8.

YAGER, ED. "Examining the Quality Control Circle." *Personnel Journal* 58 (October 1979): 682–84, 708.

YAGER, ED. "Quality Circle: A Tool for the '80s." *Training and Development Journal* 34 (August 1980): 60–63.

YAGER, EDWIN G. "The Quality Control Circle Explosion." *Training and Development Journal* 35 (April 1981): 98–105.

YAKABE, KATSUMI. *Labor Relations in Japan: Fundamental Characteristics*. Tokyo: International Society for Educational Information, 1974.

YAMADA, MITSUHIKO. "Japanese-Style Management in America: Merits and Difficulties." *Japanese Economic Studies* 10 (Fall 1981): 1–31.

YANG, CHARLES Y. "Management Styles: American Vis-a-Vis Japanese." *Columbia Journal of World Business* 12 (Fall 1977): 23–31.

YANKELOVICH, DANIEL. *New Rules: Searching for Self-Fulfillment in a World Turned Upside Down*. New York: Random House, 1981.

YOSHIDA, MITSUKUNI. "The Concept of 'Labor' in Japan." *the wheel extended: A Toyota Quarterly Review* (Tokyo), Spring 1980, 2–8.

YOSHINO, M. Y. *Japan's Managerial System: Tradition and Innovation*. Cambridge, MA: MIT Press, 1968.

YOST, JOHN C. "Quality Circles: Is Everybody Ready and Willing?" In *IAQC 1st Annual Conference Transactions*. Cincinnati: International Association of Quality Circles, February 1979.

YUKOSAWA, TOSHIHARU. "The QC Circle Movement Applied to Shop Requirement." *Japan Quality Control Circles*. Tokyo: Asian Productivity Organization, 1983.

ZAGER, ROBERT, and MICHAEL P. ROSOW, eds. *The Innovative Organization: Productivity Programs in Action*. New York: Pergamon Press, 1982.

ZANDER, A., and T. CURTIS. "Effects of Social Power on Aspiration Setting and Striving." *Journal of Abnormal and Social Psychology* 64 (1962): 63–74.

ZEMKE, RON. Quality Circles: "Can They Work in the U. S.?" *Journal of Applied Management* 5 (September–October 1980): 16–21.

ZWEIG, PHILIP L. "Quality Circles—A Kind of Employee Brainstorming—Helping Banks Solve Problems, Improve Performance." *American Banker* 146 (January 19, 1981): 1–4.

INDEX

Page references in italics are to tables and figures.

291